The Complete Book Of
BONSAI

To my father Harry Tomlinson Snr
from whom I inherited
my love of art and horticulture

A DORLING KINDERSLEY BOOK

First published in Great Britain in 1990 by
Dorling Kindersley Limited
9 Henrietta Street, London WC2E 8PS

Managing editor Jemima Dunne
Managing art editor Derek Coombes

British Library Cataloguing in Publication Data

Tomlinson, Harry
The complete book of bonsai.
1. Bonsai
I. Title
635.9772
ISBN 0-86318-484-7

The Complete Book Of
BONSAI
was produced by
NIGEL OSBORNE
115J Cleveland Street
London W1

Art Director	*NIGEL OSBORNE*
Project Editor	*JUDY MARTIN*
Editor	*JILL THOMAS*
Design Assistant	*PETER SERJEANT*

Typesetting by Midford Typesetting Ltd., London W1
Reproduced by Reprocolor International, Milan
Printed and bound in Italy by Graphicom

CONTENTS

INTRODUCTION

I am often asked when it was and why that I first became attached to bonsai. My earliest recollection dates back to a rainy holiday around 1950 spent visiting my aunt and uncle. I would like to be able to say that they employed a scholarly, kind, elderly Japanese gardener who entrusted me with the ancient oriental secrets of bonsai culture and set me on a path of spiritual enlightenment. However, the truth is more prosaic. Out of boredom, kept indoors by the wet weather, and being an avid and compulsive reader of everything from cereal packets to the complete works of Charles Dickens, I started on the only reading matter in the house — a set of rather decrepit encyclopedias. Luckily, the rain lasted for several days, long enough for me to complete all the As and most of the Bs (for many years I was a child prodigy on any subject from A to B).

The only distinct impression I retain from this industrious study is that of bonsai. My imagination was stirred, and for weeks my parents had to contend with plant pots full of seeds and saplings on windowsills all around the house. I scoured the local library for any more information about bonsai, without success. The initial interest, without further fuel, subsided.

About ten years later, I came across *"The Japanese Art of Trees and Landscapes"* by Yuji Yoshimura and Giovanna M. Halford (first published by Charles E. Tuttle in 1957 and still a valued work, with its thirty-first printing in 1987, this was the first major book on bonsai published in English), and the flame of my earlier interest was rekindled and I was soon addicted. As the interest in bonsai in the West grew, more and more books in English became available and I bought and studied every one. Gradually, but inevitably, bonsai took over my life — to such an extent that in 1979 I resigned, after almost twenty years, my executive post in the Civil Service to devote my life to bonsai.

A classic bonsai subject
*Satsuki azalea
(Rhododendron) 'Kaho' is
excellent bonsai material. It has
a graceful and adaptable
structure, evergreen foliage and
spectacular summer flowers,
making a beautiful image at any
time of year.*

Nature and art

It is unlikely that anyone browsing through this book would be completely unaware of what constitutes a bonsai, if only by virtue of the wealth of illustrations in these pages. But I have delivered talks on the subject to groups that included people expecting to see a demonstration of martial arts or hear about the problems of breeding long-haired dogs. Even those who identify the term correctly often have misconceptions about what bonsai is.

Bonsai, although a Japanese word, is used and understood throughout the world, There is no convenient English translation: "a tree or shrub trained and pruned in such a way as to resemble a full-size tree, grown in a shallow container for artistic effect and as an impression of nature" is an accurate but not very concise definition. "Bonsai" is actually composed of two words: "bon", meaning a shallow tray or container; and "sai", a plant or planting. This is literal, but "bonsai" implies much more than the literal translation. It implies the element of art that distinguishes a bonsai from a potted tree.

All my life I have been interested in and dabbled in arts and crafts, including oil painting, photography, pottery and wood carving. But for me, bonsai fulfills the creative urge as no other artform can. My love of nature, and of trees in particular, is also satisfied by the unique blend of art and horticulture that is bonsai.

Living as I do in the centre of England in an area that once formed part of Sherwood Forest, and close to the Derbyshire hills and valleys of the Peak District, I am very much influenced by the scenery I see around me. My work tends to have a strong landscape feel, with an emphasis on group plantings, rock plantings and saikei ("tray landscape").

I do believe in the importance of careful study of trees in nature, which provides a stimulus and challenge to recreate natural impressions. Impression is the correct word, as it is useless to aim for a realistic approach where every branch and twig is reproduced. An idealized recreation of nature is the goal.

Greenwood Gardens, England
The author's own bonsai collection, here displayed on benches in the nursery, reflects the beauty and variety of its surroundings at the centre of England. Many of the bonsai express aspects of the character of the local landscape.

Evocation of landscape
This Chinese elm (Ulmus parvifolia) *has been trained in clump style to create a natural multiple-trunk effect. The rounded silhouette of the tree, which is planted on a low base of Cornish slate, evokes the tranquil feeling of a mature tree growing in open countryside.*

Learning about bonsai

I often feel, when addressing an audience of newcomers to bonsai, that I should issue something in the nature of a health warning. Not that bonsai are likely to damage your health (unless you drop a particularly large specimen on your foot), but the love of bonsai can and does become an addiction.

During my thirty years of addiction to bonsai, I have become heavily involved with the bonsai world, both nationally and internationally. As well as growing countless bonsai and selling them (as many as I can bear to part with), I run classes and workshops in my studio and tour the world demonstrating bonsai techniques.

My approach to teaching has always been the same, based on an almost simplistic view that anyone can appreciate bonsai and that creating bonsai is easy – anyone can do it. I totally disagree with the attitude that bonsai is a "mystical" art that requires years of skill and dedication to achieve results (implying that some people can never aspire to this level). Bonsai does require enthusiasm and commitment, but it can be approached at many different

Art in nature
Nature imitating art is represented in the atmospheric effect of erect Scots pines emerging from the morning mist in England's beautiful Sherwood Forest.

Mood in landscape
Within the same location, a very different, eerie atmosphere is expressed in the frosted landscape by the dramatic silhouettes of old hollow-trunked oak trees and slender birches.

levels of interest, ambition and ability. I welcome the wide range of interest that exists, from the person with only one or two trees that provide appreciation of the changing of the seasons, to the skilled and dedicated grower whose collection of trees exemplifies bonsai's status as a fine art.

My love of books is incorporated in my fascination with bonsai. I have a comprehensive personal library of bonsai books from all over the world, but I also attempt at my studio to retail the widest possible range of suitable books on bonsai. Over the years, through customers' comments, I have come to realize that the existing books do not completely satisfy their needs. Although there are a few titles that represent an authoritative introduction to the art, some books are written by authors who sell bonsai but never create any, others by authors whose business it is to write books but who have no practical involvement with bonsai.

I have no aspirations to become a professional author, but I am a professional bonsai grower and teacher of the techniques. My aim with this book is to provide a practical reference work of equal value to the beginner and the more experienced enthusiast. I seek to encourage people to try bonsai for themselves and this is the attitude I have tried to foster throughout the book. By following the projects in the chapter entitled Creating a Bonsai, you can be assured of a reasonable result. But remember that this is just a beginning – even the most famous artists had to begin with small steps that simply taught them their craft. Your own progress in both the technical and artistic aspects of bonsai can be tailored to your specific interests, the time you wish to put in, and the enjoyment that you get from growing bonsai. As with a bonsai, which matures and improves with the passing years, your pleasure and satisfaction in growing bonsai can only increase over time.

Planting in rock
A group planting of dwarf Japanese cedars (Cryptomeria japonica 'Yatsubusa') acquires a sense of long-established naturalism through being planted in the rock. Soft tufa rock can be hollowed out to create pockets of planting space.

Landscape through the seasons
A mixed planting on tufa rock includes a range of species that contribute to year-round colour interest. A Japanese white pine (Pinus parviflora) stands at the apex of the design, flanked by the red Deshojo maple, flowering quince and azalea, with low cover provided by acaena heathers and mosses.

A natural perspective
A handmade ceramic slab forms the perfect base for a group of stewartias (Stewartia monodelpha), creating the spacious feeling of open landscape.

CHAPTER ONE

THE ART OF BONSAI

Bonsai is an art of infinite range. A bonsai is never "finished" – it changes with the seasons and matures and improves with the passing years. The traditions and practices of growing trees and shrubs as bonsai are adaptable to all levels of skill and interest. In the following pages, the fascination of this long-established artform is explained in terms of the aims and intentions of growing bonsai, the relationship of bonsai to the natural world, and the artistic traditions and design principles that form the basis for individual practice of the art. This chapter includes valuable information on the sources of material for bonsai and ways of displaying your bonsai for personal enjoyment and formal appreciation.

WHY BONSAI?

Bonsai is a unique artform because it is a blend of art and horticulture. The bonsai grower uses the kind of creative skill and aesthetic sense that might be put into producing a painting or sculpture, but can combine this directly with an interest in nature – in the variety of natural forms and the changing patterns of growth throughout the seasons.

The unique feature of the art of bonsai is the element of time. Unlike other works of art that, once completed, retain a fixed form, bonsai introduces a fourth dimension in that the design naturally alters with the seasons and with age, and is in a state of continual development. A comparison can be drawn with a painter working on a woodland scene, who at some stage must decide that the painting is finished. For the bonsai grower who creates a wooded landscape, there is the satisfaction not only of producing a good composition initially, but then also of watching it change and mature over the seasons and years and continuing to

take a hand in both the cultivation of the trees and the development of the design.

Many artists are attached to bonsai because of this element, but the growing interest in the art of bonsai is due to its broad appeal – it can be pursued at many levels and for a variety of reasons. To some it is a fine art, to others it is of more interest as a specialized form of horticulture. It can be a totally absorbing interest or a part-time hobby. Dedicated growers can develop a bonsai collection that occupies a vast amount of space and time and rivals the impression of natural landscape, whereas a person living in a small apartment can maintain a direct contact with nature through growing just one or two trees on a balcony or patio in close view.

Bonsai growers can also enjoy their craft at many different levels of skill. The pleasure obtained from cultivating bonsai does not necessarily correspond to the excellence of the

The individual specimen
A single tree encapsulates the beauty of nature. The foliage of this graceful maple, Acer palmatum 'Dissectum Atropurpureum', opens in spring to a soft greenish-purple, develops a deep purple hue through summer and turns to brilliant orange in autumn. The elegant structure of its twiggy framework can be appreciated in winter when the branches are bare.

tree. The effort put into care and development of bonsai can be just as satisfying applied to two or three young trees as to a mature collection, and not everyone has the ambition to progress to a more rigorous or time-consuming level of interest. In this respect, bonsai is also available to all age groups and to people in all walks of life.

Bonsai cultivation
It could be said that an outstanding bonsai is ninety per cent art and ten per cent horticulture. But artistic ability alone cannot be a hundred per cent effective, because a degree of horticultural skill is necessary to keep the tree alive and growing and to enable the design to progress from good to excellent. Not all bonsai growers are experienced gardeners and so may have little knowledge of plant cultivation initially. On the other hand, it is possible to come to bonsai through an interest in horticulture, without much confidence in artistic skills, but this enables the grower to apply skills of cultivation very effectively while the more creative aspects of bonsai design can develop gradually. This is particularly the case in the western view of bonsai, whereas the artistic basis is more rigorous and completely integrated in the eastern tradition.

Growing trees as bonsai can be a therapeutic pastime, because of the combination of creative thought and contact with nature. Care of bonsai requires daily acquaintance with the trees through watering, feeding and grooming routines, a constant reminder of natural processes, and this means that the grower is continually obtaining a fresh appreciation of them. However, there is a common misunderstanding of the techniques of bonsai that often leads people to suspect that there is something unnatural about this form of cultivation. It is not a process of stunting or in any way damaging the trees; although bonsai are small-scale in comparison to trees growing in the garden or in the wild, the size is almost incidental, a means to an end that makes cultivation of the trees a more practical prospect. Bonsai is akin to the ways in which garden trees and plants are trained – fruit trees cultivated as cordons or espaliers, a fuchsia trained as a standard on a long single stem with a cascading head of branches, evergreens trimmed as topiary, and so on. In bonsai, the tree is pruned and trained in a way that exposes its natural beauty. The aim is to recreate an impression of a tree in nature using living, healthy material. Above all, it must look like a tree, retaining all the best of its natural characteristics.

Seasonal changes
The bright green of the larches'
summer foliage (right) gives way
to a rich straw-yellow colouring
of the needles in autumn.

Group planting
A group of trees creates a natural
woodland effect. During 18 years
of cultivation, this group of
Japanese larches (Larix
kaempferi) has been extended by
introducing additional trees to
increase the depth and
perspective of the design.

BONSAI TRADITIONS

Although the art of bonsai is now commonly associated with Japan, it was in China that it originated, and the general principle of growing trees in containers may even have been brought there much earlier from India. The influence of Chinese culture was strong in Japan during the eighth century AD and it seems likely that it was at that time that the Japanese adopted bonsai as an artform and adapted it to their existing cultural and horticultural traditions. There is not much documentary evidence for the beginnings of bonsai cultivation or its development in the early stages. An apparent reference to bonsai appears in a sixth-century document, and painted scrolls of the thirteenth century feature trees growing in containers that certainly correspond to the art of bonsai as it is now known. Many references appear later in Chinese and Japanese visual art and literature.

There have been different philosophical influences shaping ideas about the purpose of bonsai cultivation. In oriental cultures, as compared to western traditions, the concepts and practices of all the arts are seen to relate to daily life and are much more fully integrated with each other and with more mundane pursuits. Art is a process of bringing order to the world, by representing real life, including landscape, within artistic frameworks that are deliberately structured according to concepts of beauty and "correctness". The arts are, in simple terms, generally more formal in eastern than in western cultures. In various contexts, bonsai has been represented as a predominantly visual and stylistic artform, as a means of more abstract or spiritual expression, or as a method of representing nature directly parallel to both painted representations of landscape and the formal design of gardens, which can be considered as a way of sculpting the landscape itself.

Bonsai has been a significant part of Japanese culture for centuries, and it is from this long practice that both the artistic precepts and horticultural methods now used worldwide have been derived. Throughout the development of bonsai in Japan, there have been many fashions and different emphases at different times. For example, in the range of trees: the pine has long been a

Style and composition
The basis of this dramatic landscape is an artificial rock made of fired clay. It is planted with a dwarf Japanese black pine (Pinus thunbergii) *and mountain maples* (Acer palmatum). *Pines and maples have long been classic bonsai subjects and the vertical, linear composition of this planting can be compared to the calligraphic character of oriental landscape painting.*

classic subject for bonsai; bamboos are also traditional bonsai material; ornamental flowering trees such as cherry and apricot were among the earliest bonsai subjects recorded, and some of the more spectacular flowering shrubs, such as azaleas and camellias, were later added to the list of desirable plants for bonsai. A true taste for trees grown for the beauty of their foliage was a relatively late development. Japanese maples, still today a very popular group of trees for bonsai and garden use, became particularly prized from the seventeenth century onwards, and this was the time when new varieties began to be developed with increasingly ornamental characteristics. In the nineteenth century, books were published on the range of hybrid trees grown for beautiful foliage. Leaf shapes and colours became major attractions in their own right.

Bonsai in the western world

In the light of Chinese and Japanese traditions, the introduction of bonsai to western countries is extremely recent. It is only within the twentieth century that bonsai has become a real interest in Europe, America and Australia and this has happened quite slowly, although the enthusiasm for bonsai is still now gathering pace. There is some evidence of exhibitions and publications on the subject appearing in European countries during the late nineteenth century. Significant interest in bonsai in England was thought to have dated mainly from a public exhibition in London in 1909, although the catalogue of an auction sale held in 1900 has come to light, which describes the items for sale as "Rare and Beautiful Japanese Floral and Arboreal Plants – Curiously and Artistically Trained".

Interest in bonsai in the United States of America spread rapidly in the period following World War II, perhaps mainly because of the stationing of American troops in Japan at the end of the war. An enthusiasm for bonsai has grown in many countries on all continents in recent decades, with an increasing number of individual growers at all levels of expertise and bonsai societies being established at local and national levels.

The western tradition of bonsai, in so far as this is an identifiable concept, takes its basis from the Japanese art, as evidenced by the vocabulary of bonsai, the classification of styles for training trees and, in purely practical terms, the origins of the specialist tools and containers used in bonsai, the majority of which are exported from Japan to other countries all around the world. Because of the diversity of interest and expertise in western countries, and also the wide variations in availability of trees, climate and the conditions for cultivation, approaches to the practice of styling trees as bonsai are perhaps more varied and less rigorously defined than in the Japanese tradition. There remains, however, a clear sense of common goals and interests that link bonsai growers worldwide and encourage the developing "communities" of bonsai enthusiasts in many different regions and countries.

Roadside tree in Omiya, Japan
This ornamental trident maple (above) is trained in exactly the same way as bonsai.

Omiya bonsai village, Japan
Many beautiful bonsai specimens are on view at a traditional bonsai nursery in Omiya (main picture).

THE ORIGINS OF BONSAI MATERIAL

Assuming your initial interest in growing bonsai, where do you find the right material, whether you intend to cultivate just one or two trees, or develop a bonsai collection? There are various sources, each with its own advantages and disadvantages. These possible methods of obtaining your bonsai also involve different levels of effort and commitment.

Buying a bonsai

The simplest way to obtain a bonsai is simply to buy one. There are specialist nurseries dealing in bonsai, and bonsai are also becoming more commonly seen in garden centres and general nurseries. The advantage of obtaining a "readymade" bonsai is the immediate gratification – there is no lengthy wait for the tree to develop to a suitable stage of growth and no effort involved in styling and training the tree as bonsai.

There are, however, a number of disadvantages to this method. The majority of bonsai are imported into western countries from Japan and the expenses of handling and transportation contribute a significant part of the price. In some areas, bonsai are not readily available and it may involve some research and a long journey for you to find a suitable source. The quality of the bonsai can also vary enormously. Some items sold as bonsai are merely trees growing in pots, not true bonsai at all.

Collecting trees from the wild

Often in nature trees become naturally dwarfed due to climatic conditions or an inhospitable situation where the tree is deprived of adequate water and nutrients. Continual grazing by sheep or deer can also keep down the size of the trees in the wild – this is a natural parallel with the process of pruning bonsai.

It is sometimes possible, if you find a dwarfed tree growing in the wild, to lift it and establish it in a container. Many of the finest bonsai in Japan have been developed from this sort of material. The main advantage is that the tree may be quite old and show its maturity in the form of the trunk and branches and the texture of the bark. It is not so easy to duplicate these characteristics of an aged tree by other means.

The obvious disadvantage is that it can take a great deal of time and effort to find a suitable tree and, having done so, you would require permission from the owner of the land where it is growing to lift it and take it away. In some areas, removal of living plant material from its natural habitat is

Garden centre tree (right)
This triple-trunk juniper (Juniperus × media 'Blaauw') has been trained over four years from a tree obtained from a garden centre, originally grown for garden use.

Collected tree (below)
The origin of this European beech (Fagus sylvatica), trained as bonsai for 14 years in informal upright style, was a beech hedge.

forbidden by law. It is also critical to collect a tree at the right time of year. It cannot be taken in full leaf: the best time for collecting is in late winter or early spring before bud break. This adds to the problems of finding and transporting a suitable specimen from, for example, a heavily forested or mountainous region.

It is difficult to re-establish a mature tree as bonsai – it is very unlikely that you could successfully transplant a collected tree straight into a bonsai pot. Usually it would need to be planted out in a garden bed or prepared container until it regained its vigour, and it might be four to five years before it could be potted as bonsai.

The above information relates only to mature trees that for natural reasons have remained small. There is no advantage to collecting seedlings or saplings that have simply sprung up where seed has been carried by the wind or dropped by birds, trees that are small simply because they are young.

With the growing interest in conservation and today's consciousness of depletion of the world's resources, the principle of collecting trees from the wild is in question. There are, however, some justifiable occasions, such as when land is to be cleared for redevelopment and the plant life would otherwise be lost completely.

Creating bonsai from garden centre stock

Methods of creating bonsai from garden centre or nursery plants can be recommended, as there are many advantages as compared to the other sources of material. Plants can be obtained quite inexpensively and there is a wide range of species to choose from. The material can be pruned to shape quickly, producing the basic structure of an interesting bonsai within hours, or even minutes. You can satisfy the creative impulse in that you can actually decide the form of the bonsai, within the limits of the material, so there is a greater level of involvement in the design and styling of the bonsai than with bought or collected trees.

The only slight disadvantage is that nursery and garden centre stock is grown to have characteristics suitable for garden use and may be unsuitable for bonsai, especially in the case of tall-growing trees. But it is possible to find useful examples of smaller trees, and there are many suitable shrubs that can readily be pruned to tree-like forms.

Growing from seed

This is an inexpensive but time-consuming way to produce bonsai material – some seed takes two years to germinate. Tree seed does not stay viable for very long and may not germinate well; even fleshy seeds, if not fresh, quickly become unreliable. However, the time it takes for the tree to develop suitable characteristics for bonsai is the main disadvantage of this method, and it is really necessary to plant the seedling into open ground and let it develop for some years before styling and potting it as bonsai. It is often the case, too, that trees grown from seed do not come true to the parent plant and in practical terms a specimen grown from seed may not show the right attributes, such as small leaves or fruits, that led you to choose the species as suitable material for bonsai.

The most reliable species for this method are the pomegranate (*Punica granatum*) and the Japanese elm (*Zelkova serrata*), which develop quite quickly and will produce an attractive small tree – about 15cm (6in) in height – within three to five years from planting seed.

Growing from cuttings

The main advantage of working with cuttings is that usually the original material is freely available – you can take it from shoots and branches that are removed in day-to-day trimming of existing trees, which otherwise would be thrown away. Cuttings can be a quick source of new stock, some rooting within a matter of weeks and achieving an amount of growth in six months that might take three or four years growing from seed. The final advantage to this method is that material grown in this way does come true to the parent plant and will have the required characteristics.

The only disadvantage is that some species – pines (*Pinus*), for example – do not root from cuttings or are difficult to cultivate in this way.

Other methods of propagation

If you use grafting, layering or air layering to obtain new plants, the correct characteristics of the parent plant are carried forward, as with growing from cuttings. You will also see results much more quickly than with growing from seed – for example, a crab apple (*Malus*) grown from seed may take twenty years to come into flower, whereas if you make a graft or layer from a 20-year-old tree, the new stock will produce blossom in the following year because the maturity of the parent, as well as its physical characteristics, is brought forward into the grafted or layered tree.

There is an advantage unique to bonsai in growing pines by grafting. One of the most commonly seen examples is the Japanese white pine (*Pinus parviflora*) grafted on the Japanese black pine (*Pinus thunbergii*). This is not only for efficient propagation but also contributes to the character of the bonsai, as the black pine produces an old-looking, rugged trunk whereas that of the white pine is smooth. The roots of the black pine are also stronger and more drought-resistant. The white pine has small, bright needles with a bluish cast but when grown on its own roots the needles have a tendency to yellow. Grafting on the stronger black pine stock seems to inhibit this tendency.

The main disadvantage of grafting for beginners or inexperienced bonsai growers is that the process requires a fairly high level of dexterity and technical skill.

Obtaining suitable bonsai material

It is difficult to make absolute recommendations here, because in theory it is possible to use any type of tree or shrub for bonsai, although some are more suitable than others. The main characteristics that you should look out for are an interesting trunk and a good arrangement of branches, with attractive bark colour and texture, compact, fine-textured foliage, preferably with small leaves – and small flowers or fruits, if you wish to include such features in the bonsai design.

Garden shrub *(left)*
*A 20-year-old garden-grown
Kurume azalea* (Rhododendron
obtusum) *about to be discarded
was "rescued" for training as
bonsai. It had been sawn off to a
stump, which was dug up and
planted in a box until it
developed new shoots.*

Many highly attractive trees, including the wide range of
colourful maples (*Acer*) and crab apples (*Malus*) and the
graceful larches (*Larix*) make admirable bonsai. Evergreens
with fine-textured or needle-like foliage also lend
themselves to bonsai – cedars (*Cedrus*), the false cypress
(*Chamaecyparis*), pines (*Pinus*), spruces (*Picea*) and junipers
(*Juniperus*). There are also many dwarf forms that readily adapt to
bonsai cultivation, particularly to small-scale designs, ranging from
the dwarf birch (*Betula nana*) to the dwarf Japanese cedar
(*Cryptomeria japonica* 'Yatsubusa') and including foliage and flowering
trees, deciduous trees and evergreens. A number of the readily
available garden shrubs – quince (*Chaenomeles*), cotoneaster
and pyracantha, for example – are easily pruned to
tree-like shapes for bonsai and will establish
quickly, producing a good display within one or
two years of planting in a bonsai container.
At the opposite end of the scale, for those who
seek a real challenge in bonsai, there are
majestic trees that in nature grow to vast
proportions, such as the English oak
(*Quercus robur*) and the wellingtonia
(*Sequoiadendron giganteum*).

Characteristics suitable for bonsai

Although the desirable attributes of bonsai are typically small leaves and fine twigs, there are exceptions to this rule that make excellent bonsai for particular seasonal effects. For example, many of the ornamental cherry trees (*Prunus*) have large, coarse leaves and twigs, but are grown for the short-lived spectacular display of spring blossom, after which they are no longer featured in a display of bonsai. Wisteria is another that is grown for the beauty of its cascading flower racemes, although the leaves are not in scale for bonsai. Satsuki azaleas (*Rhododendron*) are highly prized despite having large flowers, as these completely clothe the branches during the flowering season. Satsukis form an attractive display beyond this period, with good trunk and branch formations and glossy, evergreen leaves that make a fine show year round.

It is also worth noting that some deciduous trees, such as elms (*Ulmus*) and maples (*Acer*), are a particularly fine sight in winter when the branch and twig structure is fully revealed after leaf fall, so you do not need to opt for evergreen species if looking for year-round interest.

Different species are grown for their different although equally desirable characteristics and the choice of particular types of tree or shrub for bonsai may depend on how large your collection will be and what you want to get out of it. If you can grow only one or two bonsai in a restricted space, it makes little sense to choose those species that provide a short-lived display in a single season and are thereafter relatively uninteresting, whereas if you have a large collection of trees, you have the option to include these species together with those that provide varied interest throughout the year.

Trees grown from cuttings (right)
This group planting of honeysuckle (Lonicera nitida) *consists of six-year-old plants originally grown from cuttings. They are planted on an artificial stone slab, a resin cast, to create a natural effect of open landscape.*

TREES IN NATURE

The natural variations of trees growing in the wild are the direct inspiration for bonsai, providing the original models from which principles of design and training in bonsai have been evolved. Many people are attracted to the art of bonsai through a love of nature, and of trees in particular. The sense of scale and perspective, the impression of strength and durability that comes from full-size trees cannot always be found in a garden setting, where space may be too restricted to grow more than one or two trees, if any, nor does everyone live within easy reach of open landscape where trees can be enjoyed in all their grandeur. With bonsai, however, the impressions of nature, including its vastness, can be recreated on a manageable scale, not with the intention of isolating bonsai from the natural conditions of trees, but by supplying a healthy environment and level of care in which their true beauty can be revealed.

Natural design

The variety of growth in nature is not due just to the range of different species found growing wild in any given region, but also to the individual ways in which the trees grow according to the character of their surroundings and the weather conditions to which they are exposed. The same species of tree, while always exhibiting basic features characteristic of its type such as leaf shape and colour, bark texture and twig patterns, will develop and mature very differently according to whether it grows by itself or in a group, is sheltered by a cliffside or a building or

Root-over-rock style (above right)
The technique of styling a tree root-over-rock (see pages 80 to 83) recreates a form of natural growth often seen in rocky or mountainous sites. The Japanese mountain maple (Acer palmatum) *is a particularly suitable species for this style.*

Exposed roots in nature (right)
The dramatic effect of this silver birch (Betula pendula), *growing wild in the mountains of Wales, owes much to the way the tree has established itself over the rocky base, extending its roots to seek moisture and nourishment from the soil. The exposed roots have hardened and gripped the rock.*

Tree silhouettes
*A striking effect of trees silhouetted
against the open sky is recreated by a
single bonsai specimen.*

stands in the open exposed to strong winds, is surrounded by plentiful resources of soil and moisture or has to extend its roots to seek adequate sustenance.

Bonsai can reflect the full range of tree growth in nature, from an impressive individual specimen to a dense forest of trees to a wooded landscape extending across grassland or growing on a mountainside. This is possible through careful attention to the elements of design that establish an impression of scale and space. You can create a sense of perspective with a single tree or in a group of trees: there are basic principles of styling and planting that can help you to do this, which will be explained in later chapters. It is important to accept the fundamental principle that what you do with bonsai should reflect your observations of nature, either in terms of a particular tree or trees that you have seen in the wild, or with regard to the logic of natural development in trees – the way branches must grow out towards the light, for example, which may make a tree growing on a lakeside extend its branches over the water while in the densest part of a forest it will cause the trees to reach upward because they are shading each other.

Styling bonsai
Recognizable style categories have been developed in bonsai (see pages 46-51) that reflect observable natural elements. Often the names of the styles explain the principle of the design and its origins. Slanting style, for example, represents a tree exposed to strong wind, in which the trunk leans at an angle: there is also a sub-category of slanting style called "windswept", in which the design is more emphatic and strongly directional, creating the impression of wind rushing through the tree branches. Some trees suggest a "style" – the Norway spruce (*Picea abies*), for example, naturally presents a formal upright arrangement, whereas an oak or beech is naturally informal. The majority of trees and shrubs suitable for bonsai can be developed in any of several styles. This reflects how the basic characteristics of a tree adapt to the prevailing conditions of its environment. The attributes of individual styles and the ways of training bonsai so that they can be adapted to a particular style are discussed in the following chapter.

Looking at trees in nature is an indispensable part of "training" yourself as a bonsai grower. An excellent bonsai is not necessarily a good model for another bonsai: the design has worked well because the individual specimen that the grower started off with has been creatively adapted to a suitable style, and the tree has been well cared for over the years that the design has developed. You cannot reproduce all of these elements to "copy" a successful bonsai. Rather, you must consider the material that you have to start with, and use your experience of both natural growth and bonsai training to bring out the full potential of the individual tree. In any situation where you see trees growing unrestrained, you can begin to analyse the natural influences that have made them form particular shapes and patterns of growth and begin to relate these to basic principles and practices of bonsai cultivation.

Natural groupings

Different tree species may be seen growing together in open country, like these Scots pines and English elms (main picture). In bonsai, the scale and horticultural requirements limit the potential for mixing species. Typically, a group is composed using a single species, but this example (right) successfully combines the Japanese larch (Larix kaempferi) with the Chinese juniper (Juniperus × media 'Blaauw').

ELEMENTS OF DESIGN

The design of a bonsai encompasses the style and condition of the tree, the size, shape and finish of the container, and the relationship of the tree and container that establishes the overall impression of the design. Whatever the species of tree chosen and the style in which it is shaped and trained, there are some basic elements of design that can be usefully applied to all bonsai. Three main factors, which are important considerations in selecting a tree or shrub for bonsai training, are inherent to the basic structure of the plant: the root spread; the form of the trunk; and the arrangement of the branches on the trunk.

Creating a balance
A good design has an overall balance that is achieved through careful training of the shape and structure of the tree and a considered relationship between the tree and its container, as in this example of a Japanese white pine (Pinus parviflora). All the elements of the design are harmonious and complementary.

Root spread

An interesting root formation exposed above the soil is one of the major factors contributing to a sense of maturity and long-establishment in a bonsai. As trees grow in nature, the roots of a young tree are typically concealed beneath the ground: with age, they begin to appear at the surface, and the above-ground root formation of a rugged, aged tree may become its most powerful feature, instantly forming an impression of the tree's character as it is viewed from ground level. In the same way in bonsai, the interesting shapes and textures of roots visible above the soil give an impression of age and stability.

Ideally, the roots should extend from the trunk in all directions, but this does not mean that they should be evenly spaced or symmetrically arranged. What you should aim for, as with all aspects of bonsai design, is a good visual balance. This can result from a combination of quite irregular or asymmetrically arranged elements that seen all together form a visually pleasing design. For example, roots can give the right impression of stability and balance even though they are heavier on one side of the tree than on the other, or have complex textures and divisions that break up the structural lines. The overall impression is what counts, in each aspect of the design and in the way individual components come together. Another element that contributes to the natural and artistic impression of the bonsai is the way the roots connect to the trunk, whether they radiate or flow from the trunk base or seem to provide a firm buttress or anchorage.

Trunk

The most important single feature of the trunk is a good taper, meaning that the thickness of the trunk diminishes smoothly and gracefully towards the top of the tree. Thickness in the base of the trunk adds to the impression of the tree's maturity, but a parallel trunk line passing into the apex of the tree destroys the balance and elegance of the design. The thickness of the trunk should also be appropriate to other characteristics of the species. Whereas the delicately cut and coloured leaves of a maple may be best displayed on a slender trunk, an English oak needs to be allowed to develop a heavy trunk that recreates the characteristic grandeur of a mature oak in nature. In some cases, bonsai material will need several years of growth and training to develop the ideal form of the trunk.

It is also important to be able to obtain a good view of the trunk line, even though the foliage masses may cut across it. As in nature, trunks of bonsai trees may be straight, curved or angled, even divided. There is no particular pattern of trunk growth that disqualifies a tree from being

The visible root spread
Exposed roots contribute to the balance of the design and add to the impression of the tree's character and maturity. The roots of this oak tree (Quercus robur) appear to have a tenacious grip on the soil appropriate to an aged, solidly structured tree. In purely visual terms, the shapes and textures of exposed roots are an interesting aspect of bonsai.

suitable as bonsai: more important to a tree's suitability for bonsai training is the overall relationship of trunk and branches.

The shape of the trunk and its bark texture and colour give the tree character. The trunk should suggest a true naturalness in which an aged or weathered appearance can be an advantage, but you should avoid selecting a tree with a distinctly scarred or damaged trunk unless this can be made into a feature – for example, a hollow trunk.

Branches

As with root spread, the arrangement of branches as they spring from the trunk should create a good balance in the tree, in harmony with its general character and forming a good visual complement to the trunk line. The branches form the basic structure of the tree's silhouette. While techniques of pruning and wiring (see Creating a Bonsai) can be used to adjust the structure and silhouette even quite radically, there are some basic features to look out for when you consider the suitability of a tree or shrub for bonsai.

A good analogy for the right arrangement of branches is a spiral staircase. The branches should create a balanced pattern around and up the trunk, although again this pattern is not necessarily symmetrical. As a rule of thumb, the first branch level should be at about one-third of the way up the trunk. The heaviest branches are at the lower levels. Branches are typically thicker close to the trunk, with a taper along the length of the branch.

Bonsai are usually pruned to a roughly conical spread, because pruning prevents the branches from thickening too much, which compromises the scale and balance of the design. The top of the tree should bear the most delicate twigs, and branches at the apex are pruned more closely: low branches are sometimes allowed to extend quite far before pruning, as this enables them to thicken near the trunk.

Certain types of branch growth are not considered to make good elements of a design, but these can be pruned out. Crossing branches are not desirable. Branches spreading out from the same point on the trunk are not visually pleasing in bonsai, nor are branches that grow directly opposite one another at the same level on the trunk. The direction of the branches can often be adjusted using wiring techniques (see pages 68 to 74). Upward growing branches, for example, can be wired to sweep downward. Although it is useful to start off with material that has a good distribution of branches, wiring can also be applied to altering the position of a branch to fill out a "gap" in the branch structure and refine the silhouette of the tree.

The front of the tree

Although bonsai, like freestanding sculpture, may be viewed from all around, they are always designed with a selected "front" view, or preferred viewing angle. While there is no given front view to a tree in nature, you will usually find that it is better appreciated from one angle than it is from others and here again, observation of the ways in which trees grow in the wild can stimulate ideas for bonsai design. However, there are a number of formal points that can be taken as guidelines to selecting the front view of a tree for bonsai.

A bonsai is designed to be viewed at an eye level corresponding to a point about halfway up the trunk. The selected front view should offer the most attractive view of the root structure, the most graceful angle and best apparent taper of the trunk, and the most pleasing arrangement of branches, which allows you to "see into" the tree while also forming a satisfactory silhouette.

Curves in the lower part of the trunk are best seen when directed to one side, not coming towards the viewer: a tree with a forward curve is described as "pigeon-breasted"; this is an undesirable trait. Branches extending directly frontwards are only acceptable in the upper third of the tree, but at the back of the tree it is important that branches extend away from the viewer to give a good sense of depth and perspective.

A common mistake of beginners who study bonsai design by reference only to photographs rather than by observing

Left side

Right side

Back view

Viewpoints
A maple (Acer palmatum 'Seigen') bare of leaves in winter shows the basic structure of the trained tree from different angles. The side views (far left) clearly show that the apex inclines towards the viewer. From the front (left), the arrangement of branches gives a clear view of the trunk, while at the back there are more branches giving fullness and depth to the design. This tree is illustrated in leaf on page 99.

live specimens is to neglect the back branches, which are not visible in photographs.

The apex, the top of the tree, should incline towards the viewer – the Japanese say the tree should "bow" to you. This is because, as you look at a tree in nature you have to look up, to take in the height of the trunk, and as you tilt your head back the top of the tree seems to come towards you. A bonsai with the apex leaning away from you always looks wrong.

Deciding on the front view is a matter of weighing up the combination of roots, trunk, branches and apex from various angles and selecting what appears to you to be the best presentation. The arrangement of branches and shape of the apex of the tree can be adjusted by pruning and wiring, so the trunk and roots are more crucial to your choice. Of all these factors, the root structure is the most important, as it is the most difficult to change.

Size and scale

The range of bonsai sizes varies from a tiny specimen that you can balance on the palm of your hand to one considerably taller than the height of a person. Many people not directly acquainted with bonsai think that it is about "making trees small", but this is not the case. The purpose of bonsai is to use the tree to create an impression of nature, and the fact that it is smaller than its natural size is mainly a convenience for handling and working with the tree. This is particularly apparent in the Japanese view of bonsai, where little distinction is drawn between the way trees in a park or garden are pruned and shaped to enhance their natural beauty, and the way that the same techniques are applied to growing trees in pots.

Given the range of bonsai sizes, it is as pointless to argue that one size is better or more successful than another as it would be to compare the merits of a portrait miniature with those of a large abstract painting. However, it is fair to say that the majority of bonsai fall within a middle range of about 15cm (6in) to 60cm (2ft). This is because the extremes of very large or very small both present special problems.

Large trees, about 2m (6½ft) or more, may require up to four strong people to transport them safely. Even moving them on a day-to-day basis to gain access for grooming is extremely difficult. There is also the expense of an appropriately sized container to be taken into account, and the question of where to display such a large item. Large bonsai are, however, extremely impressive and there is a definite fascination to accepting the challenge of growing a massive tree in a container.

With very small trees, there is a practical problem of watering. With a tiny container, the bonsai may need watering several times a day in warm or dry weather. Design of very small bonsai is also difficult. Whereas in a middle-sized bonsai, one leaf may represent a cluster of leaves in scale with the natural size, in a tree only 8cm (3in)

Establishing a sense of scale
Dwarf tree forms are excellent for small-scale rock plantings, as in this example of the dwarf Japanese white pine (Pinus parviflora 'Yatsubusa') on Ibigawa rock. The small foliage and compact silhouette creates a greater impression of distance than could be achieved with a full-size tree.

tall, one leaf must represent a branch or the whole apex of the tree. It may only be possible at this size to represent two branches and the apex – very small bonsai require a minimalist approach taking the principle of "less is more". However, for many people, the scale of extra-small bonsai (also called miniature or *mame* bonsai) allows them to create an extensive collection that can be accommodated in a relatively small space, as these bonsai are usually displayed all together.

Whatever the size of the bonsai, considerations of scale must be geared to creating a natural impression. This is why small-leaved trees are preferred, because they are more adaptable in terms of scale. The larger the leaves and the coarser the foliage and twigs, the more difficult it is to make them work effectively as a representation of a full-size tree. Some trees are simply not adaptable to very small bonsai, others are quite unsuitable for extra-large specimens, but there are many species that comfortably adapt to the middle range of sizes.

In group and landscape plantings, there is often more scope for manipulating the sense of scale, because the trees relate to each other and to other elements of the design, such as rocks or ground cover plants that might be included to enhance the naturalism of a landscape planting. The principles of establishing scale in a rock planting are further explained on page 76.

TREE AND CONTAINER

In styling bonsai, you will naturally be giving much attention to initial shaping of the tree and the grooming that helps to refine the design over the years. It is important not to neglect the question of a suitable container for the tree. This is an equal part of the bonsai design and selection of the right container to create a harmonious relationship with the tree completes the overall effect of the bonsai.

There are practical points to be considered (as discussed on pages 52 and 53), but these are straightforwardly resolved. The aesthetic value of the bonsai pot is a more difficult consideration, because it depends both upon the individual species of tree that you are potting and the way you have styled it and, to some extent, on your own subjective sense of what makes a good design. The following are some basic guidelines that may help in your selection. Experience of both creating and appreciating bonsai will also help you to develop a good instinct for the types of container possibly suited to a particular style and species of tree.

Size, shape and finish

The size and proportion of the pot in relation to the tree are among the first things you should consider. The container must be in scale with the tree, in practical terms forming an adequate reservoir for soil and water, but in design terms enhancing the balance of the tree's height and spread. For an individual specimen, the tree should not appear to be floating in an over-large pot, nor cramped into a tiny container that appears to form an unstable base for the size of tree. As an approximate guideline, for a tree with a mainly vertical emphasis, the measurement across the container could be between two-thirds and three-quarters of the tree's height, whereas for a tree with a strongly horizontal spread, these proportions can apply to the relationship between pot length and the overall width of the tree. (With initial potting of a newly styled deciduous tree, it is important to allow for the larger spread and mass that it will have when it comes into leaf.) Traditionally, bonsai containers are shallow in relation to length and width. There are aesthetic reasons for sometimes choosing deeper pots for certain types and styles of trees.

Pots shapes vary quite widely and many styles are available in a range of sizes (see pages 54 and 55). The most

Landscape planting
The feeling of natural landscape in this design is enhanced by contrasting the colour and texture of the trees with an unassuming container of simple shape and discreet tone. The wide lip of the pot casts a shadow that makes the landscape appear to be "floating".

Space within the container
The sense of movement in this group is emphasized by the clean, open shape of the container.

basic shapes are rectangular, oval and round; the sides of the pot may be straight and vertical, curving, or slightly flared. There are also basically rectangular pots with angled or sculpted corners, varying the overall impression of the shape. Some pots have minimal, unobtrusive "feet" while others have distinctive, ornate "feet". Likewise, the rim of the pot may be plainly finished in line with the direction of the sides, or may be turned inward or outward.

Most pots have an unglazed finish and the colour is the colour of the clay after firing. In general, subdued or subtle earth colours are considered more appropriate to bonsai than light or brightly coloured glazes. A smooth, undecorated surface is quite common, but there are pots with embossed or impressed designs or bands of relief decoration.

The character of the design

When matching the pot to the tree, you should take into account not only matters of size and proportion, but the overall character of the design. This is influenced both by the style of the bonsai, which may be formal or informal, and the characteristics of the tree – such as whether it is delicately branching or heavily massed, slender or rugged, features only foliage or also bears flowers or fruits, is green-leaved throughout the growing season or has a range of colour variation through the year.

A rugged forest tree demands an unfussy, earthy style of pot. A pine or larch, for example, is best suited by a subdued brown, grey or black container in a simple uncluttered shape – oval or rectangular, with discreet feet. An ornamented pot with highly coloured glaze, painted decoration or elaborately sculpted feet would be quite wrong for a forest tree. Trees with a heavy mass of foliage, solid trunk and textured bark may also need to be matched to the deeper bonsai pots that can balance their visual weight. Depth is an important consideration in selecting the container for a fruiting tree. A tree in fruit may create a heavy visual mass that needs to be balanced by a relatively deep container, which also provides the reservoir of moisture required to swell the fruits.

A light, graceful tree with seasons of brilliant foliage colour, such as a maple, requires a shallower, more dainty pot. A pale colour or brighter, more decorative glaze may be more appropriate here. The vivid reds and oranges of a maple's autumn foliage appear particularly intense against a white or cream glazed pot, and a shallow oval shape offsets the slender elegance of the maple. In choosing the style and colour of the pot, you should take into account the different features and colours of the tree in different seasons – flowers, fruits and changing leaf colours. Examples of some particularly fine seasonal characteristics are shown on pages 32 to 39, while further details of the seasonal features of individual species are described in the Species Guide (pages 90 to 167).

In general terms, a rectangular pot with sharp corners and straight sides is very formal, an oval less formal. Oval and round pots suit trees with a rounded mass. A delicate tree requires an elegantly shaped pot that reflects its delicacy, while a tree with a strong, forceful shape and texture needs a pot with an emphatic, powerful shape. A tree with very angular movement might be better presented in an angular pot with distinct edges to the shape, rather than a smoothly curved oval pot.

The best way to become aware of the nuances in the relationship between tree and container is to study many examples of quality bonsai, both live specimens and in photographs, and apply a critical analysis to the various aspects of the design. Consider the size, shape, proportion, colour and finish of the pot in relation to the size, shape, style, texture and colour of the tree, and try to identify the links that have led the grower to choose a particular pot for a particular tree. This way you will gradually acquire an eye for what is right or wrong.

Colour harmony
The soft green foliage of the Swiss willow (Salix helvetica) is echoed in the coloured glaze of the cascade pot.

Positioning the tree in the pot

Having chosen a suitable pot, you should also keep in mind that the way the tree is presented in the pot affects the impression of the design. The container gives a balance to the silhouette of the bonsai and the overall impression of the composition includes the link between the shapes of the pot and the tree. The position of the tree within the pot should take into account the general balances of the composition and the flow of the design – whether the movement of the trunk line is slanted or curved to left or right, and the balance of the branches on either side of the tree that creates outline and mass.

It is not usual for the tree to be placed centrally in the pot. A more natural effect is obtained if it is off-centre, nearer to one side than the other usually in a ratio of 1:2, although it may be roughly at the mid-point of the front-to-back dimension of the pot. As the pot forms the base of the design, the tree should be positioned in a way that leads the eye to appreciate the overall relationship between tree and pot, not to be drawn out of the composition. For example, a tree with an extended lower branch on the right-hand side would be positioned towards the left-hand side of the pot, forming a balance between the branch spread and dimensions of the pot: a tree with a slanted trunk would be placed with the base of the trunk to one side so that the apex of the tree would be positioned above the approximate centre of the pot.

In a group or forest planting (see pages 84 to 87), the spacing of the tree trunks within the container is a very important aspect of the naturalism of the design. Free spaces at either side of the planting is an essential feature of the design, but these spaces should be unequal, forming an asymmetrical composition.

SPRING COLOUR

Spring can be the most colourful time of year and is a very exciting period for all aspects of bonsai cultivation. On a practical level, you see how the trees have survived the period of dormancy over the winter months. New buds begin to swell and break, providing fresh new foliage and, in some species, the earliest flowers of the growing season. Gradually the growth rate increases and becomes very intense, until all of the trees have resumed full vigour.

One of the first trees to come into new leaf is the Japanese larch (*Larix kaempferi*), whose bright green new needles can be relied upon to provide an encouraging sight in early spring. Brilliant foliage colour comes from the many varieties of Japanese maple (*Acer palmatum*), particularly the red-leaved cultivars 'Deshojo' and 'Seigen'. There is a great variety of colour and texture even among the green-leaved deciduous and evergreen species.

The autumn cherry (*Prunus subhirtella* 'Autumnalis') provides flushes of white or pale pink blossoms from winter through spring when the weather is mild, and flowering quinces (*Chaenomeles japonica, C. speciosa* and *C. × superba*) contribute strong reds and pinks, as well as white flowers in early spring. As the season progresses, in addition to the beautiful sight of the developing leaf cover, there are further blooms to be enjoyed from hawthorn (*Crataegus*), wisteria, crab apples (*Malus*) and cherries (*Prunus*) and, in late spring, from any of a number of spectacular azalea cultivars (*Rhododendron*).

The Deshojo maple
Brilliant red spring colour is a feature of Acer palmatum *'Deshojo', one of the many beautiful maple cultivars that provide colour and interest throughout the year. The technique of leaf-cutting a bonsai (see page 179) can be used to bring on a second crop of these vivid leaves in late summer.*

Wisteria blossom
The cascading racemes of wisteria are a particularly fine example of colourful spring blossom.

Crab apple blossom (above)
The flowers of Malus cerasifera are attractive and highly fragrant.

Dwarf willow in catkin (above)
Yellow catkins are an attractive spring feature of Salix repens, here offset by the light tone of the cream matt-glazed container.

The Ukon maple (above)
Acer palmatum 'Ukon' is at its brightest in spring, although the intense lime green is maintained throughout the growing season. The fresh colouring also extends to the trunk and twigs of the tree.

Double red hawthorn blossom
Crataegus oxyacantha 'Paul's Scarlet' produces a generous display of vivid flowers.

SUMMER COLOUR

During the summer, all bonsai are growing very vigorously and changing constantly. Deciduous trees are in full leaf and evergreens, too, have developed a discernible freshness of colour with the new foliage that has formed.

The variety of greens is one of the finest aspects of summer, although coloured foliages may provide a counterpoint or a different but equally lush effect. Flowering trees provide particular points of attraction in this season. Early summer is the time for the spectacular blooms of Satsuki azaleas (*Rhododendron*). The summer-flowering pomegranate (*Punica granatum*) offers scarlet, white, pink or yellow forms and the small flowers of potentilla provide a similar variety from which to choose. Cotoneaster and pyracantha also flower in summer, and by late summer these and varieties of crab apple (*Malus*) have begun to form their colourful fruits.

Some deciduous trees can be leaf-cut early in the season (see page 179), particularly maples (*Acer*), to bring on a repetition of the glorious spring foliage colour with new leaves appearing by late summer.

Multi-coloured Satsuki azalea
Many of the Satsuki cultivars have multi-coloured or striped flowers making an intensely colourful effect on a single plant. This example shows the range of colour variation that can be displayed in the blossoms of a single specimen.

Satsuki azalea 'Kaho' in flower
Although the flowers of most Satsuki azaleas are relatively large in terms of bonsai scale, they clothe the branches completely, thereby creating a richly colourful mass. The graded pinks of the cultivar 'Kaho' make the plant look like an elaborate confection.

Potentilla in flower (right)
Extremely popular as garden
shrubs, potentillas are equally
desirable bonsai material. This
example is Potentilla fruticosa,
a yellow-flowering species that is
brightly contrasted with a blue-
glazed pot in this design. The
flower colours of potentilla range
from white through cream to
yellow, pink and orange.

The Sango Kaku maple (above)
As this beautiful Acer palmatum cultivar shows,
it is not only foliage and flowers that provide the
diversity of summer colour. A striking feature of
this tree is the coral-pink bark and twigs,
attractively echoed in the pink-tinged green
foliage. The compact growth habit of the tree is
also a good characteristic for bonsai.

Maple foliage
The foliage colours of the many
different maples provide a
spectacular display from spring
through autumn. The overall
impression is enhanced by the
attractiveness of the leaf shapes,
which are finely cut or divided.

AUTUMN COLOUR

This is a season as colourful as spring but whereas the brilliance of spring seems to come through very quickly, with everything happening at once, in autumn it is more drawn out, giving time to appreciate the many changes. As the leaves of deciduous species change colour and begin to fall, some trees are already bare before others have begun their most spectacular colour changes.

Maples (*Acer*) are truly spectacular in autumn, with a range of rich, strong colours – yellow, orange, red and purple. Some of the brightest reds come from euonymus and stewartia, while the leaves of the gingko turn to a distinctive buttercup yellow and the needles of the larch (*Larix*) change from bright green to vivid gold. Beech (*Fagus*) and birch (*Betula*) are also among the species that have particularly fine characteristics in autumn. The rowan (*Sorbus aucuparia*) has a decorative autumnal display with red berries set among its gold and orange foliage. Other fruiting species, including crab apples (*Malus*), Japanese deciduous holly (*Ilex serrata*) and some cotoneasters, produce a new kind of visual interest as the leaves fall and the structure of the branches is more clearly seen, vividly decorated with bright fruits.

English elm in autumn leaf
*The characteristic silhouette of the English elm (*Ulmus procera*) here displays the mellow autumn foliage colour. The soft yellow of the leaves shows well against the dark grey-brown of the trunk and is nicely complemented by the green-grey shallow oval pot.*

Beech leaves (above)
The effect of a beech wood turning colour in autumn is captured in this group planting of Fagus crenata, *with leaves shading from yellow to brown against the pale trunks.*

Colour gradations (above)
In this large group of trident maples (Acer buergerianum), individual trees are in different stages of turning colour, creating a spectacular display from green through orange to brilliant scarlet.

Autumn fruits (left)
Berries provide additional colour in autumn, as in this cotoneaster growing on lava rock. The bright red of the berries and leaves is contrasted here with the blue-green glaze of the pot.

Long-lasting colour (below)
The spectacular autumn display of berries produced by pyracanthas can persist all through winter, standing out vividly against glossy evergreen foliage. Different varieties offer red, orange or yellow berries.

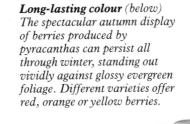

WINTER DISPLAY

Winter is the season in which the Japanese traditionally display bonsai. They hold their major exhibitions at this time of year. It is considered that many bonsai can be truly appreciated when the structure of the trees is unobscured by foliage. It is a prime time for viewing evergreens, which seem to express an air of strength and perseverance throughout the harsh conditions of winter. But particularly striking are those deciduous trees that display very fine and delicate twigs, such as the Chinese elm (*Ulmus parvifolia*) and trident maple (*Acer buergerianum*). Bare of leaves, trees with interestingly coloured and textured bark, such as crape myrtle (*Lagerstroemia indica*) and stewartia, take on a new attractiveness. Some trees also retain their fruits right through the winter, adding touches of strong colour to the more subdued hues. Chinese quince (*Chaenomeles sinensis*) makes a good display in winter with a combination of these features, having a strong pattern of branches, decorative bark and bright fruits. In late winter, the first sign of the luxuriance to come is signalled by the flowering apricot (*Prunus mume*) producing its pale, fragrant blossoms on bare wood, soon followed by the flowers of winter jasmine (*Jasminum nudiflorum*).

Winter colour
Few trees flower in winter, but Prunus mume *is a welcome exception late in the season, especially this colourful cultivar (below) bearing a combination of flower colours on the single plant. The deep red flowers of another cultivar of the same species (above) are as fragrant as they are decorative.*

Colour and mass
Evergreens such as this Japanese black pine (Pinus thunbergii) *can be relied upon for an interesting display through winter. The erect bright green needles and rugged bark on this species create a forceful, persistent image. It makes a particularly striking effect at a time when so many other trees are sparse-leaved or bare.*

Twig traceries *(below)*
Fine-twigged species such as the Korean hornbeam (Carpinus turkzaninowii) *present a very delicate and refined image when they are leafless during the winter months. An interesting pattern is created by the interlaced twigs of a group planting.*

Structural interest *(above)*
The more mature deciduous trees, such as this aged oak (Quercus robur) *often form a dramatic silhouette after leaf fall.*

DISPLAYING BONSAI

Where you choose to keep your bonsai and the kind of informal display that you make of them in normal day-to-day conditions depends on a variety of factors, such as the size of the bonsai collection and the available space for siting the trees; the appreciation and enjoyment that you wish to get from viewing and working with them on a daily basis; and the requirements of the trees for conditions that encourage healthy growth.

The height at which bonsai are displayed is usually a compromise between the best position for viewing — ideally, the trees should be viewed at eye level — and a practical height for reaching the bonsai easily to carry out watering, grooming and other routine tasks (see also pages 170 and 171). Commonly, bonsai are arranged on benches at about tabletop height; alternatively, they can be placed on shelves attached to a wall, such as the wall of a garage or

A background of bamboo (above)
Bamboo screens in Osaka, Japan.

A water basin (above)
Rock plantings in Oyima, Japan.

Monkey poles (right)
Garden display in Toronto, Canada.

house extension. If they are sited close to the house, in a patio area for example, and are normally viewed from a sitting position, the display can be at a slightly lower level to take account of the usual eye level. Another possibility is to position the bonsai on a low garden wall.

One rule for display is never to place a bonsai in a position that means you have to look down on a tree. A large specimen can stand on the ground only if it is meant to be seen from a distant view (there are also practical reasons for keeping bonsai off the ground, to avoid mud splashes during rainfall and to discourage insects from entering the pots). Closer to the house, a large tree displayed on a patio might be arranged at quite a low level on a paving slab mounted on blocks or bricks. Another possibility for displaying individual specimens is the arrangement known as a "monkey pole" — a vertical pole with a platform at the top.

Traditional tokonama-style display
The main tree is featured in its own space together with accessory.

Outdoor conditions
Ideally, the trees should be viewed against a plain background so that the silhouette and internal spaces of the design can be fully appreciated. However, this is rarely possible in a garden setting and is less crucial for informal display than for formal exhibition, as in your own surroundings you can view the bonsai at close quarters with less distraction from the background elements.

If your collection includes rock plantings, these appreciate more humid conditions. For one or two examples, adequate humidity can be maintained when the plantings are kept outdoors in their water trays. For a large collection of rock plantings, you may need to create special conditions, constructing a bench or shelf that forms a water basin so that there is a larger surface area of moisture to provide adequate humidity through the summer months.

How you arrange the bonsai individually or as a group is mainly a matter of your personal interest in creating a good view of the style and design of each specimen and the seasonal features of the trees. If you grow flowering bonsai, for example, you may wish to feature the trees during the flowering season and then move them to the back of the benches if they are not particularly interesting after the flowers have faded. If you are considering the collection as a whole group, then questions of height, scale and the overall perspective of the arrangement will come into your siting of the individual trees in relation to one another.

Keep in mind the requirements of the trees for good light and protection from the elements. An exposed position in an area frequently subject to fierce winds, for example, is obviously not ideal. If the bonsai are displayed on shelves against a wall, this may seem a good solution because they have a flat background to be viewed against and a sheltered position. However, the wall should receive good light and not cast its own shadow on the trees, and you will need to rotate the bonsai from time to time, as the back branches

can die because of lack of light and the intensity of heat reflected from the wall if the trees are permanently kept with the front view on display.

Indoor display
Although the vast majority of bonsai are hardy trees that must live permanently outdoors, there may be occasions when you wish to bring one indoors for a day or two, for your own enjoyment or to make a temporary decoration for a special occasion. If you have a good choice of trees, you can select something appropriate to the time of year. A spring-flowering tree, for example, in the right season provides a beautiful display of blossom comparable to a carefully crafted flower arrangement, and may also fill the room with fragrance.

Place the bonsai in a light position, but avoid a window that receives full sun at midday, as this may scorch the leaves. Keep the tree away from sources of heat, such as an open fire or a radiator, and be aware also of lesser heat sources from electrical appliances — for example, if you place the tree on top of the television, it is exposed to heat coming from the back of the set.

Even the most informal display indoors requires space for the shape of the tree to be appreciated and a muted background that shows off the design and colours of the bonsai. The best background is a plain, pale-coloured wall. Patterned fabrics or wallpapers detract from the natural beauty of the tree. In Japan, the traditional method of displaying bonsai was the tokonoma, an alcove in which the bonsai was displayed usually together with a smaller accent plant or rock and a scroll decorated with calligraphy or a painted image hanging on the wall of the alcove behind, the three elements arranged to create a triangular composition. This is not particularly relevant to display of bonsai in modern western homes, but it does illustrate a sound basic principle of giving the bonsai its own uncluttered space where it can be fully appreciated.

On a practical level, you may be concerned about the problem of watering the tree while it is indoors. As the tree and container together form the design, you should not consider altering this relationship by standing the pot in a tray or dish to allow for drainage. You can simply take the bonsai outdoors or to the kitchen for watering and allow it to drain well before returning it to its indoor location. A rush mat or similar discreet base can be used to protect the furniture from the feet of the pot.

All the above considerations also apply to tropical and sub-tropical tree species that are sold in countries with temperate climates for cultivation as indoor bonsai. It can be difficult to maintain even these trees in indoor conditions (see page 170), and the way in which they are permanently displayed must take account of their cultural requirements for bright light and sufficient humidity to offset the drying effect of interior warmth.

SHOWING AND JUDGING BONSAI

In the context of formal display of bonsai on exhibition, there are more clearly defined guidelines as to what is or is not appropriate than with regard to informal display for your own interest and pleasure. The opportunities to exhibit bonsai specimens are not many, and the context will vary according to the activities of organized bonsai and horticultural societies in your region. For exhibitions at national level, it is most likely that experienced bonsai growers will be invited to submit their best specimens and the selection and arrangement of the exhibition will be the responsibility of experienced organizers. At the other end of the scale, it is possible you may find a class for bonsai exhibits in a local horticultural show, where the criteria for displaying and judging the bonsai will be very different from those of a specialist society or institution.

Preparing bonsai for exhibition
If you get the opportunity to show bonsai formally, at whatever level, it is important to prepare both the tree and container to ensure that the bonsai is in the best condition when it goes on display. This includes grooming the tree to refine the silhouette and remove any dead leaves; tidying the soil surface to eradicate weeds and take out any plant debris that has collected in the container; freshening or renewing mosses, grasses or ground cover plants if these are included in the design; and cleaning the pot to take off dirt

Bonsai exhibits
These pictures show the bonsai display in successive years at the Chelsea Flower Show, London, UK.

Exhibition arrangement
The stands accommodate the heights and spreads of the trees.

and water marks and rub up the surface to a smooth, unblemished finish. You can leave wiring (see pages 68 to 71) in place on the tree if trunk or branches are being trained. This does not detract from the overall impression as long as the wiring is neatly and effectively done.

When you enter one or two specimens for exhibition, you are unlikely to have any influence on how or where they are displayed, so this preparation is your final chance to present the bonsai at its best. If you grow and exhibit *mame* (miniature) bonsai, you may be given a space within which you can arrange the grouping of the display.

Outdoor exhibition, Osaka, Japan
The bonsai are displayed outdoors at table height against a pale, plain backround. Because of the visitors' high regard for bonsai no barriers are needed around the exhibit, although it includes some extremely valuable specimens.

Arranging an exhibition

There are basic requirements for a full-scale exhibition that contribute to a good overall impression of the show and to doing justice to the individual exhibits. With regard to positioning the bonsai, there should be enough space around each tree for its shape to be fully appreciated. All the trees should be easily visible from the front view – they should not be arranged so that one is standing in front of another. An important aspect of the exhibition is the background against which the trees are seen. This should be of a plain, light colour and high enough to accommodate the full height of the largest bonsai. If the backdrop is created using screens rather than a solid wall, it is paticularly important to take account of the height and width of the screens in relation to the heights and spreads of the trees.

The bonsai may be displayed on tables or on individual stands. If tables are used to form the main display area, they should be plainly covered to create a uniform surface. White or pale, neutral-coloured cloths are suitable – patterned fabrics confuse the effect. The flat horizontal and vertical surfaces against which the trees are displayed must be light-coloured, although it is acceptable to use a dark cloth for the drop that hides the table legs and the view below the tabletops.

Positioning of the bonsai on a flat surface or on plinths or stands should take into account both the actual size of the trees and an appropriate level for their display. For example, trees that naturally inhabit high regions can be placed higher than trees that are normally found in lowland areas. A grouping of bonsai should create contrasts of scale, form, texture and colour, but dramatic contrasts of scale detract from the effects of the individual specimens. Generally, bonsai can be grouped in terms of sub-groups according to size – large and extra-large specimens, small to medium sizes, and extra-small bonsai as another separate group. *Mame* bonsai are usually displayed together as a group, otherwise they tend to get lost in the overall display. If you have a collection of *mame* bonsai, it may be possible to devise a special stand with suitable "compartments" for the individual trees.

Judging bonsai

Bonsai are living sculptures and, as with any works of art, comparative judgements are rarely appropriate and never very effective. At national level, bonsai are not typically judged by any system of competitive marking. It is more usual for awards of merit to be made that enable certain specimens to be singled out for their individual merits. The criteria for such awards can range across a variety of considerations: the bonsai might be a specially fine example of a particular style, or show effective use of difficult material, or it may be an unusual species that has required very careful cultivation and training. This system of judging can focus on the specific intentions of the grower and the success of the bonsai purely on its own terms. Specialist growers can be judged by their peers from an informed point of view.

At regional levels, a comparative marking system may be employed, particularly in horticultural shows where bonsai is included as one category among many and the element of competition is already established for other classes of entry – notably flowers and vegetables. This can be an opportunity to have your work seen and appreciated publicly, and for you to meet other local bonsai growers and view their work, but the awarding of prizes will most likely be the task of judges with no specialized knowledge of the art of bonsai, so it is not necessarily a valuable yardstick for your own progress.

Another reason why bonsai exhibitions are not often judged in comparative terms is that it is difficult to create distinct categories for the entries, or to be sure that they are applicable. Amateur growers are not always precisely informed about the age or origin of a "bought" bonsai, for example. Most ways of categorizing will inevitably involve judging different species against each other, or different styles, so there is no clear-cut and obvious way to systematize the judging process.

If you do become involved in a system of judging that requires points to be awarded, the fairest method that you can employ is to devise sub-categories that can be judged individually proportionate to the possible total of marks. You should pay attention to both the horticultural condition of the bonsai and the design elements: the way basic attributes of the tree – roots, trunk and branches – have been enhanced by the styling and training; the arrangement of foliage; the relationship between the tree and the container; and the presentation of the bonsai. In effect, this may enable you to judge each item more or less independently; the competitive element will occur when you come to total the marks for each entry and see how the different totals compare.

CHAPTER TWO

CREATING A BONSAI

Every bonsai is a unique combination of the character of the original plant material and the creative skill and judgement of the bonsai grower. The practical techniques for shaping and training a tree or shrub as bonsai are fully explained in the following pages with clear step-by-step examples. These are related to design considerations – selecting a style, developing the character of the bonsai, establishing the natural impression of a forest or landscape planting. Using the basic methods described in this chapter, you can create a bonsai from a garden centre plant in a matter of minutes. You can then apply your technical skills to improving and refining the design as the bonsai matures.

BONSAI STYLES

The classification of recognizable styles provides a set of basic guidelines for assessing a tree's potential as bonsai and setting the aims of your design. There have been many attempts to reclassify and redefine bonsai styles over the years, and many variations and subdivisions exist. The fifteen styles shown here represent the full range of bonsai design in single-trunk, multiple-trunk and group plantings. These styles can be created using the techniques demonstrated in this chapter; the techniques required to shape the tree in a chosen style depend on the individual specimen selected for the bonsai.

The most important principle of bonsai styling is that all the styles are based on the ways trees grow in nature. By careful observation of trees growing in the wild, you can design realistic bonsai without knowing the names of accepted styles; but it is useful to be able to identify them, so that you can describe them to others and understand references in books and magazine features. It is not

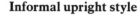

Informal upright style

This style is probably the most commonly seen both in nature and in bonsai and is suitable for most species. Due to environmental factors – wind, shade and competition for light or moisture from other trees or from buildings – the trunk of a tree curves, bends and changes direction. The growth of the trunk is basically upright – vertical or occupying an angle within about 15 degrees of the vertical — and the silhouette is well balanced. A pronounced bend or slant in the trunk should be seen from the front view to travel to right or left, not towards the viewer.

FORMAL UPRIGHT STYLE
Larix kaempferi

BASIC STYLES

Five basic styles are recognized in bonsai design and these are classified according to the angle of the trunk. They are formal upright, informal upright, slanting, semi-cascade and cascade styles. These represent different angles of the trunk, from straight and vertical in the formal upright to a trunk that bends right over and falls below the horizontal to form a full cascade.

INFORMAL UPRIGHT STYLE
Betula pendula

Formal upright style

The name is self-explanatory, the tree grows straight and upright. This occurs in nature where a tree is growing in an ideal open situation with no deprivation due to shortage of water or nourishment, and no harsh, adverse weather conditions. In a formal upright, the trunk of the tree should ideally have an even taper from base to apex, which creates a more elegant effect than a uniform thickness. The spread of branches is not strictly symmetrical, but the tree's silhouette should be well balanced around the vertical axis of the trunk.

Recommended species for this style include larches, junipers, pines and spruces. Fruiting trees and those species with a naturally informal habit are inappropriate.

necessary to learn their Japanese names and origins, nor to adhere rigidly to a specific interpretation of a style.

Choosing a style

You should always keep in mind that you are working with live material when designing a bonsai. The natural characteristics of the tree or shrub will sometimes suggest suitable styles and you must consider how you can train and adapt the original material to produce a good example of the style you have chosen.

While it is possible to grow bonsai in a style totally opposed to a tree's typical growth pattern, this is inadvisable for the beginner. Whether you base your design on the naturally upright habit of a beech or birch, the rugged, gnarled trunk of an oak or pine, or the slender, graceful habit of the maple, there is still a great deal of choice between different styles suited to that plant or the way in which you can interpret a style for the particular specimen. If you choose to work with a shrub, such as azalea, cotoneaster or pyracantha, that does not have a naturally tree-like form, you have in some ways fewer restrictions, but in order to make a shrub look effective as a bonsai tree you have to base your design on the style of a tree in nature.

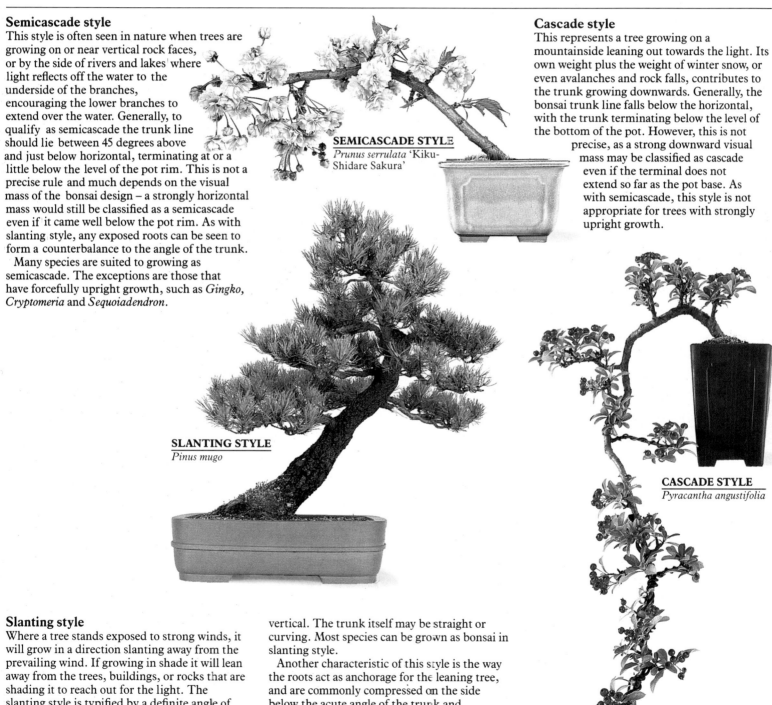

Semicascade style

This style is often seen in nature when trees are growing on or near vertical rock faces, or by the side of rivers and lakes where light reflects off the water to the underside of the branches, encouraging the lower branches to extend over the water. Generally, to qualify as semicascade the trunk line should lie between 45 degrees above and just below horizontal, terminating at or a little below the level of the pot rim. This is not a precise rule and much depends on the visual mass of the bonsai design – a strongly horizontal mass would still be classified as a semicascade even if it came well below the pot rim. As with slanting style, any exposed roots can be seen to form a counterbalance to the angle of the trunk.

Many species are suited to growing as semicascade. The exceptions are those that have forcefully upright growth, such as *Gingko*, *Cryptomeria* and *Sequoiadendron*.

SEMICASCADE STYLE
Prunus serrulata 'Kiku-Shidare Sakura'

SLANTING STYLE
Pinus mugo

Cascade style

This represents a tree growing on a mountainside leaning out towards the light. Its own weight plus the weight of winter snow, or even avalanches and rock falls, contributes to the trunk growing downwards. Generally, the bonsai trunk line falls below the horizontal, with the trunk terminating below the level of the bottom of the pot. However, this is not precise, as a strong downward visual mass may be classified as cascade even if the terminal does not extend so far as the pot base. As with semicascade, this style is not appropriate for trees with strongly upright growth.

CASCADE STYLE
Pyracantha angustifolia

Slanting style

Where a tree stands exposed to strong winds, it will grow in a direction slanting away from the prevailing wind. If growing in shade it will lean away from the trees, buildings, or rocks that are shading it to reach out for the light. The slanting style is typified by a definite angle of the trunk followed through from base to apex, usually to a maximum of 45 degrees from the vertical. The trunk itself may be straight or curving. Most species can be grown as bonsai in slanting style.

Another characteristic of this style is the way the roots act as anchorage for the leaning tree, and are commonly compressed on the side below the acute angle of the trunk and smoothly extended on the opposite side to help support the weight of the tree.

LITERATI STYLE

Also called bunjin, this style of tree is often seen at the seashore or in areas where trees have grown up reaching for the light in competition with other trees that have since died or been felled. Characteristically, the trunk line flows or twists through several curves. Some trees grow this way with old age – the Scots pine naturally assumes this style in maturity. Most conifers can be recommended for growing as literati, and rugged deciduous trees such as flowering apricot and hawthorn.

Difficult to define precisely, this style breaks many rules but nevertheless the trees have an air of refined elegance. Curiously, the name literati (Latin, meaning 'educated' or 'literate people') is used in the absence of an English equivalent for the Japanese *bunjin*, which in turn is a translation of the Chinese *wenjen*, the name for Chinese scholars practised in the arts. The slender trees in their paintings had an abstract, calligraphic quality that was the inspiration behind cultivating bonsai in this style.

LITERATI STYLE
Pinus thunbergii

STYLING ON ROCK

Rock-plantings of individual bonsai specimens divide into two types. In root-over-rock style, the roots of the tree grow over the rock and extend into the soil, whereas in clasped-to-rock style the tree is actually planted on the rock. The way the tree itself is styled depends on how the grower sees the overall relationship between tree and rock in the design. A single tree or a group or landscape planting (see also pages 76 and 88) may be grown on rock.

ROOT-OVER-ROCK STYLE
Acer buergerianum

Root-over-rock style

This style occurs in nature in areas where trees establish themselves on rocky ledges and crevices and as they grow send out roots that snake over the rocks to find more moisture and nourishment in deeper soil. Having found the soil, the roots fatten up as they become the major pipelines for water and nutrients that sustain the tree. Exposure causes the roots to harden and flatten themselves to the surface of the rock, and they effectively become an extension of the tree trunk.

This style in bonsai design gives a "close-up" or "near" view of a tree or trees on rock, as the main feature of interest is the web of roots embracing the rock. The roots grow into the potting compost and care is the same as for any other bonsai; when repotting, the rock is treated as if it were part of the trunk of the bonsai.

Trees for root-over-rock styling must have naturally strong roots. Maples, particularly the trident maple, the Chinese elm, pines and junipers can all be recommended. As well as choosing a strong root structure, you should consider whether the specimen "looks right" growing on rock, with the tree and rock forming a natural complement.

BROOM STYLE
Zelkova serrata

BROOM STYLE

Whereas a conifer grown in an ideal situation is likely to grow in formal upright style, many of the fine-branched deciduous trees, such as elms or maples, in the same situation are likely to become broom-style trees. These species are recommended for growing as bonsai in broom style, but coarse-branched deciduous trees and evergreens are not suitable.

The name derives from the fact that the shape of the tree resembles an upturned Japanese broom. The straight section of the trunk supports a symmetrical domed head of twiggy branches – deciduous broom-style trees create a beautiful display through winter, seen at their best when the structure is bare of leaves. This is a very restrained, classic bonsai style, but arguably the most difficult to achieve.

ROOT-CONNECTED AND MULTIPLE-TRUNK STYLES

This classification combines styles where several trunks grow up from a single root system. The term "multiple-trunk" is used generally for root-connected styles where there are three or more trunks.

All species can be grown in twin-trunk, clump or straight-line styles. Species suitable for sinuous style are recommended on the following page. In some cases, the design of root-connected bonsai may appear similar to group style, but the essential feature is that the trunks arise from a common root and do not represent individual trees as in a group planting. A major advantage to root-connected styles is that all the trees, springing as they do from one rootstock, exhibit the same features such as leaf shape, texture and colour, which is not necessarily the case with group plantings.

CLASPED-TO-ROCK STYLE
Pinus parviflora 'Kokonoe'

Clasped-to-rock style

This differs from root-over-rock in that the roots are confined to the rock alone and do not extend into soil contained in a conventional bonsai pot. The style represents trees in nature growing on mountains and cliffs and can be designed as a "near" or "distant" view. Depending on the design and the size and scale of the trees used, the same piece of rock can be made to appear to be several feet or several miles away. Because of the small amount of soil available for the bonsai, watering is even more critical than usual.

In this style, a flat piece of rock or slate can be used for planting in the same way as a pot, or the tree can be planted on a more upright or rugged rock which is usually displayed in a shallow tray (*suiban*) of sand or water.

As with root-over-rock styling, it is important to consider whether the tree presents a natural appearance growing on rock. Spreading beech trees, for example, do not grow in rocky mountainous areas.

TWIN-TRUNK STYLE
Acer palmatum 'Deshojo'

Twin-trunk style

This is a familiar sight in nature, occurring when a tree develops two trunks from the base. Usually, one trunk predominates and this is essential in your bonsai design to avoid an ugly catapult shape. In China and Japan, such designs are called "father-and-son" or "mother-and-daughter" styles. The smaller trunk grows in close proximity to the larger and more dominant trunk, and is protected and influenced by it. The trunks may divide at or just above soil level, and sometimes a low branch is trained and styled as a second trunk.

Twin-trunk is the most commonly seen multiple-trunk style, but the principle applies to three, five or seven trunks, and so on.

Clump style

This is where several trunks arise from the same root in a clump formation, spreading out from the base as each one reaches out for its own light. Many examples of this style exist in old English woodlands where coppicing was practised. This was an early method of timber production whereby trees were sawn off at ground level and the resulting vigorous new shoots that developed provided straight, slender poles suitable for fencing and other construction work. Some trees have a natural tendency to develop multiple trunks in clump style.

CLUMP STYLE
Rhododendron obtusum

SINUOUS STYLE
Chaenomeles japonica 'Chojubai'

STRAIGHT-LINE STYLE
Ilex serrata

Straight-line style

Also called raft style, this is based on a tree in nature that has fallen or blown over but has continued to grow, with the original branches reaching up vertically to become trunks. In bonsai, this gives scope to make an interesting design from a poor tree with one-sided branches, material that would not be suitable for a single specimen bonsai.

Sinuous style

This style in nature can occur when suckers arise from surface roots or where a very low branch rubs on and roots into the ground, thereby layering itself and producing extra trunks. The best species to use to create this style are those with flexible trunks and branches (such as pine and yew) or a tendency to throw up suckers from exposed roots (as do the elm and quince). Trees that do not have these characteristics are less suitable.

The word "sinuous" implies that the ground-level pattern of the trunks can be curving or twisted because suckering growth may be random, whereas with the straight-line style, the original trunk line dictates the above-ground relationships of the new trunks.

GROUP PLANTING

This planting method recreates the effect of several trees growing together, or a spinney, wood or forest. The look must be natural and uncontrived and this is easier to achieve if odd numbers of trees are used.

Group or forest plantings contain a minimum of three or five trees. Odd numbers are used until a sufficiently high number is reached to demand concentration in counting the trunks. In practice, this means that a group would never be composed of four trees; fourteen could form an acceptable design, and forty would create a natural forest effect.

Most species are suited to group style. As with all bonsai designs, the group should represent something that you would see in nature: for example, a beech wood makes a striking effect, whereas a forest of wisteria trees would look incongruous.

GROUP PLANTING
Acer palmatum 'Ukon'

SAIKEI

Also described as "tray landscape", saikei is a way of representing a landscape in detail. Trees, rocks, grasses, mosses and sands can be used to create the natural variations of landscape which appear in nature. Saikei can be enjoyed as an instant short-term composition, which can then be dismantled. The materials can then be re-used for another landscape view, or the trees can be "promoted" to become individual bonsai as they mature.

Saikei as a "training ground" for bonsai trees was the original idea of Toshio Kawamoto of Japan, who invented the word saikei – usually interpreted in English as "living landscape" – to differentiate tray landscapes with living plants from designs with artificial or no plants. "Bonkei" means tray landscape, in which real or artificial plants may be used, or no plants at all. In saikei, there must be living plants.

Saikei has come to be recognized as an individual style category of bonsai, and the plantings are typically enjoyed as permanent displays. With careful choice of material and attention to the scale and proportion of the design, saikei forms a literal recreation of landscape in miniature.

SAIKEI
Chamaecyparis obtusa 'Yatsubusa'

CONTAINERS

The container is part of the bonsai design and it is usual to choose the pot for the tree after styling, to find one that complements it in size, shape, colour and finish. The size as well as the shape of the pot should create a good balance with the height and spread of the tree. Its colour and finish should be appropriate to the character of the tree, either harmonizing with or complementing the natural colours and textures.

There are a few essential practical points to consider when selecting the container. It should drain easily, having adequate drainage holes finished flush with the interior of the pot base, and it must be frost-proof. It must hold enough soil to accommodate the tree's roots and allow for the development of the root system that will take place over one or two years of growth before the tree needs repotting.

Traditionally, bonsai pots are shallow as compared, say, to pots used for houseplants or patio shrubs, but the container must allow enough moisture to be retained to keep the tree healthy. For practical reasons a relatively deep pot is sometimes necessary – for example, for a fruiting tree that has a particularly high requirement for moisture during the period when the fruits are swelling. The depth of the pot also relates to the visual mass of the tree. A dense evergreen with a thick trunk demands a deeper pot than a slender-trunked maple with a crown of delicate leaves. The

relationship between tree and pot creates balance in the composition (see also pages 30 and 31).

There is no advantage to planting a tree in a bonsai container over-large for the tree's size and requirements, in the hope of saving time on watering. If the tree cannot use all the moisture retained in the pot, the roots may become waterlogged and rotten. The size, shape and depth of the pot also establish the base of the overall composition, and you should be aware of sympathetic proportions between the tree and the pot, an essential aspect of bonsai design.

The interior of a bonsai pot is unglazed, although the exterior may be glazed or unglazed. Natural earth colours and an unglazed finish are usually preferred, as these characteristics coexist most easily with various different styles and characteristics of many species of tree or shrub used for bonsai.

Very bright or pale-coloured pots are usually inappropriate, but sometimes a well-chosen colour forms a striking complement to a tree with distinctive colouring, perhaps a species with bright autumn foliage colour or brilliant flowers. Ceramic glazes can produce very subtle colour combinations, however, and there are some discreet but lustrous effects in more subdued hues that correspond well to the colours of nature. There are interesting effects of colour and texture such as speckling and crackle-glaze.

Rectangular pot with sculpted corners

"Cloud"-shaped pot

Hexagonal cascade pot

Round cascade pot

Incurved "drum" pot

Rectangular pot with flared rim

Small "drum" pot

Small rectangular pot

Oval water tray (suiban)

Mame pots

"Burnished" rectangular pot

Shallow round pot

SIZE OF CONTAINER

Just as bonsai can be small enough to balance on your hand or large enough to stand higher than a person, so it follows that container sizes must vary to the same extent. The aesthetic considerations vary somewhat with the scale of the pot. A pot 75cm (30in) long by 10cm (4in) deep presents a solid visual mass which needs to be subdued in colour and texture in order not to dominate the entire composition of the bonsai. Conversely, a 5cm (2in) tree in a pot only 2.5cm (1in) by 1.2cm (1/2in) can be easily overlooked on exhibition, and in this case it is appropriate to have a more brightly coloured pot that makes the bonsai more noticeable.

There is a different emphasis in the proportions of large and small pots for practical reasons. In a small pot, greater depth is required in proportion to the overall size in order to provide an adequate reservoir for soil and water, whereas larger pots that give more room for root spread can be relatively shallow.

Pot sizes
An attractively coloured glazed pot (above) is acceptable in small-scale bonsai. Bonsai pots vary widely in size, shape and colour (right).

PREPARING A POT

The first step towards potting up a tree as bonsai is to choose a container suitable for the particular size, style and species of tree. It is then essential to prepare the pot adequately to receive the tree. A good bonsai pot has large drainage holes to allow free drainage of moisture, but these must be covered in a way that prevents the potting soil from being washed out in watering. The old-style method of crocking a container with pieces of broken pot is inappropriate to bonsai, as the pieces take up too much room in the shallow containers and can shift out of place as the tree roots are settled into the pot.

The usual solution is to secure small squares of vinyl mesh over the drainage holes, held in place with twists of wire to prevent movement. With round drainage holes, the wire twists are secured on either side of the hole. If the holes are rectangular, set the wires diagonally across them, otherwise they can slip out of place.

It is a common mistake to save time by covering the whole base of the pot with mesh. But the roots of the tree become entangled in the mesh, causing unnecessary difficulty and damage when it comes to repotting the bonsai.

Inserting anchorage wires

It is always advisable to anchor the tree securely in the pot. This is particularly critical with evergreens, because the dense foliage is wind-resistant and the tree may be rocked in the pot by heavy winds. Newly potted trees that have not had time to establish a rootball are also very vulnerable if not tied down within the pot.

The simplest method of anchorage is a single wire running underneath the pot base and up through the drainage holes. The ends of the wire are twisted together at the back of the tree after the rootball has been settled. The larger the pot, the more wires you may need, for example, at front and back of the tree. (For repotting technique, see pages 173 to 175).

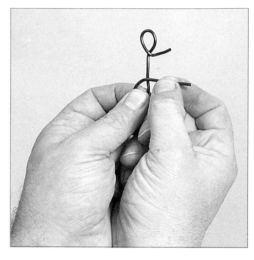

1 Cut a length of wire and form each end into a loop with a short tail. The width between loops equals the diameter of the drainage hole.

2 Cut small rectangles of plastic mesh of a size to fit over the drainage holes. Make enough mesh squares and wire twists to cover all the holes.

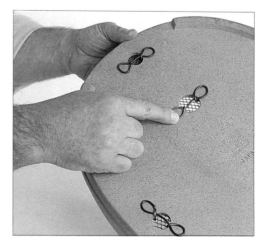

3 Place mesh over the hole inside the pot, turn it over and push the ends of the wire twists through the hole, opening them out on the inside.

4 Cut a long piece of wire. Push one end through a drainage hole at one side of the pot, take it under the base and up through a hole on the other side.

CONTAINER STYLES

The choice of containers includes wide variation in size, shape and detail. Any specialist bonsai supplier should be able to offer an attractive range of container styles and sizes. Currently, Japanese manufacturers dominate the worldwide market for good-quality mass-produced and handmade bonsai pots, with potteries in the Tokoname region holding the major market share. It is a relatively recent development that bonsai pots of equal quality have become available from ceramicists in western countries. There is still little scope for mass-produced containers in the west, because the home markets are as yet relatively small, but there are now many designers in countries around the world who are producing interesting handmade bonsai pots and gaining a wider reputation for their products.

This "catalogue" of bonsai pots illustrates a general selection from the range of containers that should be readily available. Many of the styles can be obtained in several sizes and are suited to variations of bonsai style and tree species.

MAME POTS

These very small pots, known as mame *pots, vary in size from only 1.2cm (¹/₂in) to 4cm (¹/₂in). The colours and finishes are designed to draw attention to the tiny containers.*

Rectangular unglazed brown Japanese Tokoname pot (left)
This is a very formal pot with sharp edges suitable for a formal tree. This example is relatively deep and would be used for a tree with a heavy trunk or strong visual mass.

"Cloud"-shaped unglazed brown Japanese Tokoname pot (right)
This shape is a hybrid between the sharp lines of the rectangle and the shallow curve of the oval pot. It is versatile, suited to a wide range of styles and species, as is the discreet unglazed finish.

Oval glazed green Japanese Tokoname pot (above)
Oval containers are very commonly used in bonsai, being complementary to most styles and species. The coloured glaze of this example would offset a flowering tree or deciduous species with brightly coloured foliage.

Round glazed green Japanese Tokoname pot (right)
A round pot is particularly complementary to an upright, slender tree. Again, a glazed finish is best suited to a more colourful tree.

"Drum"-style unglazed red Japanese Tokoname pot (above)
This shape of pot is named after the shape of a Japanese drum. It provides a simple masculine style suitable for rugged bonsai, for example, a literati-style tree.

Oval unglazed red-brown Japanese Tokoname pot (left)
The crisp lines of this oval pot give it a slightly formal style while the horizontal band visually reduces the depth. The colour would be a good choice for a Chinese juniper, picking up the bark colour.

Oval matt-glazed "onyx" pot by Petra Engelke (below)
This is a quietly dramatic pot with subtle lines that would spectacularly offset a red-leaved maple or similar bright-foliaged or flowering tree.

Oval "Schilf"-glazed pot by Petra Engelke (right)
The beautifully subtle colouring of this container would look good with hawthorn, birch, beech, hornbeam and other such strong-looking, green-leaved trees.

Oval unglazed grey Japanese Tokoname pot (right)
A softly elegant but formal shape provides a versatile pot that could be used for a range of trees from a heavy-trunked maple to an informal pine.

Oval unglazed brown Japanese Tokoname pot (below)
This simple shallow oval is designed for group or saikei plantings. The surface area allows the necessary feeling of space for a landscape effect.

Rectangular matt-glazed brown pot by Bryan Albright (below)
This is an unassuming design with clean lines that would not detract from a gently formal tree.

Rectangular glazed brown pot by Bryan Albright (left)
This relatively deep pot has an old-looking, Chinese-style effect that would be equally suited to a heavy-trunked hornbeam, hawthorn or crab apple.

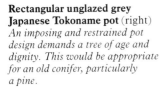

Rectangular unglazed brown Japanese Tokoname pot (right)
This is a classical, formal shape, although its starkness is somewhat softened by the impressed panel. This style and proportion of pot is becoming less popular with the current taste for informal bonsai.

Rectangular matt-glazed grey pot by Bryan Albright (above)
This solidly masculine shallow pot would provide a stable base for a broom-style tree or a rugged group planting.

Rectangular unglazed grey Japanese Tokoname pot (right)
An imposing and restrained pot design demands a tree of age and dignity. This would be appropriate for an old conifer, particularly a pine.

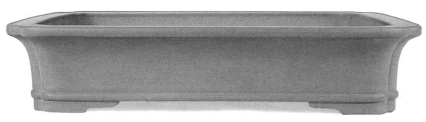

Rectangular unglazed grey Japanese Tokoname pot (below)
The effect here is very similar to that of the example far left, but the shallower depth requires a tree of less weight and mass.

Rectangular unglazed grey Japanese Tokoname pot (left)
This modified rectangle has a softened effect due to the sculpted corners and incurved lip. It would be suited to an informal tree, but one with a thick trunk and strongly massed silhouette.

Unglazed brown Tokoname cascade pot (left)
In cascade-style bonsai the height of the pot must accommodate the fall of the tree. In the proportions of this clean-lined rectangular shape, the height is twice the width of the pot at its rim.

Irregular "rock"-shape unglazed brown Tokoname pot (below)
An irregular design of this type is usually used to display a rugged slanting, windswept or semicascade tree, but can alternatively hold small herbaceous or alpine plants forming an accessory or accent planting.

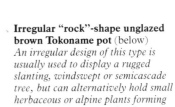

Unglazed brown Tokoname semicascade pot (above)
The depth of the semicascade pot relates to the horizontal or downward spread of the tree, this example having a very clean, strong shape and plain surface finish.

Unglazed grey Tokoname cascade pot (left)
This cascade pot has a softer effect than the previous example due to the hexagonal cross-section and flaring lip.

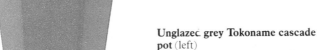

TOOLS

To the beginner, there seems to be a bewildering number of tools available. Over the years, many of these tools have been designed for specific purposes and although you may feel that you will not need them all, it is useful to know the different types of tools and what they are used for.

If you are concerned purely with maintenance – that is, grooming and repotting existing bonsai – you will need a much less comprehensive tool kit than if you are about to create a bonsai from, say, a large overgrown trunk lifted from the ground, that requires sawing and sculpting.

Similarly, if your trees are all small or extra-small, you have no need of heavy duty wire cutters, but if you work with large trees these cutters are essential.

Most of the specialized tools for bonsai are designed and made in Japan, but they are readily available in most parts of the world. There are some items for which you will be able to find domestic equivalents. As with all types of tools, quality varies considerably across the range. Good quality tools are expensive, but poor quality tools usually turn out to be a false economy.

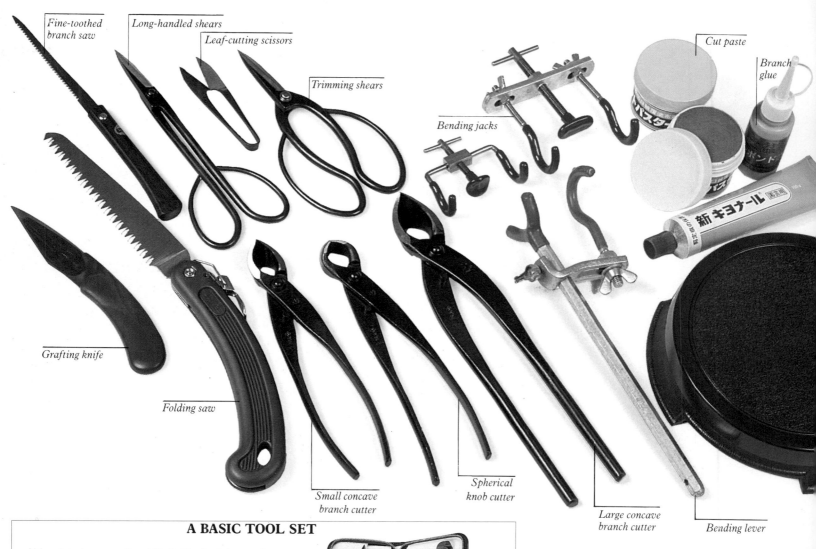

Fine-toothed branch saw

Long-handled shears

Leaf-cutting scissors

Trimming shears

Cut paste

Branch glue

Bending jacks

Grafting knife

Folding saw

Small concave branch cutter

Spherical knob cutter

Large concave branch cutter

Bending lever

A BASIC TOOL SET

Although tools are usually sold individually, it is sometimes possible to buy selected tools as a set. This example is a basic first tool set including the two essential pruning tools, trimming shears and a concave branch cutter, together with a wire cutter. More comprehensive sets are available for advanced work, but many bonsai enthusiasts prefer to buy an empty tool case and build up a collection of tools to suit their own range of work.

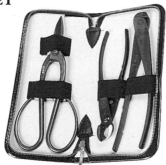

Pruning and cutting tools
When you buy tools, consider the type and size of bonsai you wish to work with. Large trees require large, strong tools, while extra-small trees demand finer, more delicate tools. Details of the essential tools and how to use them are shown on page 58.

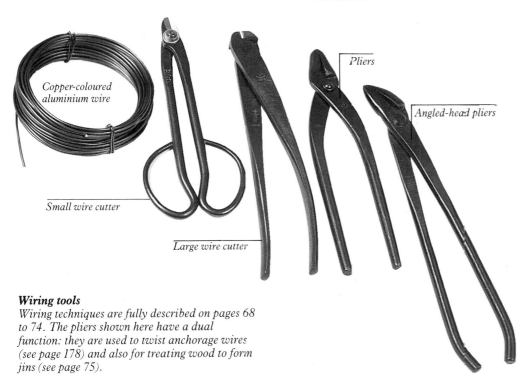

*Copper-coloured
aluminium wire*

Small wire cutter

Large wire cutter

Pliers

Angled-head pliers

Wiring tools
Wiring techniques are fully described on pages 68 to 74. The pliers shown here have a dual function: they are used to twist anchorage wires (see page 178) and also for treating wood to form jins (see page 75).

POWER TOOLS

POWER TOOLS

Sometimes heavy-duty power tools are required but the tools shown here are the most versatile and useful. A reciprocating saw cuts easily through tough roots, trunks and branches where space is restricted. A die grinder makes an extremely useful and controllable carving tool. A rotary tool with flexible drive is used to refine carving done by the die grinder, or can be used instead of it for work on small trees.

Die grinder

Rotary tool with flexible drive

Potting tools and equipment
These tools are required for potting trees as bonsai initially and for the regular repotting that is an essential part of routine maintenance of the bonsai (see page 173).

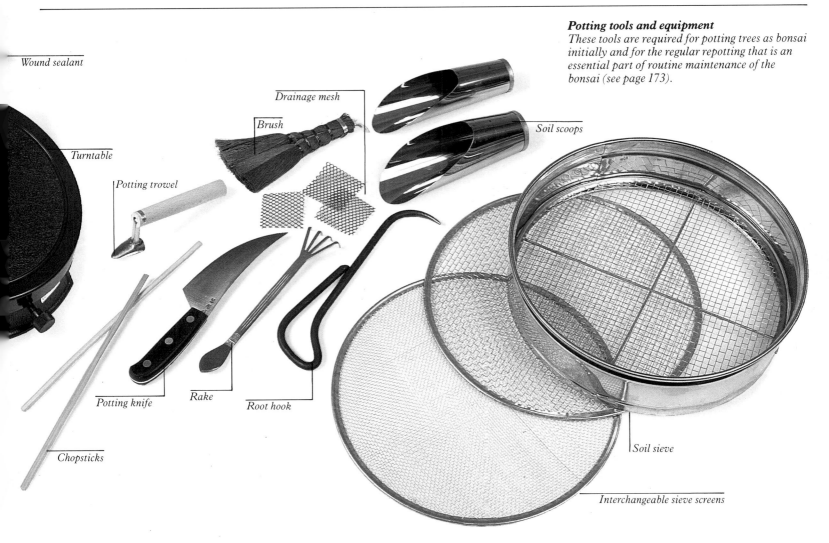

Wound sealant

Drainage mesh

Brush

Soil scoops

Turntable

Potting trowel

Potting knife

Rake

Root hook

Chopsticks

Soil sieve

Interchangeable sieve screens

USING THE ESSENTIAL TOOLS

As with any art or craft, you can begin at quite a simple level with only the most essential tools and materials and decide how to increase your stock as you develop your experience of bonsai and become more ambitious in your designs.

The six tools demonstrated here are those that you will find most useful when you begin. They include tools used in pruning, wiring and root pruning. Trimming shears and a concave branch cutter are the most important and should be the first that you buy. It is possible to grow and train bonsai using only these two items, perhaps with the addition of wire cutters, if you intend to use wiring as part of the bonsai training.

TRIMMING SHEARS

This is the basic cutting tool for trimming branches, twigs and roots. The large handles allow you to use all your fingers in the cutting motion, giving maximum power and control. It is also possible to use your fingers independently to remove pruned twigs without putting the shears down.

When correctly adjusted, the rivetted joint of the shears should not be too tight: the handles should fall open in your hand, without you having to pull them open. Blades are sharpened to a fine knife-edge, rather than a scissor-edge, which enables them to cut cleanly without crushing the stem. The tips of the blades are used for delicate twig trimming. Heavier branches, up to approximately 6mm (¼in) diameter should be cut closer to the joint of the blades where the metal is stronger and thicker. Take care when using the shears for root trimming, as potting soil containing grit can chip the blades.

When using trimming shears to cut shoots, take care to introduce the blades in a way that ensures you cut only the stem, not the foliage.

Cut cleanly through the stem in a single motion, leaving no ragged edges. A clean cut promotes sound healing of the stem.

CONCAVE BRANCH CUTTER

This cutter is used to remove a whole branch at the trunk. It leaves a concave cut so that, as the tree heals and the new cambium forms, the edges of the cut roll over and fill the concavity to heal flush with the trunk. If the branch is cut away flush with the trunk initially, as happens if you cut a branch with shears, the healing process creates an ugly bulge.

Ideally, the elliptical cut should run vertically up the trunk, as rising sap promotes stronger healing in a vertical cut than in one cutting across the trunk. For heavy branches, you may need to make the cut in two stages to get better control of the angle.

The concave branch cutter is available in various sizes. Whatever size you have, it should be used only on branches with a diameter of no more than half the width of the cutter's blades.

This angle of approach is most effective, shown here in cutting a branch growing at right angles from the trunk, but you can vary the angle.

The best angle of approach leaves a vertical concave cut as this heals more efficiently than a cut made across the trunk line.

SPHERICAL KNOB CUTTER

Also described as a wen cutter, this tool leaves a perfect spherical cut on the trunk or branch which will heal flush. The tool is a more recent development than the concave branch cutter and it leaves a better-shaped cut, but it cannot always be used to remove a branch as the angle of approach is limited. You must hold the knob cutter at right angles to the trunk, and surrounding branches often prevent this.

This tool can also be used both to whittle away at stubs too large to cut in one movement and for initial rough shaping of jins and dead wood (see page 75).

Take off most of the branch before using this tool, so that you can approach the branch stub at right angles to the trunk.

BUD-TRIMMING SHEARS

These long-reach shears are designed for trimming buds on pines and needle junipers, but are also extremely useful for light training work on trees with delicate twigs, such as maples and _Zelkova_. If you only grow small bonsai

This tool, used for trimming of buds and delicate twigs, give easy access due to the elongated, slender shape of blades and handles.

sizes, these are the best choice for basic shears.

You must be careful not to damage the blades by using the shears on twigs or branches that are too heavy for them. If you cannot cut easily through the stem with the normal action of the shears, this tool is not suitable for the work.

The sharp blades cut cleanly, leaving no ragged edges, enabling accurate cutting; as here, just above a pair of buds on the trident maple twig.

WIRE CUTTERS

Ordinary domestic wire cutters are inexpensive and can be used to cut bonsai wires to length, but are rarely accurate and strong enough to provide the precision needed when cutting wire from the tree without damage to the bark. Various qualities of Japanese purpose-made wire cutters are available and the best-quality tools are durable and dependable, provided that

they are not forced to cut wire too strong for their capacity.

When selecting wire cutters, ask for details of the maximum wire diameters recommended for the particular tool. The type of wire is also important: for example, an average pair of wire cutters may cope with 5mm diameter aluminium wire but only 3mm copper wire.

ROOT HOOK

The tool shown here is a proprietary brand metal root hook. Many growers make themselves a similar type of tool to help in combing out the roots of larger bonsai prior to root pruning. The hook has a rounded end which, when used in a radial motion from the trunk, disentangles the roots without damaging them. For smaller trees, you can use a small pronged rake, a chopstick or a round-tipped length of wooden dowel.

When using wire cutters to remove wiring from a tree, approach the cut with the blades at right angles to the wire.

The snub-nosed design of purpose-made wire cutters allows the wire to be cut close to the bark without injury to the stem.

Use the root hook in a "raking" motion to disentangle circling roots on the outer layers of the rootball.

BASIC METHODS OF CREATING BONSAI

Bonsai is often described as a form of living sculpture, recreating the impression of a tree in nature but using live material to achieve the effect. The two main methods used in creating a bonsai can be compared to the basic sculpture techniques – carving and modelling.

In carving a sculpture from a solid mass of material, the stone or wood is cut away to reveal the general shape, then surface form and texture are refined. In bonsai, a similar technique is applied to shaping a tree or shrub by pruning. This can be described as the "subtraction" method.

In modelling with a malleable material such as clay, a form is built up by adding and shaping pieces of clay until the final image is complete. In bonsai terms, this is equivalent to starting from seed or a cutting and encouraging the plant to develop gradually into the required shape. This technique can be described as the "addition" method.

The comparison with sculpture techniques provides a useful analogy for the basic practices in bonsai, but because the raw material of bonsai is alive and growing, the two methods are not mutually exclusive. Most bonsai are formed by a combination of the two; for example, a tree grown from seed is allowed to develop freely for a number of years, and is then severely pruned to reduce and shape the material. This is followed by a period of new growth, which in turn is pruned to shape. Alternatively, a young tree or shrub obtained from a garden centre or nursery is drastically pruned, allowed to develop freely over one or two growing seasons, and then is shaped and refined by less radical pruning. These processes can be repeated any number of times and with each stage, the bonsai becomes more detailed and refined.

While you can obtain good results by pruning only, you will often find that further shaping is required to achieve the best expression of a design. Wiring allows you to alter the basic structure of the bonsai by training trunk and branches into a different form or relation from that of their natural growth pattern. This is not harmful to the tree and the technique is easily acquired with practice (see page 68).

PRUNING TO SHAPE

A quick and easy method of achieving the basis of a bonsai design almost instantaneously is to acquire a well-shaped, vigorous young shrub from a garden centre and cut away the branches to create a more refined image. For this, you apply the basic "subtraction" method.

This example shows a pyracantha, the original shrub a mass of freely developed, slender branches densely clothed with glossy green foliage. With pruning, an attractive slanting trunk line emerges. The branches have been thinned out and shortened to create a graceful triangular silhouette with a slightly domed apex and extended lower branches providing asymmetrical balance. With the roots trimmed, the bonsai is potted in a speckled cream glazed oval container to complete the design.

Using this simple approach, you can create a bonsai in minutes from suitable nursery or garden centre stock. A more detailed explanation of the method is shown on pages 62 and 63.

Six-year-old garden centre plant

The same plant after pruning and repotting

FIRETHORN
Pyracantha 'Teton'

GROWING FROM SEED

The "addition" method gives maximum control over the bonsai, as the grower supervises every stage of the tree's development. When you propagate a plant from seed, or a cutting, you can encourage it to develop characteristics suitable for bonsai which nursery-grown stock intended for garden planting may not have.

The seedling is cultivated in a pot until it has achieved sufficient size and resilience to be planted in open ground, where the trunk and branches will grow stronger and thicker over a period of years. This is more efficient than continuing to grow the plant in a container, as two years in open ground can achieve an amount of growth that may take twenty years if it is pot-grown. While the tree or shrub is in the ground, the branches are trimmed back to encourage bushy growth. The roots are also trimmed back every winter, either by using a sharp spade to cut them while the plant is still in the ground, or by lifting the plant to trim the roots and then replanting. This practice is important, as it causes a fibrous root system to develop close to the trunk.

The tree or shrub can then be lifted and the roots and branches pruned to design the basic form of the bonsai. It will then continue to develop in the bonsai container, pruned and trained as necessary to refine the design. The stages of this process are demonstrated by the example of a Japanese white pine grown from seed, on pages 66 and 67.

Ten-year-old tree

Six-year-old tree

Three-year-old tree

Two-year-old tree

JAPANESE LARCH
Larix kaempferi

WIRING TECHNIQUES

The trunk and branches of a tree can, if reasonably flexible, be trained into a different shape or direction by wiring. Wire is wound in a spiral, at an angle of 45 degrees, along the length of a trunk or branch. The shape of the tree can then be adjusted by, for example, twisting a branch into a different position or bending the trunk into gentle curves, and the wire will hold the new arrangement in place.

The wire is bound tightly enough to encourage the branch or trunk to accept the new curve or angle – wiring may be left in place for any period from a few months to a year – but must be removed before it cuts into the surface, as this causes disfiguring scars which may take many years to grow out.

You can apply wiring to bonsai created by either of the basic methods described here or, as is more common, formed by a combination of the two methods. Detailed information on types of wire and techniques of wiring is given on pages 68 to 71.

The same plant after pruning and wiring

Six-year-old garden centre plant

CHINESE JUNIPER
Juniperus × media 'Blaauw'

PRUNING TO SHAPE

The simplest and quickest method of creating a bonsai is to buy a healthy small shrub from a garden centre and prune it back to give it a distinctive shape and style. This method is highly recommended for the beginner in bonsai. Instant results are possible – the sequence of pruning shown here was completed in only 15 minutes. The material is comparatively inexpensive and if your first attempt is not successful, your second may produce a masterpiece. It gives you an immediate introduction to bonsai as compared to techniques of growing from seed or cuttings, with which you will have to wait years to see the effectiveness of your bonsai design.

The success of this method naturally depends on obtaining suitable material. Choose a shrub with a sturdy, thick trunk, and a good trunk line that can form the basis of the design. It should also have plenty of branches in good proportion to the trunk and compact twigs or foliage growing close to the trunk.

You will need a hardy and adaptable species with small leaves suited to bonsai scale, and small flowers or fruits, if you want a bonsai with these seasonal features. Cotoneasters and pyracanthas are ideal for this treatment, and other suitable material includes *Chaenomeles japonica*, *Jasminum nudiflorum* and the smaller shrubby varieties of *Lonicera*. For a first attempt, it is helpful to select a deciduous species in which the basic structure can be clearly seen when the branches are bare of leaves. You can prune it to shape in late winter, or in early spring just before the leaf buds unfurl.

PRUNING A COTONEASTER

The rockspray cotoneaster (*Cotoneaster horizontalis*) is an excellent subject for a first attempt at bonsai. It is strong-growing, with prolific shoots and branches that respond well to clipping. It breaks buds from old wood and often forms an interesting trunk without training. In a young plant, the branch structure develops in a flat herringbone arrangement, but after pruning the branches soon send out new shoots in all directions.

The specimen used for this demonstration was originally bought from a garden centre but has been planted out in a growing bed for some years to thicken the trunk. The cotoneaster, six to eight years old, has just been lifted from the growing bed. Bare of foliage in late winter, it shows a strong, twisting trunk line and a mass of crossing, twiggy branches. The nodes from which new shoots will emerge in spring are closely spaced, giving the branches a "serrated" appearance.

As well as pruning the branches to shape the bonsai, it is necessary to cut back the mass of roots that the shrub has developed in open-ground or container growing in the nursery. Root pruning (see page 173) encourages the growth of new feeder roots and the trimmed roots settle easily into a shallow bonsai container. You should aim to produce a shallow root system while preserving as many fibrous roots as possible.

The bonsai material
The rootball of the lifted shrub is still clogged with soil from the growing bed. The branches are slender and extended, some showing the typical herringbone pattern of the fine twigs.

1 Gently loosen the soil in the rootball and use a metal root hook to comb out the roots. Disentangle them carefully, working in a radial pattern from the trunk base.

2 Cut back the longer roots and remove heavy downward-growing ones. Rotate the shrub, preferably at eye level, to find the view most suitable for the front of the bonsai.

3 Prune away the twiggy growth to expose the trunk line. Leave an interesting arrangement of shortened branches on which new foliage can develop close to the trunk.

The bonsai in leaf
*Within a few months, the bonsai has become
attractively clothed with small, fresh green
leaves. Now that the silhouette has filled out, it
can be seen that the design holds a good balance
in the alternating directions of the branches
springing out from the trunk and the way the
visual weight of the foliage is distributed between
the lower trunk and apex of the bonsai. It is
surprising how easily this elegant tree-like form
has been created out of the sprawling mass of
branches seen in the bare-stemmed shrub.*

Foliage *The fresh green new foliage
grows close to the trunk.*

Trunk *The natural curve of the
trunk has been made clearly visible
through selective pruning, creating a
good example of informal upright
style.*

Structure *The major branches and
foliage masses are concentrated on
the outer curve of the trunk, giving a
balanced silhouette.*

4 Select a suitable container, prepare the pot
and plant the bonsai (see page 174). A
shallow oval container is used here, balancing
the height and width of the tree.

CLIP AND GROW METHOD

This is a two-stage process, longer term than simple pruning to shape. The technique involves a more radical adaptation of the original material. Drastic pruning precedes a period of regrowth that produces results in the following growing season – the full sequence shown here represents the development of the bonsai over a little more than one year from the original pruning.

The clip and grow method is a combination of subtraction – cutting away unwanted material – and addition – allowing new branches to develop which form the structure of the bonsai. It can be used to develop a more dramatic design than will be achieved only by pruning, emphasizing sharp angles between trunk and branches and encouraging an aged or rugged appearance.

STYLING A FLOWERING CHERRY

Prunus subhirtella 'Autumnalis', the autumn cherry, is a an excellent choice for bonsai. Unlike many other cherries that have coarse twigs and leaves and a short flowering period, the autumn cherry has a branching pattern of delicate twigs, fine leaves, and small flowers that appear in successive flushes during mild spells from late autumn to spring. The autumn leaf colour – shades of yellow and orange – also provides a good display.

The material used in this demonstration is a grafted cherry bought from a garden centre. Two to three years after grafting it is a slender, bushy plant. The branches are cut to leave a small stump or shoulder, rather than cutting right into the trunk, because cherries throw new shoots at the required downward angle from underneath each shoulder. Once each new shoot has gained in vigour, the shoulder can be trimmed back more neatly.

1 Choose a plant with a sturdy trunk and vigorous growth. Find the view that will make the front of the bonsai (see page 28).

2 Prune back the fibrous roots and shorten heavy roots to create a compact root system radiating from the base of the trunk.

3 Tilt the plant and cut away heavy roots on the underside of the rootball, to leave a flat root system to fit the bonsai pot.

4 Use concave branch pruners to remove branches. Leave a small shoulder each time from which new shoots can develop.

5 Apply cut paste or other suitable wound sealant to preserve moisture in the trunk and prevent the bonsai from drying out.

6 When the pruning is completed, plant the tree in a ceramic training pot. This ensures good drainage and healthy root development.

The bonsai after one year
One year later, in late winter, a cherry shows a considerable amount of new growth, with slender straight branches extending from points where previously branches were cut away. Flower buds are forming on the new stems.

Flowers *Flower flushes are successive through winter into spring. Future pruning will cause twiggier growth to form, producing more flowers.*

Branches *The branches are beginning to form a balanced, tree-like structure.*

Trunk *An advantage of this method is that a sturdy trunk exists from the start, although the bonsai itself is only one year old. It would take years to get to this stage growing a tree from seed.*

Seasonal interest *The flowers will be followed by a mass of small, oval, bright green leaves that will turn to orange in autumn.*

Container *The relatively deep training pot has provided moisture, ventilation and frost protection over the year, while the severely pruned roots developed new growth. The tree can now be potted into a shallow bonsai pot.*

The bonsai in flower
Two months later, the tree has come into flower and will soon break leaf. In future seasons, the tree will be potted into a bonsai pot and the branches wired to refine the shape and style of the bonsai and encourage more prolific flowering.

PRUNING AND WIRING

Creating a bonsai by pruning only is easily done with shrubs, such as cotoneaster or pyracantha, or with dwarf conifers, but it is seldom possible with taller-growing trees. It is unlikely that you will find suitable material for bonsai among garden centre stock, so it may be necessary to grow the tree yourself from seed or a cutting. As you work on styling the bonsai, you will discover that simply pruning the tree does not necessarily create a well-balanced design. In this case, you need to apply wiring to give you more control over the structure of the bonsai.

This demonstration of pruning and wiring a Japanese white pine shows how wiring can improve and refine a design initially created by pruning. Full explanation of wiring techniques is given on pages 68 to 71.

GROWING A JAPANESE WHITE PINE FROM SEED

A typical pine from a garden centre will be a relatively large tree with a straight, parallel-sided trunk, and "wheel-spoke" branches spaced at intervals of about 60-90cm (2-3ft), carrying the foliage at a similar distance from the trunk of the tree. These characteristics are quite unsuitable for bonsai.

The ideal material for bonsai should have a tapered trunk, numerous branches with short intervals between them, and compact foliage growing close to the trunk. Usually the only way to obtain a pine tree that provides these features is to grow it yourself. Growing a tree from seed (full details of sowing seed are given on pages 184 and 185) is a lengthy process, but it ensures that you have suitable raw material for bonsai styling. After several years, the young tree can be trimmed and shaped by pruning and wiring to create a pleasing arrangement of branches and a balanced silhouette. Further refinement of the design may extend over a period of several more years after the bonsai has been potted and styled.

The bonsai material

This sequence shows the development of a Japanese white pine (*Pinus parviflora*) from a one-year-old seedling to a tree of suitable age and size for bonsai training.

After one year, the seedling is transferred from the seed tray to a 6.25cm (2½in) diameter pot. This is allowed to grow on untrimmed for three years, potted on into successively larger pots as the roots develop.

In the four-year-old seedling, the trunk is still very slender but the internodal distances – the spacing of branches and foliage – are very short. The next priority is to fatten the trunk, so the pine is planted in open ground in a prepared growing bed.

After five years in open ground, with adequate watering and feeding, the tree has developed a sturdy trunk and branch structure. New candle growth, compact young shoots that develop all over the tree, has been cropped back each spring to encourage a dense mass of foliage.

One-year-old seedling   *Four-year-old tree*   *Nine-year-old tree*

1 Comb out the roots with a metal root hook to eliminate crossing roots. Shorten them as little as is necessary to make a shallow root system that will fit a bonsai pot.

2 Select the front view of the bonsai (see page 28). Prune surplus branches to refine the structure, using concave branch cutters to cut branches a short distance from the trunk.

3 About half of the foliage mass has been removed by this stage. A stub has been left near the base of the trunk which can be used to form a jin (see page 75).

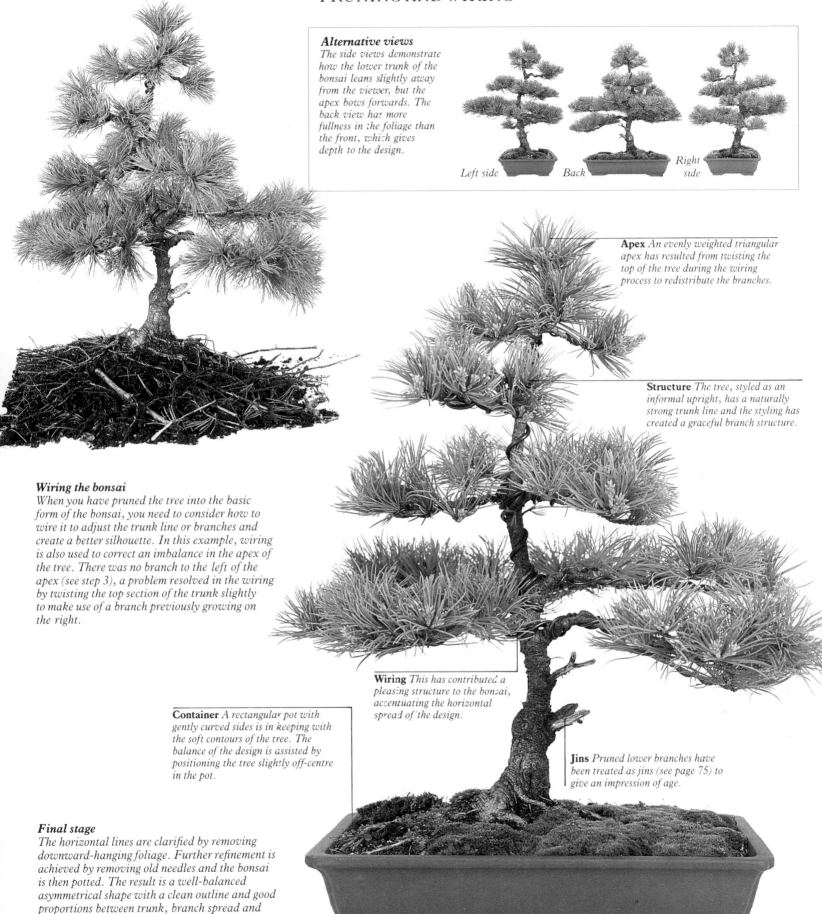

Alternative views

The side views demonstrate how the lower trunk of the bonsai leans slightly away from the viewer, but the apex bows forwards. The back view has more fullness in the foliage than the front, which gives depth to the design.

Left side   Back   Right side

Apex *An evenly weighted triangular apex has resulted from twisting the top of the tree during the wiring process to redistribute the branches.*

Structure *The tree, styled as an informal upright, has a naturally strong trunk line and the styling has created a graceful branch structure.*

Wiring the bonsai

When you have pruned the tree into the basic form of the bonsai, you need to consider how to wire it to adjust the trunk line or branches and create a better silhouette. In this example, wiring is also used to correct an imbalance in the apex of the tree. There was no branch to the left of the apex (see step 3), a problem resolved in the wiring by twisting the top section of the trunk slightly to make use of a branch previously growing on the right.

Wiring *This has contributed a pleasing structure to the bonsai, accentuating the horizontal spread of the design.*

Container *A rectangular pot with gently curved sides is in keeping with the soft contours of the tree. The balance of the design is assisted by positioning the tree slightly off-centre in the pot.*

Jins *Pruned lower branches have been treated as jins (see page 75) to give an impression of age.*

Final stage

The horizontal lines are clarified by removing downward-hanging foliage. Further refinement is achieved by removing old needles and the bonsai is then potted. The result is a well-balanced asymmetrical shape with a clean outline and good proportions between trunk, branch spread and foliage masses. From wiring to completion, the final stages have taken just over one hour.

WIRING

This is a technique which enables you to shape a tree by changing the direction of trunk or branches. It can be used to create or refine a bonsai design. Once the technique of wiring has been mastered, many more design possibilities are revealed. For example, branches with naturally upward growth can be wired to spread horizontally, or sweep downwards to give an impression of age in a relatively young tree. Initially, wiring is applied to shaping of the trunk and main branches. Subsequent new growth needs wiring and rewiring for maintenance and refinement.

Wiring is a technical skill that requires practice, but with some care it is easily learnt. It is often more difficult for the bonsai enthusiast to accept the need for wiring, although many famous and beautiful bonsai could not have been created without using this important technique. The examples on these pages, and throughout the book, demonstrate the various ways in which wiring makes the final contribution to the beauty and refinement of the bonsai image.

WHEN TO WIRE

In theory, wiring can be done at any time, although trees are more liable to be damaged by the process in spring and summer when they are full of sap and have young, soft shoots, or in early autumn when the wood is likely to be thickening. As a general rule, you can wire evergreen trees at any time, but the best time for wiring conifers is between late autumn and early spring when the tree is in its dormant period, and while it is still too early for new buds to appear.

With deciduous trees, it is easiest for the beginner to see what changes are needed in the structure during winter when the branches are bare, but in cold weather the wood may be brittle and susceptible to damage. The best time to wire deciduous trees is as they become active in spring,

Before wiring

After wiring

Apex *The branches have been opened out to create a more balanced shape.*

Foliage *Detail wiring has been applied to spread the foliage horizontally, creating the flat planes typical of the mature cedar.*

Silhouette *A branch previously growing on the left-hand side of the tree has been taken to the back to give depth to the design.*

Direction *Lower branches have been wired and brought downwards to create a more natural and elegant effect.*

Shaping the tree by wiring
*This slanting-style specimen of the blue cedar (*Cedrus atlantica glauca, *above) was last wired five years previously. Branches that were trained in a downward direction have now begun to lift up towards the light, the typical tendency of an unwired tree. Wiring is again applied (right) to refine the shape, adjusting the directions and growth pattern of the branches.*

before the delicate leaf buds have opened, or in autumn, just before dormancy. However, deciduous trees that have been leaf-cut, such as elms and maples, are best wired immediately after the leaves have been removed. The branches are more flexible at this time, and there is less chance of the wire biting in, as the growth is not so vigorous as in spring.

Stop watering two or three days before wiring. A trunk or branch retaining moisture is more difficult to manipulate, so the tree is more flexible if it is not recently watered.

HOW LONG TO LEAVE THE WIRE

The period for which the wire should be left on the tree varies according to a number of factors – the thickness of the trunk or branch, the type of tree, the quality and age of the wood. A thick branch is more resistant to training than a slender one; young and pliable trunks or branches set in place more easily than old wood.

You need to check the wiring regularly to make sure it does not begin to cut into the bark as the tree continues to grow and thicken. For deciduous trees, wiring can be left in place for three to six months, for evergreens, six months to a year.

REMOVING THE WIRE

You can remove the wire by unwinding it or, preferably, by cutting it away in small pieces. Cutting lessens the risk of damaging the tree. If you have left the wire too long and it has cut into the bark, unwind it carefully, following the direction of the original wiring. If the bark is deeply cut, apply a wound sealant.

After removing the wire, you must again be watchful, as some trees are more likely than others to revert to the original position. This occurs slowly, but once it has started to happen, you will have to rewire. The second wiring can follow the direction of the first, but if the tree is wire-scarred, you should wind the wire in the opposite direction from the previous wiring.

TYPES OF WIRE

The two most common types of wire used for bonsai are aluminium and copper. Copper wire must be annealed to soften it so that it bends more easily, and it is sometimes possible to buy pre-annealed copper wire. Non-annealed wire is freely available: the process of annealing involves heating the wire in a low-temperature fire until it glows a bright cherry red colour, then allowing it to cool slowly. If it is overheated it becomes brittle.

Copper wire has been traditionally preferred for bonsai wiring for its strength, which enables relatively small-gauge wires to be used, and its sympathetic colour. Both of these characteristics make copper wire less obtrusive than aluminium. Copper is recommended for wiring conifers because it holds the comparatively elastic wood quite securely. It does have disadvantages: it tends to harden with time, increasing the risk of damaging the bonsai when the wire is removed; it is not always possible to buy the wire pre-annealed; and if it is to be re-used, it must be re-annealed.

Aluminium wire is recommended for deciduous trees. It is less likely to damage the bark, being lighter and softer than copper wire, but it is less strong, so a thicker gauge must be used to apply the necessary control to the trunk or branch. However, the softness makes aluminium easier to remove than copper wire, and it can be re-used.

The bright, silvery colour of aluminium is inappropriate to the natural colouring of trees, so it is preferable to use aluminium wire which has been treated to give it a duller, copper-coloured finish. This is readily available and is the most widely used type.

Gauge and length of wire

There are many different thicknesses of wire, and you should carefully match the wire gauge to the size and vigour of the trunk or branch to be wired. As a rule of thumb, a wire gauge between one-sixth and one-third the diameter of the wood is recommended, but you must also take into account the age and resistance of the wood and how drastically you have to bend it when shaping the bonsai.

To estimate the length of wire that you need, allow one and a third times the length of the trunk or branch that you are wiring. This allows for the wire to be wound around the branch at a 45 degree angle, the best angle for effective wiring. It is very important not to cross the wires, not only because this looks unattractive, but because if by chance the wires do bite into the wood, the crossing creates a "tourniquet" that cuts off the supply of sap, killing the trunk or branch beyond that point.

Removing the wire
The wire is cut away in small sections to avoid damage that might be caused by unwinding it.

Wire biting in
Wire left too long on this Japanese white pine is causing the branch to swell.

Wire scarring
When the wire is removed, the disfigurement is evident. This can take years to grow out.

WIRING TECHNIQUES

It is important to learn how to wire a tree neatly and accurately. Many people seem unconcerned about neatness, but careless wiring will be reflected in unsatisfactory shaping of the tree. When you begin to practise the technique of wiring it is very time-consuming to get it right, but once you achieve neatness and accuracy, speed will follow.

Before you start, make sure that you have adequate supplies of wire in the gauges you are likely to need. Equip yourself with wire cutters of sufficient strength to cut the wires. You may also need pliers to hold the wire and help you to finish off at the ends.

If you are working on a tree with heavy branches that may need to be bent quite drastically, you may require raffia to wind around the branches before wiring, which will protect the bark surface. It is also sometimes advisable to wrap the wire with strips of paper when you are working on delicate or soft twigs.

The wire must be securely anchored to be effective. For a trunk or low branch, the wire can be anchored in the soil. With higher branches, it is usual to wire two branches with one piece of wire, taking a turn around the trunk for anchorage. The sequence of wiring typically progresses from the heaviest to the most delicate parts of the tree. If you need to

wire the trunk, start with this. Wire branches by working from the lowest level upwards. Some people prefer to wire the length of each branch alternately until the whole tree is wired, then to return to the finer twigs to apply the detail wiring. Other growers prefer to complete one branch at a time with both the main wire and the subsidiary wiring before moving on.

Other methods of shaping are often advocated, including tying branches down with strings or wires, suspending weights from them, or tying them to canes. All these methods are possible, but are inefficient compared to the wiring techniques shown here, and are seldom used.

STARTING TO WIRE THE TRUNK

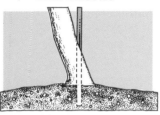

1 Cut a length of wire of the correct thickness and push one end into the soil behind the tree trunk.

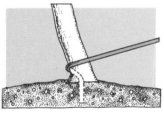

2 Bend the wire around the base of the trunk almost parallel to the soil for maximum anchorage.

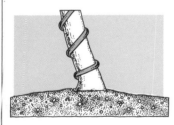

3 Take the first coil around the trunk base, then proceed to wind at an angle of 45 degrees.

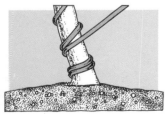

4 Where more than one wire is needed, apply the second wire close to the first, but not crossing it (see right).

Reshaping by wiring

This illustration shows wiring applied to bend the trunk of a tree into a curve and to direct the branches downwards. Details of individual techniques used on trunk and branches are shown opposite.

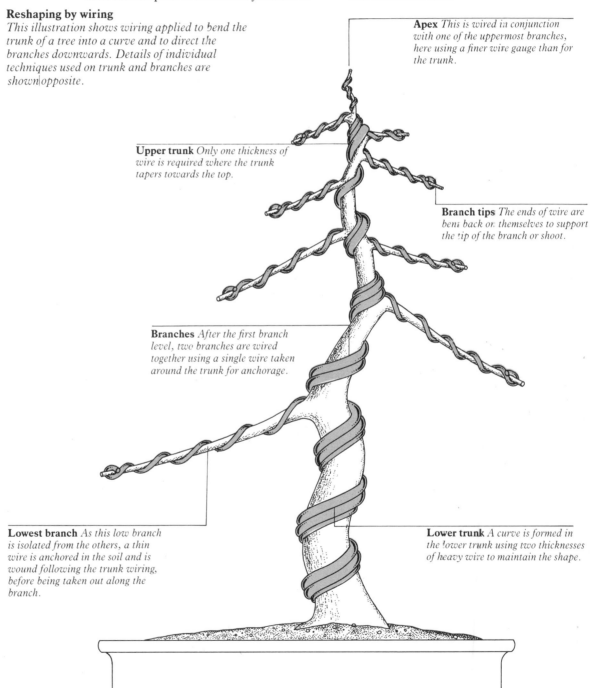

Apex *This is wired in conjunction with one of the uppermost branches, here using a finer wire gauge than for the trunk.*

Upper trunk *Only one thickness of wire is required where the trunk tapers towards the top.*

Branch tips *The ends of wire are bent back on themselves to support the tip of the branch or shoot.*

Branches *After the first branch level, two branches are wired together using a single wire taken around the trunk for anchorage.*

Lowest branch *As this low branch is isolated from the others, a thin wire is anchored in the soil and is wound following the trunk wiring, before being taken out along the branch.*

Lower trunk *A curve is formed in the lower trunk using two thicknesses of heavy wire to maintain the shape.*

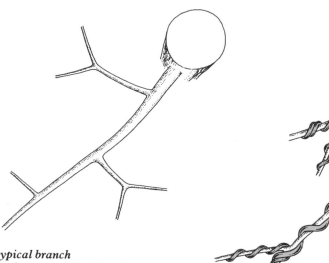

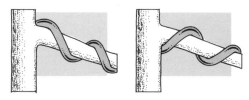

Starting to wire a branch
Take the first turn of wire over the branch (left). If it passes underneath (right), the branch is more likely to snap when bent.

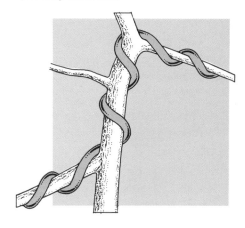

Wiring a typical branch
The branch, shown extending from the cross-section of the trunk, has been wired to close up the arrangement of the twigs.

Anchoring branch wiring
It is usual to wire two branches at the same time with one wire, taking the wire around the trunk in between to give it anchorage.

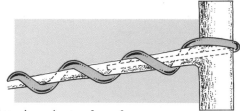

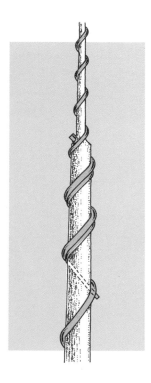

Changing the wire gauge
As the thickness of a trunk or branch tapers towards the tip, you will need to continue the wiring with a smaller wire gauge. Run the thinner wire adjacent to the thick wire for several turns so that it becomes effective support for the tapering section of the trunk or branch. This technique is commonly used in bringing a thin branch up to form the apex of the tree.

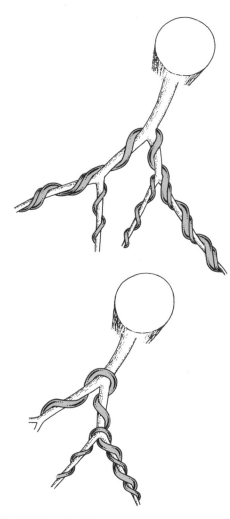

Securing wire to a branch
Where a branch is too isolated to be wired in conjunction with another, secure the end of the wire by trapping it under the first few turns.

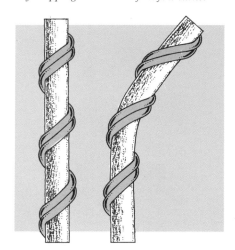

Anchoring subsidiary wiring
Where it is necessary to wire only twigs, not the full branch, the wire is not anchored at the trunk (shown in cross-section) but at the division of the branch, supporting the join evenly (top) not spiralling around it (above).

Bending the trunk
When a trunk is bent into a curve, the wire should provide maximum support at the outer point of the curve. Between spirals, the support of the wiring is weaker.

WIRING A JUNIPER

This demonstration shows wiring of *Juniperus × media* 'Blaauw'. All junipers provide good material for a first attempt at wiring, because the wood is flexible and unlikely to snap when bent into shape. Because of the evergreen foliage, the effect that the wiring has on the design is immediately visible.

The intention of the bonsai design is to simulate an appearance of age. In an old tree, the weight of the branches and each winter's snow contribute to a downward sweep and this is mimicked by wiring the branches into a downward direction. At the same time, the branches can be positioned in the best way to achieve visual balance.

Junipers have either prickly, needle-like "juvenile" foliage or fine-textured, scale-like "adult" foliage, or a mixture of both. Although the needle-like foliage can give the bonsai design a dramatic, rugged appearance, it can also be unpleasant to handle. For first attempts at wiring, you will find it easier to work on a juniper with scale-like leaves.

The bonsai material

This juniper is typical nursery stock, grown in the open ground for garden use. It has been planted in a plastic container for one year and no bonsai training has been applied during that time. The typical upward growth of the young tree is clearly visible. The mass of branches must be thinned out to reduce the density of the silhouette before the shape is refined by wiring.

Before wiring
The tree has a straight, upright trunk with a sturdy base and good taper, strong but flexible upward-growing branches and dense scale-like foliage.

After wiring
Three hours of work on pruning, wiring and repotting the juniper results in the skeleton of a handsome bonsai, which will be developed over the next few seasons.

STAGE ONE: WIRING THE TREE

1 Select the front view of the tree. Remove heavy branches near the base of the tree and thin out the upper branches. Stubs that are left on the lower part of the trunk can be treated to form jins (see page 75).

2 Start with the lowest branches. Wire the first two with one piece of wire, making a turn around the trunk for anchorage. Measure and cut the wire to one and a third times the combined lengths of the branches.

3 Hold the wire against the trunk and make the first turn over the top of the lowest branch. Anchor the wire around the trunk and take it over the top of the second branch. Then wire the length of each branch.

DETAILED WIRING

As well as wiring the branches in a downward direction, it is necessary to thin out the foliage and wire the subsidiary growth to create flat foliage pads, giving a more refined image to the tree. This temporarily creates an artificial look, but within one year the foliage will have filled out considerably.

After wiring, the tree is groomed. Downward-growing shoots are totally removed, and upward growth is finger-pruned. This kind of maintenance pruning continues throughout the growing season and in following seasons. It has the effect of recreating the "cloud-shaped" foliage pads that occur on this tree in nature.

Branch structure
This shows the structure of a typical branch, from directly above looking down, before any refinement takes place.

After pruning
This is the same view after surplus foliage has been trimmed away and longer shoots pruned back to create a more balanced shape.

After wiring
The branch has been wired with 2.5mm copper-coloured aluminium wire and the shoots with 1.5mm wire. The previously straight stem has been wired into gentle curves.

Profile view
This shows the shape of the wired branch as it appears on the bonsai, leading downward from the trunk but with a slight upward movement at the tip.

4 The result so far shows the first two levels of the branches wired in their approximate positions. When the basic wiring is complete you can make further refinements to the shapes of the branches and foliage.

5 Continue wiring the upper branches, bending them carefully into place and supporting them while the wire is applied. Work on two branches at a time where possible to take advantage of the trunk for anchorage.

6 At this stage, the wiring is almost completed. The longer branches have all been shaped and only the apex is to be wired. No attempt has yet been made to tidy up the foliage masses.

The intermediate stage
When all the branches have been wired, giving each one a separate shape and direction, you can make final adjustments to their positions and then groom the tree to clarify the lines, giving special attention to removing leaves that hang down below the main foliage pads.

STAGE TWO: POTTING THE TREE

1 Remove the wired tree from its original pot and use a metal root hook to comb out the roots in a radial pattern. Prune them back in proportion to the trunk and the pot to be used. Trim downward-growing roots to create a shallow root system (see page 173).

2 Prepare the pot with mesh over the drainage holes and anchorage wires (see page 53) and put in a layer of potting mixture. Position the tree in the pot facing front and secure it by twisting the anchorage wires over the roots. Fill up the pot with soil.

The overall design
The wiring remains in place on this species for about one year. It must be regularly inspected and the wires removed if they begin to bite into the bark. The tree will be rewired at two- to three-year intervals to take in new growth. There will be many adjustments and amendments to the tree as it grows and becomes more refined. For example, after three to five years, it may become necessary to prune out some of these branches to open up the design.

Foliage *Well-shaped foliage pads will gradually fill out with further seasons' growth.*

Branch structure *This now creates a well-balanced framework around which the foliage will quickly develop.*

Jins *Stubs left after removal of the lower branches are treated as jins (see opposite) to give the tree an aged, weathered appearance.*

Trunk *The naturally graceful trunk line, improved by careful wiring, is now clearly visible*

Container *A red-brown unglazed Tokoname oval is appropriate to the rugged character of an evergreen forest tree and highlights the reddish colour of the tree bark.*

JINS, SHARI AND DRIFTWOOD

These are all terms referring to treatment of dead wood on bonsai. Trees in nature, particularly those that grow in a harsh environment, often have areas of dead wood that add a sense of drama to their appearance. The bristle-cone pines (*Pinus aristata*) of the south-western United States of America are excellent examples, but on mountains everywhere in the world, it is possible to find trees that feature dead wood.

If the bonsai design has dead wood as a dominant feature, it is described as a "driftwood" design, from the resemblance to weathered driftwood found on the sea shore. An extensive area of dead wood carved or torn down the trunk of the bonsai is referred to by the Japanese word "shari"; similarly, carved or torn branches are called "jins". The word "jin" is, after "bonsai", the most commonly used Japanese word in the vocabulary of bonsai – there is no easy English equivalent. It is used as a noun, as a verb – "to jin" – and as an adjective, as in "jinning pliers".

Treating the wood

You can incorporate any of these effects in your bonsai design by carving the dead wood and treating it with lime-sulphur solution to bleach and preserve it. The wood need not be naturally dead. Jins are often created from live branches that are not wanted in the bonsai design. If these branches were removed completely, the trunk of the tree would be scarred, and this tends to make the bonsai look "man-made". A surplus branch, or stub of a pruned branch, stripped of bark and torn or carved to create a natural effect, as if it has been damaged by high winds or heavy snow, adds to the impression of age in the bonsai and also contributes a strong visual element to the design.

CREATING JINS

This sequence shows the process of carving jins from pruned branch stubs before wiring the tree, the treatment applied to the juniper (*Juniperus × media* 'Blaauw') shown in the demonstration of wiring on the previous pages. The lower branches were pruned to leave sturdy stubs standing clear of the tree trunk. These stubs were stripped of bark, torn and cleaned to leave rugged, natural-looking jins near the base of the tree and at the level of the lowest branches left on the bonsai.

For this you need concave branch cutters, jinning pliers, and a wire brush. In this example, an electrically-driven rotating wire brush is used, but you can do the work by hand with an ordinary wire brush of suitable size.

1 Use a concave branch cutter to score the bark around the base of the stub close to the trunk.

2 Use jinning pliers to grip the bark and crush it, separating the bark from the wood underneath.

3 Grip the loosened bark with the jinning pliers and pull it away, exposing the white wood underneath.

4 To create a more natural effect, grip the wood with the pliers and tear it downwards to expose the grain.

5 When you are satisfied with the shape of the jin, use a wire brush to clean up the surface of the exposed wood.

PLANTING ON ROCK

Rock brings an extra dimension to the art of bonsai. The introduction of this solid, elemental material increases the range of bonsai design in both the immediate visual impact and the different associations with landscape that it can contribute.

The success of a rock planting depends on finding a beautiful rock and enhancing it with a suitable and attractive planting, to create a bonsai design in which all the materials are fully integrated. You can approach the design of a rock planting in many different ways. A large slab of slate or flat rock can be used instead of a man-made container, giving an impressive naturalism to the composition. Rocks can be positioned as outcrops from the surface of the soil in a bonsai container to suggest the rocky terrain in which the tree lives. A single rock can be treated as a magnificent mountain, a craggy cliff or rocky island.

The demonstration on these pages represents clasped-to-rock style, with the roots of the bonsai confined to the rock. In root-over-rock style (see page 80), the rock serves to feature the roots of the bonsai. In saikei, or tray landscape (see page 88), rocks are often used to create rugged and dramatic landscapes.

Selecting the rock

Of the many different types of rock that occur in the world, some are more suitable than others for bonsai rock plantings. You should avoid the bright, glittery textures of quartz or marble, as these detract from the trees. Sedimentary rocks, such as sandstone, are unsuitable as frost may cause the rock to split along its strata lines. Soft rocks erode too easily and quickly to be useful for clasped-to-rock and root-over-rock styles. However, soft non-sedimentary rocks, such as tufa and lava rock, have the advantage of being easy to shape and can be effective if you plant the tree in the rock, by hollowing out a section and treating it as if it were a pot.

The best type of rock is hard-textured, so that it will not crumble away over the years, and visually interesting in shape, texture and colour.

The type and shape of rock are particularly important for clasped-to-rock style compositions. The rock should be an interesting shape in its own right, as it is not likely that you will produce an interesting rock planting if you use a boring piece of rock. The shape should look natural, but as there are so many incredibly convoluted forms of rocks, boulders and mountains in nature, this is not restrictive. Good colour and texture are important elements; generally, dark colours such as blacks and greys create the most impact.

Designing a clasped-to-rock planting

The rock is the "foundation stone" of the composition. It dictates the type of tree, the tree's size and style. A rugged mountain-like rock requires a species and style of tree that you could expect to find in a mountainous locality – pine, birch, juniper, spruce – while smooth, rounded rocks suggest the presence of water and can be used with waterside trees, such as willow.

You should first examine the rock from every angle to determine the best view, which then becomes the "front" of the rock. Then, it is important to establish an idea of scale when making your choice of plant material. The rock could represent a boulder, a cliff or a mountain. A single tree about two-thirds the size of the rock would make it seem comparatively small, as if it were a boulder supporting the tree, and this suggests a near view. Whereas a forest of tiny trees would totally change the perception of the rock, making it seem a large-scale element seen from greater distance – a forested mountain.

A planting on rock can be displayed just as it is, but it is more usual for the rock to be placed in a shallow tray of sand or water, which adds another element to the scale and perspective of the design.

PLANTING CLASPED-TO-ROCK STYLE

The rock used in the demonstration is a collected piece of Japanese Ibigawa rock. In substance it is a volcanic conglomerate; that is, a mixture of different types of rocks welded together by volcanic activity.

This material already has a particularly interesting combination of colour and texture. It has been cut and chiselled to refine the shape, and treated with acid, which eats away the softer parts of the rock to make the surface more irregular. The base has been sawn flat to give stability.

After careful study of the form of the rock, it was decided to create the impression of a rocky island or outcrop with small trees clinging tenaciously to the sides. To establish the correct sense of scale, several young, partially trained white pines were chosen to form the basis of the composition.

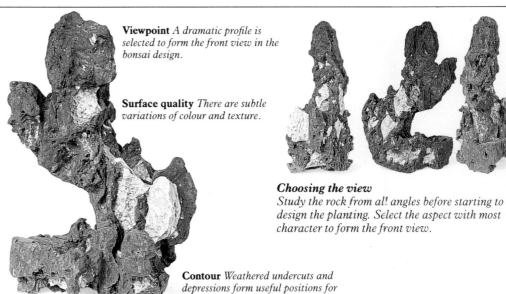

Viewpoint *A dramatic profile is selected to form the front view in the bonsai design.*

Surface quality *There are subtle variations of colour and texture.*

Contour *Weathered undercuts and depressions form useful positions for planting the trees.*

Choosing the view
Study the rock from all angles before starting to design the planting. Select the aspect with most character to form the front view.

Materials for the rock planting

The three white pines (*Pinus parviflora*) are each only about 10cm (4in) high. Other living materials are included in the design to create the impression of an isolated island – a small cotoneaster, a bright yellow heather to contrast with the colour and texture of the pines, and dwarf thyme, acaena and mosses. Moss must be allowed to soak in water for several hours before it is used to complete the planting.

When you make a planting in clasped-to-rock style you need anchorage wires (see below) to secure the trees on the rock, and a strong, waterproof adhesive to hold the wires in place. Epoxy resin is a suitable adhesive, but it takes a day or two to harden fully. You can alternatively use a quick-drying adhesive made in Japan specifically for use on rock plantings – this is readily available from bonsai suppliers worldwide. It eliminates the waiting time involved with epoxy resin, but you must take great care when using it and be aware that it is dangerous – it will just as quickly glue your fingers together as stick wire to rock.

All the plants are planted in peat muck spread on the rock surface. This consists of one part clay to one part black sedge peat, soaked and kneaded together to form a sticky, moist mass.

Preparing anchorage wires

Cut a length of wire and hold the centre of the wire against a fine chopstick or knitting needle — any tool of about 6mm (¼in) diameter, with a tapered end, will do. Take it under the chopstick, over the top, and underneath again, leaving a long end on either side. Slip off the circle of wire and hold it flat with pliers while you pull the ends up vertically. When you attach it to the rock, stick the circle of wire to the rock's surface, leaving the ends free.

You need enough anchorage wires to make a network that will secure the roots of all the plants. When you take the wires over the roots bring together individual wires from different anchorages, rather than securing the two ends of one anchorage wire to each other.

Anchorage wire
Leave long ends of wire on each side of the circle for securing the planting.

1 Hold up the trees to the rock and check their shapes and proportions to find the most suitable planting places, where they will emphasize and complement the rock's features.

2 Attach prepared anchorage wires to the rock in the appropriate positions for securing the trees after planting. Use enough wires to make a web-like framework over all the roots.

3 Press a layer of peat muck onto the rock at a position chosen for one of the trees. Put the tree in place, spread the roots on the peat muck and use more muck to cover them.

4 Cross the anchorage wires over the roots. Grasp the ends of the wire with pliers and twist them together to secure the tree in its position on the rock.

5 Apply more peat muck and press it in place. Keep the peat muck moist until moss is applied in the final stages; have a mist-sprayer handy to prevent drying out.

6 Secure the other plants in their positions in the same way, placing the other pines first, followed by the smaller plants. Spray if necessary, to keep the peat layer damp.

The finished planting
The rock planting gives an immediate impression of maturity. Although the plants are comparatively young, they look as though they have been established on the rock for years. In this style of bonsai, a dramatic effect is achieved in a short time and can only be enhanced with age.

7 Apply soaked moss to the peat muck to cover the surface. As well as providing a more attractive finish, this helps prevent erosion.

8 Position the rock in a shallow water tray, adding fine gravel and water. The water enhances the design and maintains a humid atmosphere around the plants.

Container *The design of the planting is set off by the grey unglazed shallow water tray with embossed detail.*

Detail *The white stripes on the foliage that give the white pine its common name add detail to the design.*

Trees *These are carefully wired so that the curves of the trunk follow the contours of the rock.*

Rock *Outcrops of white quartz provide interesting texture, breaking up the form and providing colour contrast.*

Contour *The rounded, irregular shapes of the cypresses echo the contours of the rock.*

Colour *The bright foliage of the evergreen cotoneaster makes a striking contrast to the autumnal colours of the other small plants and the blue-green of the pines.*

Contour *A specially interesting feature is the shape of the rock under the overhang, which encourages water to collect and form the impression of a cascading stream.*

PLANTING ROOT-OVER-ROCK STYLE

In nature, trees that grow in rocky and mountainous areas sometimes deposit seeds into crevices in the rock. As new trees grow from these seeds, their roots snake out over the rock searching for moisture and nourishment. When they find soil, the exposed parts of the roots fatten up and hold tightly to the rock. This feature is frequently mimicked in root-over-rock style bonsai, particularly with trees that readily form strong surface roots, such as the trident maple and Chinese elm. Although these species are prime candidates for this treatment, there is a wide range of possibilities, especially in smaller bonsai sizes where it is not necessary for exceptionally heavy roots to form.

Because the rock is a permanent feature of the planting, and the roots of the tree become as one with it, the type of rock you choose is important. It should be very hard and frost-resistant, with an interesting craggy texture. Avoid soft rocks that will crumble in frost, or types that have a flat, visually dull surface.

The type most commonly seen in root-over-rock planting is Japanese Ibigawa rock (see page 76). It satisfies all the criteria, being hard, rugged and interestingly coloured and textured. It is available from bonsai suppliers worldwide, but in some areas you may be able to find indigenous rocks that provide a suitable equivalent.

TRAINING A MAPLE IN ROOT-OVER-ROCK STYLE

This demonstration, using a Japanese mountain maple (*Acer palmatum*), shows how an effective, small root-over-rock planting can be created over just one year. The first stage is to attach the tree to the rock, then to provide conditions in which the roots can thicken and take a grip on the rock. The tree is then potted in soil in a bonsai container, treating the tree and rock as a single unit.

The amount of time it takes for the roots of the tree to thicken adequately depends on the size of the tree. One year is usually enough for small to medium bonsai, but a tree intended to make a large bonsai may need two to three years to develop strong roots that firmly grasp the contours of the rock. You can judge by eye whether the roots are thick enough to make an

interesting element in the bonsai design, but you should also check that they are permanently trained on the rock and do not pull away when released from the binding material that initially attached them to the rock (see page 82).

Designing root-over-rock style
Root-over-rock styling gives more dramatic interest to a young tree used for bonsai. This elegant maple, no more than three years old, gains impact from the appearance of maturity in the overall design.

Materials for the bonsai

The essential element in choosing materials is that the rock should be the right shape to fit the root structure of the tree. In this case the tree, a two- to three-year-old mountain maple seedling, field-grown and bare-rooted, has already been selected and several suitable

pieces of Japanese Ibigawa rock have been assembled.

For the first stage, you require plastic grafting tape, or strips cut from a plastic bag, to bind the roots to the rock, sharp sand and an ordinary plant pot in which the tree can grow on. For the process of binding roots to rock,

you will need someone to help you, as it is difficult to both hold the roots firmly over the rock and apply the plastic strips using only two hands.

For the final planting, which takes place one year after the first stage, you will need to select a suitable bonsai container and potting soil.

STAGE ONE: ATTACHING ROOTS TO ROCK

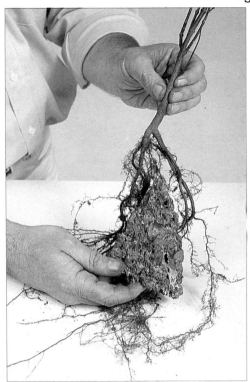

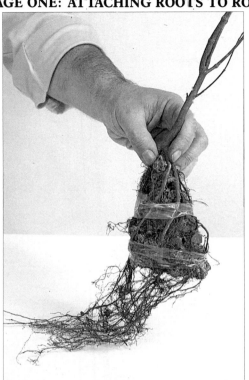

1 Comb out the roots and shake loose any remaining soil. Select a suitable rock by holding several samples to the tree's roots to see which has the correct shape.

2 Wrap the roots over the rock and hold them firmly while your helper starts to bind plastic tape around the roots. To begin with, secure them at top, centre and base of the rock.

3 Bandage the roots tightly to the rock, covering them completely to prevent new roots developing horizontally, as they should only grow downward. Leave the longer roots free at the base.

4 Trim the tree back hard, pruning each branch to within no more than one or two buds from the trunk.

5 Seal the cut ends of the pruned branches to prevent drying out; it is essential to keep in the moisture for new bud development.

6 Plant the rock and roots in a pot of sharp sand, covering up to the base of the trunk. No other growing medium is needed.

STAGE TWO: POTTING THE TREE

The intermediate stage
Allow the tree to grow vigorously in the pot for one year. Water daily throughout the growing season and feed every two weeks in summer; reduce watering in winter, but keep the sand lightly moist. New shoots may grow to as much as 90-120cm (36-48in) in one year. In this example, the year's new growth has been cut back to within one or two buds of the trunk.

1 After one year, in late winter or early spring, trim the branches roughly and remove the tree from the pot of sand. Wash off the sand with clean water, using a hosepipe, watering can or bowl of water.

2 Use small, sharp scissors to cut away the plastic tapes, being careful not to cut into the roots. Cut the strips and unwrap the plastic to free the roots and rock completely.

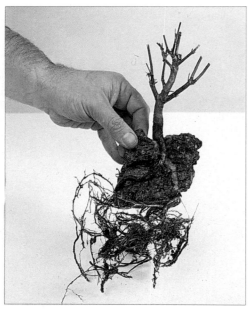

3 Once the rock is freed and the roots cleaned, you should see that the roots have thickened and are clinging securely to the rock. If not, bind them again and replant the tree in sand for another year.

4 If you are satisfied with the way the roots have developed, examine the tree and rock to select the front view (see page 28). Give the branches a final trimming according to this view. Plant the tree in a prepared bonsai pot (see page 53), treating the rock as an extension of the trunk.

Structure *Hard pruning at the potting stage has created a good basic shape from which the graceful, arching leaves create an elegant silhouette.*

The final result
After three months in the bonsai container, the tree has come into leaf. The young tree has the basis of a good design and will be allowed to develop more twiggy growth over the next few years. The rock adds an interesting extra element to the small bonsai, which is shown here at life size. The soil surface has been covered with sand and planted with mosses to enhance the naturalism of the design.

Rock *The rock contributes balance to the design as well as textural interest, giving weight to the slender form of the young tree.*

Roots *The root system grips the rock tightly, with one strong root seen very prominently from the front view.*

Container *An oval pot with a soft blue-green glaze speckled with cream enhances summer foliage colour and will form a striking complement to the tree's spectacular scarlet autumn colour.*

GROUP PLANTINGS

Group or forest plantings are a way of extending the beauty of one tree, as encapsulated in a bonsai specimen, into the natural beauty of a stand of trees, a wood or a forest.

If you study trees in nature you will see how they have adapted to their environment. A solitary tree in the middle of a field, in fertile soil and not subjected to extreme weather conditions, will grow large and strong, with a heavy trunk and spreading branches. In a group of trees in the same situation the growth pattern of an individual is different. Each tree competes with the others for water, food and light. The trees shade each other, and therefore reach upwards instead of spreading outwards, developing tall, slender trunks rather than short thick ones. Only trees on the ouside of the group will receive enough light for spreading branches to grow well. The strongest or oldest trees dominate; the subordinate trees lean away from their taller neighbours to reach out towards the light.

You need to be aware of these natural influences if you are to produce effective bonsai, and effective group plantings in particular. Limiting your ideas to impressions obtained from existing bonsai, whether real or in photographs, is likely to result in unconvincing designs.

Materials for group plantings

When you design a bonsai group, you can exploit the variations in shape and form that tree groups in nature exhibit. For example, young trees tend to be slender and are unsuitable as single bonsai specimens, but they can be used in a group planting to represent forest trees that have grown tall and thin. Similarly, some trees growing close together fail to develop side branches, or their branching is one-sided. Trees with these characteristics may not make individual bonsai, but can have a natural place in a group.

Many varieties of trees provide suitable material for group planting, especially those that have a naturally upright habit. They include both evergreen and deciduous species. Small-leaved, fine-textured forms of either type are suitable for small to medium-sized bonsai groups, but coarse-growing and large-leaved varieties should be used in taller, larger group plantings to achieve the right sense of scale. The following are particularly recommended: beech, birch, cedar, *Cryptomeria*, elm, hornbeam, juniper, larch, maple, spruce. In the case of maples, elms and *Cryptomeria*, you may need to grow and train the plants yourself, from seedlings or cuttings. Training consists of pruning each tree to create a more slender, upright shape than would be appropriate for an individual bonsai specimen.

Group plantings are usually composed of trees of the same species, as this gives the most natural look to the arrangement. It is possible to include more than one species

---

PLANTING A GROUP OF JAPANESE DWARF CEDARS

The bonsai material consists of five specimens of Japanese dwarf cedar (*Cryptomeria japonica* 'Yatsubusa'). These have been grown from cuttings and pre-trained for group planting over a period of about eight years. They show variations of height and thickness of trunk judged to be a suitable combination for a small group.

Use an odd number of trees, for a natural effect, and remember that you need more stock to choose from than you will actually use.

ROOT PRUNING

Remove the first tree from its training pot and comb out the roots with a metal root hook. Trim the roots with large-handled shears. Repeat this for each tree, then work out a rough arrangement of the group before selecting a suitable pot large enough to accommodate the group. Cover the drainage holes (see page 53) and insert a shallow layer of grit covered with a layer of potting soil.

1 Position the tallest tree first. Select the front view of the tree (see page 28) and place it in the pot about a third of the way in from one side and towards the front of the pot. This tree stands closest to the viewer.

---

in a group, although this is rarely seen, but it is difficult to achieve a satisfactory result when mixing species, and beginners should avoid the temptation to try this approach. There are problems in making the design work well if you are using different types of material, and most combinations look unnatural. Consider the end result of the demonstration on these pages, showing a group planting of *Cryptomeria* – the trees look as if they would grow this way in the wild, whereas it would be impossible to create a natural effect with, say, one specimen each of pine, cherry, beech, oak and wisteria, however effective they might be as individual bonsai.

With more than one type of tree, it is more difficult to achieve a realistic sense of scale. A large tree in the foreground of the design and a smaller tree of the same species set in the background immediately establish the depth and perspective of the planting. This effect would be destroyed if the background tree were a different species with, for example, larger leaves than the foreground tree. Using the same species enables you to set up direct visual links and contrasts throughout the design.

You may also invite horticultural problems if you try to design a mixed planting. Different species have different requirements as to soil type, watering and feeding.

Designing a group

The eye is easily deceived and a bonsai group can create an illusion of perspective by the same "visual tricks" as those used in drawing or painting to render impressions of space and distance. The relative scale of different elements in the composition establishes a perspective. Tall trees at the front and smaller trees at the back create a feeling of depth in the landscape, even if the actual measurement across the container is only a few inches. Another trick for creating perspective through scale is to stagger the arrangement slightly so that the group is, in effect, composed of two or three smaller groups successively diminishing in height.

The treatment of detail in the design can also assist the illusion. If you keep the silhouette of the background trees simple and draw attention to the trunk lines and branch structure of trees in the foreground, the eye registers the silhouetted forms as being less distinct and therefore further away than the more detailed area of the design.

Trees in a forest vary in height and in the thickness of their trunks, and there are irregular spaces between them. Symmetry is undesirable in group planting, particularly in the spaces between the trees and the open spaces left on either side of the pot, which should be irregular. Although you may put a lot of thought into positioning the trees, the overall effect of the design must look natural and uncontrived.

An impression of space within the composition is very important. You must be able to imagine that you could walk among the trees. A large, shallow pot contributes to the sense of space. Sometimes, instead of a pot, a flat slab of rock or slate is used.

2 Select a shorter and more slender tree and position it close to the first tree. Let it lean slightly away from the taller tree as if competing for light.

3 Position the third tree on the opposite side of the first and slightly further back in the container. Make sure the spacing is varied between the central tree and those on either side to give a natural asymmetry.

4 Place the fourth tree, a thinner-trunked specimen, at the back of the container to increase the perspective, and the fifth leaning out slightly on the extreme right of the composition to complete the five-tree group.

The intermediate stage
At this stage, the five-tree planting is well balanced, giving a good impression of depth and perspective.

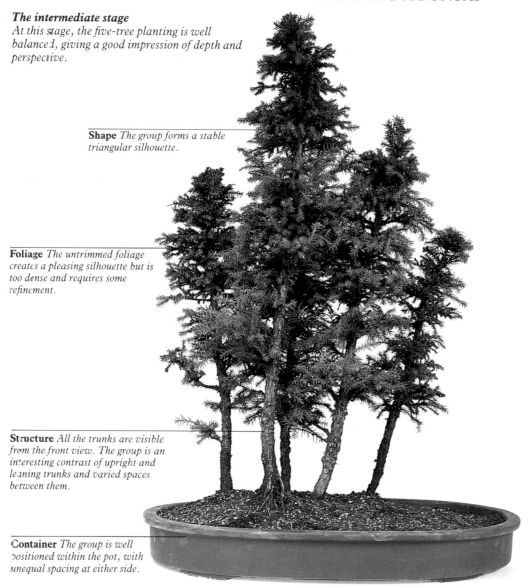

Shape *The group forms a stable triangular silhouette.*

Foliage *The untrimmed foliage creates a pleasing silhouette but is too dense and requires some refinement.*

Structure *All the trunks are visible from the front view. The group is an interesting contrast of upright and leaning trunks and varied spaces between them.*

Container *The group is well positioned within the pot, with unequal spacing at either side.*

Viewpoint *The dominant tree inclines slightly forward near its apex.*

Height *The tallest tree is at the front and the smallest at the back.*

Placement *The space is more open in the foreground of the design.*

Side view
This shows more clearly the spacing of the trees between front and back of the pot which creates the perspective in the design.

STAGE TWO: GROOMING AND FINISHING

1 Using shears or scissors, remove downward growing shoots and crossing branches to open out the structure of the design.

2 Groom the foliage as necessary to create a balanced silhouette. This can also have the effect of letting light into the design.

3 As the final stage, water the soil well and apply fresh moss, pressing it firmly into place with a spatula.

Silhouette *The asymmetrical triangle formed by the trees is pleasing to the eye.*

The finished group
The five-tree group has been completed within two hours, from preparation for planting to final grooming. The arrangement works well because there is a natural logic governing each aspect of the design.

Foliage *The pruning has created a good initial shape. Further trimming will be repeatedly applied, as the foliage grows rapidly. Branches may be wired at a later stage to refine the shape.*

Structure *A balanced arrangement of trunk lines, with the eye being led through the design by the inclination of two trunks towards the open space at the right of the pot.*

Spacing *All trunks are clearly visible but not evenly spaced, creating a natural effect.*

Soil surface *Velvety green moss provides the finishing touch to the landscape of the design.*

Container *The unglazed brown Tokoname oval is large enough to allow a feeling of space within and around the group.*

SAIKEI PLANTING

In keeping with the English term used to translate the Japanese concept of saikei – "living landscape" – the components of a saikei planting can vary in kind and extent as much as the forms of natural landscape. Although saikei is a means of representing landscape naturalistically on a small scale, it is not necessarily strictly realistic. A saikei planting may be a reconstruction of a view familiar to the bonsai grower, using materials commonly to be seen growing together in a particular type of location, or it can be a more exotic or imaginative representation. In either case, the individual elements must be able to coexist easily within the design, the living plants being able to flourish under the particular conditions of cultivation as saikei. The combination of plants and inert materials such as soil, rocks or sand should create a convincing atmosphere of natural landscape.

Elements of design

Rocks are not an essential feature of saikei plantings, although they tend to contribute a dramatic mood to a design, adding height and rugged contours that emphasize the sense of space and distance. The Ibigawa rocks used in the demonstration of saikei planting shown here are Japanese, which might suggest a theme based on their own natural landscape, but their shapes equally conjure an association with the rocky outcrops that form small islands off the coastlines of south-western England or Brittany in France. Those islands were, in fact, the inspiration behind this particular design. A gentler effect, and a quite different impression of landscape, would be achieved with low, horizontally stratified stones, such as those sometimes seen emerging from health or moorland.

Alternatively, an undulating, open landscape could be created with low banks of soil, covered with mosses, grasses or low ground cover plants, within which trees could be arranged to create a broad perspective. A container with a water reservoir is sometimes used for a design evoking a coastal, lakeside or river view, but more often an impression of water is created by skilful use of sand or grit. Saikei planting has infinite possibilities allowing the grower a very free means of expression.

For the live material in saikei, you can use trained plants, garden centre plants that you prune and shape as required, or even young seedlings or cuttings.

CREATING A SAIKEI PLANTING

To set the scale of the landscape, two large pieces of Ibigawa rock are selected, together with some smaller pieces. The featured trees are two specimens of dwarf Hinoki cypress (*Chamaecyparis obtusa* 'Yatsubusa'). These have been lightly trimmed and thinned, just enough to expose the trunk lines, but they maintain their natural forms.

The landscape is filled out with smaller plants – two heathers (*Calluna vulgaris* 'Foxii Nana'), mosses (pre-soaked for some hours beforehand) and low-growing ground cover plants, including *Acaena, Cotula* and *Thymus*. Fine-textured plants have been chosen to preserve the scale of the design. Ground cover plants not only increase the visual range of the design but have a practical purpose in that their roots help to prevent erosion of the soil on rock. The dwarf heathers are to be used in this planting to create the impression of tiny trees standing on the smaller and more distant rock.

The container chosen for this saikei planting is an unglazed brown Tokoname shallow oval pot. This gives a broad base for the design and the pot's low rim creates a clean edge that leaves the landscape open to view, assisting the sense of perspective. The dark colour is a suitable complement: a brighter, glazed container would seem inappropriate to the mood of a rugged landscape.

Fine gravel is used to surround the rocks and the plants are planted behind the rocks in basic soil mix. Peat muck – one part clay to one part sedge peat kneaded into a moist mass – is used in the final stage for planting the mosses.

Positioning the rocks

The key to a successful composition is the positioning of the rocks. These are arranged to be visually attractive, and should ideally form an interesting composition in their own right. Sometimes you can arrive at a good result by instinct, simply by placing the rocks in the container and adjusting their positions by eye. But there are various elements to be considered and, with practice, it is possible to analyze why the basic features of the design are working well, as in this example.

Proportion *The highest point in the design is not central, but positioned at about one-third of the measurement from side to side of the pot, as seen from the front.*

Shape *From the front, the composition is basically triangular, but with an asymmetrical balance, one side of the triangle being more than twice the length of the other as measured from the apex.*

Structure *The natural formation that creates an impression of caves and inlets at the base of the larger rock is to be an important aspect of the overall design.*

Surface detail *The strata of the two rocks run in the same direction, as they would in nature.*

Perspective *The large rock is close to the front of the container and the smaller rock is placed near the back, to establish a sense of depth.*

1 With the rocks in position, hold up the plants in their containers against the rocks to find suitable positions establishing the perspective of the design. Site the trees first, then choose positions for the mosses and low-growing plants.

2 Put a shallow layer of fine gravel across the base of the container, surrounding the rocks. Pour potting soil between and behind the rocks: smaller stones are positioned as "retaining walls" to support the soil behind the rocks.

3 Plant the trees in the soil behind the large rock. Then add the ground cover plants, selecting those of the most suitable height and texture for each area of the design and planting them in the soil around the base of the trees.

4 Trim the dwarf heathers to tree-like shapes. These should be shaped to echo the style of the trees, so they appear to be the same species seen at greater distance. Plant the heathers behind the secondary rock.

5 Cover the soil with a layer of peat muck as the base for moss planting. Press the soaked moss gently into the muck. U-shaped pieces of wire can be pushed through the moss to secure the soil surface in vertical areas.

Back view
The mossy surface layer runs to the edges of the small rocks used to form the retaining wall for the soil, suggesting that they are outcrops of the larger rock and creating a more gentle landscape impression from this viewpoint, with the trees seeming closer to the viewer.

The finished planting
From the front view, the rocks provide a dramatic focal point with their textured, craggy surfaces. The trees rising from behind the rocky peaks enhance the impression of distance.

Scale *Careful attention has been paid to the relative scale of all the components of the design, to create a naturalistic effect.*

Perspective *The heathers, being similar in form and colour to the cypresses, successfully represent trees growing on the more distant rock.*

Container *The rocks stand on gravel in an unglazed shallow oval pot. Water cannot be used to surround the planting because it would saturate the soil behind the main rock.*

CHAPTER THREE

BONSAI SPECIES GUIDE

An extremely wide range of trees and shrubs provides suitable material for bonsai. This guide includes detailed information on over 60 species. The trees and shrubs are ordered alphabetically by their botanical names and are also identified by their common names. An introductory text describes the characteristics of the tree or shrub, its background, and special features that make it suitable as bonsai. Full details on cultivation are provided. Each entry is illustrated by a fine bonsai specimen. Related species and cultivars are also illustrated in several entries to show the range of styles, characteristics and seasonal attractions.

USING THE SPECIES GUIDE

In the following pages over sixty different tree and shrub species grown as bonsai are catalogued in order of their botanic names. There is advice on how to create and care for a bonsai specimen, as well as recommendations for the most suitable styles and sizes for the species. All the entries are illustrated with photographs of top-quality bonsai of the named species and, in some cases, of related species, varieties or cultivars. The photographs are extensively captioned, and for every entry there is a separately photographed leaf detail.

There is a further compendium of trees and shrubs suitable for bonsai cultivation on pages 190 to 217. This has a much larger range of entries, including many additional varieties and cultivars, as well as further garden trees and shrubs that can be grown as bonsai.

The species information

The species guide is arranged in alphabetical order by genus and species name. Those species that are generally known by two different botanic names, or that have been reclassified, are included under their most widely used name, with the synonym given in brackets. The introductory text details any points of interest on the origins and history of the species, both in the wild and in bonsai cultivation, and its native habitat. It also outlines the natural growing pattern, describing inherent characteristics of shape and structure, since these are important elements to consider when planning your bonsai. Any outstanding features of the species, such as attractively textured bark, or particular seasonal effects, such as flowers, fruit, or colourful autumn leaves, are described here. The names of any interesting varieties, cultivars, or related species recommended for bonsai cultivation are also given. Some of these have a striking visual characteristic that makes them noteworthy, such as unusually coloured foliage or spectacular flowers. Some are naturally more suited than the species to different styles or sizes. Dwarf forms, for instance, have naturally finer twigs and leaves, allowing them to be used for smaller sizes. An alternative species or sub-species may be more frost or drought resistant, making it tolerant of a different climate than that required by the species.

Suitable styles

Each of the species described may be suited to a number of different bonsai styles, such as formal or informal upright, cascade or multiple-trunk. A range of appropriate styles for each is therefore recommended. The choice of a style for any bonsai is a case of individual considerations and must depend on the form of the particular plant material at the outset. The recommended styles cover what observation shows to be practical and likely to give satisfactory results: for example, a species that tends to a formal upright style in nature will usually be successful in this style as a bonsai. For detailed descriptions of the bonsai styles see pages 46 to 51 of *Creating a Bonsai*.

Suitable sizes

Just as the inherent shapes of different species dictate the styles that suit them best, so their leaf size, twig structure and rate of growth make them naturally suited to different sizes: a species with large leaves, for instance, will be difficult to grow as a tiny bonsai. The sizes that are generally suitable for each of the species are recommended in the following general categories: extra-small, small, medium, large and extra-large. The measurements to which these correspond are: extra-small, up to 10 cm (4 in); small, 10-20 cm (4-8 in); medium, 20-45 cm (8-18 in); large, 45-90cm (18-36 in), and extra large, over 90 cm (36 in). These are approximate sizings, however, and not a formal classification. They are included simply as a consistent and convenient guide as to the height of tree that you are trying to achieve.

Cultivation techniques

Concise notes on cultivation cover all aspects of caring for the bonsai. These are the points essential to the needs of the tree or shrub: more detailed information on the methods and techniques of caring for bonsai can be found in the chapters on *Routine Maintenance* on pages 168 to 181, and *Propagation* on pages 182 to 189. The notes are grouped under six headings: *Position* (see pages 170 and 171), describing the preferred level of light and any special care that may be necessary in summer or winter; *Watering* and *Feeding* (see page 172), giving the correct frequency, amounts and type of water and fertilizer; *Repotting* (see pages 173 to 175) recommending the appropriate time of year and how often it is necessary to repot as the tree matures; *Pruning* (see pages 176 to 179) giving the most appropriate times for maintenance pruning such as leaf-cutting or finger pruning, and *Propagation* (see pages 184 to 189), recommending the most reliable methods and suitable times of the year to carry them out.

The main captions

The captions to each photograph contain much additional information. This relates directly to the bonsai shown, although the information they give may be useful in considering the design of your own tree. It is impossible to "copy" a successful bonsai, and pointless to try; your own starting stock must be looked at and dealt with as an entirely unique plant requiring individual training to become an entirely unique bonsai.

The age, height and style of every tree are detailed. Any special features of the bonsai, to do with its structure or seasonal display are also captioned, explaining what is unusual about them or the methods that were used to achieve the effect.

Choosing pots

Since the choice of container is an essential part of creating a good bonsai, the styles and materials of the containers are also identified. These range from Japanese Tokoname ware to individual handmade pots and, in one case, a slab of rough Cornish stone. The particular reasons behind the choice of a certain size, shape, and finish of container for the bonsai are explained, being points that you might consider when you come to make your own choice. Further advice on selecting containers can be found in the *Art of Bonsai*, on pages 30 and 31. In *Creating a Bonsai* there is a catalogue of the different types available on pages 54 and 55, and instructions on how to prepare a pot for planting on page 53.

The leaf boxes

As a further reference for identification and size, individual leaves from the bonsai featured in the guide have been separately photographed. They are shown in special detail boxes, where they are reproduced at either life size or a specified reduction. These leaf detail boxes are included for every entry in the section. They assist in the identification of the species, as the bonsai example shown may have been photographed in spring to illustrate flowers which obscured the leaves, or after the leaves had fallen in autumn, to show an interesting twig structure. They are an additional indication of the actual size of the bonsai, since in many cases these have had to be shown quite considerably reduced.

Identification *The botanical names, by which the section is ordered, are given in italic type, with synonyms, if applicable, in brackets. The common name is given in bold type.*

Description *A general introduction to each species covers the history and special features of the tree, and lists varieties, cultivars and related species that are also suitable for bonsai.*

Seasonal effects *Each bonsai is photographed at the time of the year which best shows the special features of the species, such as spring flowers or autumn berries.*

Bonsai styles *This lists the styles and sizes for which the plants named in the entry are considered most suitable.*

Cultivation *A summary of the particular needs of the species when grown as a bonsai, from its most advantageous positioning through to the most effective methods of propagation.*

Symbols *Each of the areas covered by the cultivation notes has an identifying symbol to provide instant access to the information needed.*

Leaf boxes *These are included for every species in the guide and show individual leaves at life size or specified reductions for identification and size reference.*

Main captions *Captions give details of the bonsai shown and comment on its particular characteristics.*

Points of interest *Any special features of the example shown or the way it was created are pointed out and explained.*

Identifying containers *The containers used are identified for reference. Particular reasons for the choice of style are explained.*

--- BONSAI SPECIES GUIDE ---

Prunus mume

JAPANESE FLOWERING APRICOT

The large *Prunus* family consists of trees and shrubs grown for their stoned fruits – apricots, cherries, peaches, plums – and a wide range of ornamental species grown for the beauty of their flowers. They are found in temperate regions throughout the northern hemisphere, although the greatest variety occurs in Japan and the Far East. *Prunus mume*, said to have originated in China and Korea, has been extensively cultivated over generations in Japan for its beautiful fragrant blossoms, which burst out on the bare branches in late winter. A small bonsai displayed indoors when in flower fills the whole room with its scent. Many cultivars are available in Japan, of which very few are seen in the West. *P. spinosa*, the blackthorn or sloe, is a common hedgerow plant in Europe but as bonsai it has a delicacy similar to that of *P. mume* and makes an excellent alternative.

Prunus mume

Leaf shown half life size

BONSAI STYLES
Suitable for all styles except formal upright or broom, and for all sizes.

Flowers *Fragrant pink and white blossoms are borne on bare branches in late winter.*

Prunus mume
JAPANESE FLOWERING APRICOT
This 30-year-old tree, 40cm (16in) in height, has an unusually dramatic design combining aspects of semicascade and clasped-to-rock styles.

Structure *The gnarled old trunk, shaped by cutting, gives the design almost the appearance of clasped-to-rock style, forming a solid base for the low branch trained as a semicascade.*

CULTIVATION

☼ **Position** Full sun. Protect from frost in winter to avoid twig die-back and damage to flowers.

💧 **Watering** Daily throughout the growing season. Water sparingly in winter, but keep the soil continuously moist from the time when flower buds start to swell, to avoid bud and flower drop.

▪ **Feeding** Heavy summer feeding results in more flowers for the winter. The amount of feed required depends upon the type of soil and watering supplied. Feed at least every two weeks throughout summer – this can be increased in amount and frequency.

▪ **Repotting** Annually in late winter, as soon as flowering has ceased. Use basic soil mix.

✂ **Pruning** Trim back hard after flowers have fallen. Allow rampant growth in summer and trim back resulting shoots in autumn.

✎ **Propagation** From hardwood cuttings in late winter. By layering in summer. By grafting in winter or spring.

Container *English brown unglazed rectangle by Gordon Duffet provides clean lines offsetting the complex textures of the bonsai.*

146

Acer buergerianum (A. trifidium)
TRIDENT MAPLE

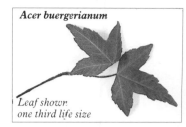

Acer buergerianum

*Leaf shown
one third life size*

The trident maple has a naturally upright growth pattern and is tolerant of pruning, dry soil and air pollution. For this reason it is used in many of the world's cities as a "street" tree, and the same characteristics make it excellent for bonsai. *A.b. formosanum* is an interesting sub-species, less tall-growing but with dense foliage growth. An unusual cultivar for bonsai is *A.b.* 'Mino Yatsubusa', a dwarf form with thick, shiny leaves that in autumn look as if lacquered scarlet and orange. *Acer ginnala*, the Amur maple, is a good alternative for cold areas, as the roots are more resistant to frost damage.

Acer buergerianum
TRIDENT MAPLE
Grown in informal upright style, this tree is 20 years old and 55cm (22in) high.

BONSAI STYLES

Suitable for all styles except broom, and for all sizes. Web-like root structure makes this tree particularly suitable for root-over-rock style.

CULTIVATION

☼ **Position** Full sun. Roots are susceptible to frost damage due to high moisture content, and need winter protection.

⚫ **Watering** Daily throughout the growing season. Keep the soil relatively dry in winter to minimize frost damage to roots.

▦ **Feeding** Once a week for the first month after leaves appear, then every two weeks until late summer.

▦ **Repotting** Annually in early spring as buds swell, but before bud burst. Cut back frost-damaged roots to older woody growth; new roots grow quickly. Use free-draining soil mix.

✄ **Pruning** Trim new growth back to one or two sets of leaves. In a vigorous, well-fed tree, leaf-cutting can also be carried out in midsummer.

↯ **Propagation** From seed in late autumn; provide frost protection. From softwood cuttings in midsummer; in late winter to early spring, hardwood cuttings (pencil, broom handle and even wrist-thick) in sharp sand are successful. By air layering in spring.

Foliage *Fresh green foliage develops spectacular and variable tints of orange and red in autumn.*

Branches *The branch structure has been developed since formation of the trunk, through five years of container growing.*

Trunk *The heavy trunk was formed by several years of growing in the ground with drastic pruning each year to achieve the taper.*

Container *Grey unglazed Japanese Tokoname ware.*

Acer ginnala
AMUR MAPLE
This hardy species is commonly substituted for
A. buergerianum in locations with harsh winter
conditions. This 15-year-old group planting
stands 60cm (24in) high.

Foliage *Three-pointed leaves
turn from green to brilliant
crimson in autumn.*

Structure *An asymmetrical
shape is created by planting the
tallest trees off-centre with
smaller specimens at the sides
and back to create perspective.*

Container *Brown unglazed
Japanese Tokoname shallow
oval, displayed on a
varnished wood base.*

Foliage *Dense, compact foliage
mass balances the weight and
texture of the rock supporting
the tree.*

Roots *The position of the tree on
the rock creates a long fall of
sturdy roots, forming a dramatic
feature in the design.*

Container *Brown unglazed
Japanese Tokoname oval pot.*

Acer buergerianum
TRIDENT MAPLE
This 25-year-old bonsai, 38cm (15in) in height, is
grown in root-over-rock style to take advantage
of the strong root structure characteristic of this
species.

Acer campestre
FIELD MAPLE

This small deciduous tree is the native European maple. It is less often grown as bonsai than its Japanese relatives but, like other maples, it is a good choice because of its pleasing leaf shape and the attractive colour of the autumn foliage, in this case a bright buttercup yellow. The twigs of the field maple are relatively coarse, so it is not suited to smaller bonsai sizes unless grown extra-small, when a single leaf can represent the mass of foliage and twigs of a tree branch.

Acer campestre
Leaf shown half life size

Acer campestre
FIELD MAPLE
A group grown from cuttings is shown here at 13 years of age. The overall height is 53cm (21in).

Foliage *Leaves are a strong, bright green in summer, turning to clear yellow in autumn.*

BONSAI STYLES
Suitable for all styles, except literati. Medium to large sizes are preferred, but this tree can also be grown as extra-small bonsai.

Structure *Visual space is achieved by variations of height and thickness in the five trunks asymmetrically arranged within the container.*

CULTIVATION
☼ **Position** Grow in full sun for best autumn colouring, but protect from hottest summer sun to avoid leaf scorch. Extra-small bonsai require frost protection in winter.

💧 **Watering** Daily throughout the growing season, sparingly in winter, but keep soil evenly moist.

▦ **Feeding** Every two weeks throughout summer.

▧ **Repotting** Every two to three years. Repot as buds swell but before they open. Use basic soil mix.

✄ **Pruning** Trim back new shoots to one or two pairs of leaves throughout the growing season. Keep internodal distances short by ruthlessly trimming back long internodes. Leaf-cut in mid summer to encourage smaller leaves and good autumn colour. Best time for wiring is immediately after leaf-cutting.

Container *A brown unglazed Japanese Tokoname shallow oval forms a broad, low base for the tree group.*

✍ **Propagation** From seed in winter. From softwood cuttings in summer. By air layering in spring or summer.

Acer palmatum
JAPANESE MAPLE

The Japanese maple, also native to China and Korea, is one of the classic bonsai subjects. It is an elegant tree which responds well to bonsai cultivation and is extremely rewarding in the range of its attractions – the graceful branch structure, the delicate shape of the five-lobed leaves and the seasonal variation of foliage colour. In older specimens, the bark develops beautiful silver colouring. This species has been cultivated in Japan for centuries and there are now over 250 cultivars.

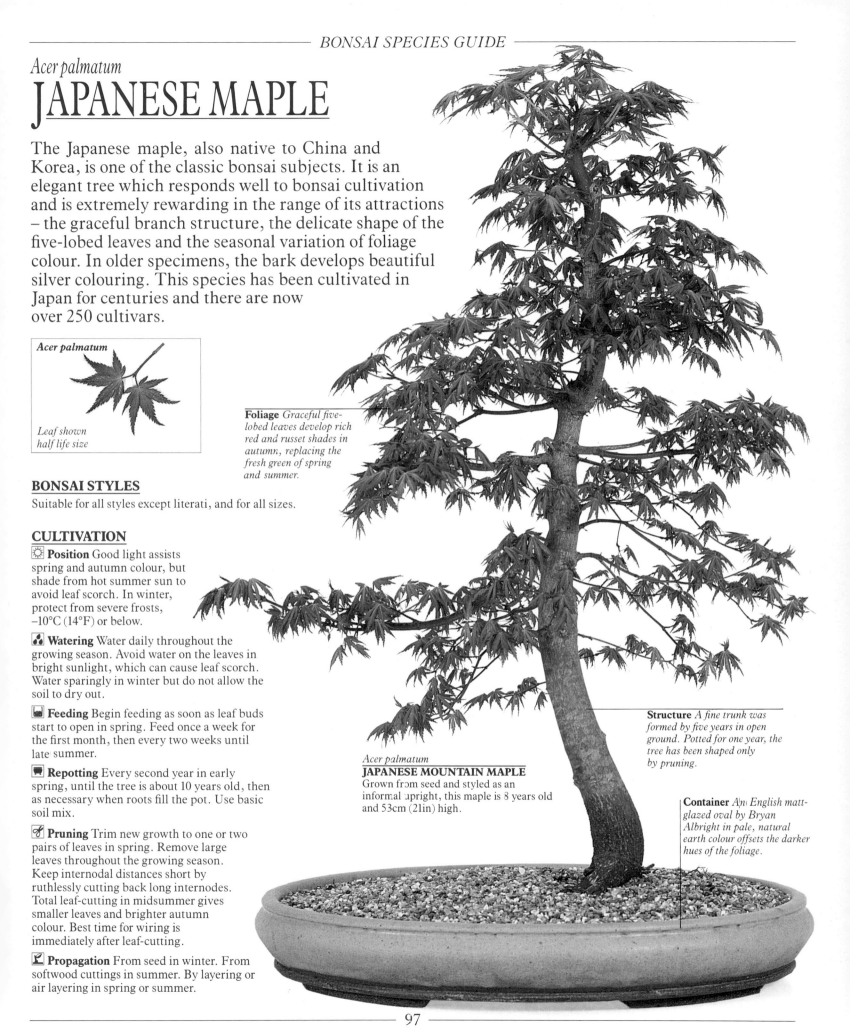

Acer palmatum

Leaf shown half life size

BONSAI STYLES
Suitable for all styles except literati, and for all sizes.

CULTIVATION
☼ **Position** Good light assists spring and autumn colour, but shade from hot summer sun to avoid leaf scorch. In winter, protect from severe frosts, −10°C (14°F) or below.

Watering Water daily throughout the growing season. Avoid water on the leaves in bright sunlight, which can cause leaf scorch. Water sparingly in winter but do not allow the soil to dry out.

Feeding Begin feeding as soon as leaf buds start to open in spring. Feed once a week for the first month, then every two weeks until late summer.

Repotting Every second year in early spring, until the tree is about 10 years old, then as necessary when roots fill the pot. Use basic soil mix.

Pruning Trim new growth to one or two pairs of leaves in spring. Remove large leaves throughout the growing season. Keep internodal distances short by ruthlessly cutting back long internodes. Total leaf-cutting in midsummer gives smaller leaves and brighter autumn colour. Best time for wiring is immediately after leaf-cutting.

Propagation From seed in winter. From softwood cuttings in summer. By layering or air layering in spring or summer.

Foliage *Graceful five-lobed leaves develop rich red and russet shades in autumn, replacing the fresh green of spring and summer.*

Acer palmatum
JAPANESE MOUNTAIN MAPLE
Grown from seed and styled as an informal upright, this maple is 8 years old and 53cm (21in) high.

Structure *A fine trunk was formed by five years in open ground. Potted for one year, the tree has been shaped only by pruning.*

Container *An English matt-glazed oval by Bryan Albright in pale, natural earth colour offsets the darker hues of the foliage.*

Acer palmatum cultivars

JAPANESE MAPLES

Acer palmatum 'Deshojo'

Leaf shown life size

A wonderful bonsai collection could be created solely from the various cultivars of *Acer palmatum*. There are spring foliage colours rivalling the intensity of most flowers, and diverse leaf shapes and sizes, from small compact leaves with a jewel-like quality to large cut-leaf forms in greens and purples, their lacy patterns providing a tranquil floating or weeping effect. Some cultivars exhibit colourful trunks and stems, others have interesting textures and muted hues. Whatever the spring or summer colours of the leaves, all cultivars respond with a startlingly varied range of autumn foliage colour, from palest yellow through bright yellows, oranges, reds and purples.

Acer palmatum 'Deshojo'
JAPANESE RED MAPLE
A 40-year-old specimen 80cm (32in) high, grown in twin-trunk style.

BONSAI STYLES

Suitable for all styles except literati, and for all sizes.

CULTIVATION

☼ **Position** Full light brings out autumn leaf colours most spectacularly, but shield from hot summer sun which will cause leaf scorch. In winter, provide protection against frosts at −10°C (14°F) or below.

💧 **Watering** Daily throughout the growing season. Make sure no water falls on leaves exposed to bright sun, or they will be scorched. Reduce watering in winter, but do not allow soil to dry out.

▦ **Feeding** As leaf buds open in spring, feed once a week for the first month, then every two weeks until late summer.

▤ **Repotting** Every second year in early spring, until the tree is about 10 years old, then as necessary according to root development. Use basic soil mix.

✂ **Pruning** Trim new growth to one or two pairs of leaves in spring. Remove large leaves throughout the growing season. Cut back long internodes to maintain short internodal distances. Total leaf-cutting in midsummer encourages small leaves and improves autumn colour. Wiring is best done immediately after leaf-cutting.

✄ **Propagation** From softwood cuttings in summer. By layering or air layering in spring or summer.

Foliage *Brilliant red spring colouring gives way to green in summer, and then to shades of red and orange in autumn.*

Structure *Strong, interestingly shaped root spread gives stability to the graceful trunk thickened by growing in open ground.*

Container *A soft green glazed Japanese Tokoname oval complements the red hues of spring and autumn leaves and enhances the summer colouring.*

Acer palmatum 'Seigen'
JAPANESE RED MAPLE
At 20 years old, this informal upright
stands 55cm (22in) high. The intense
pink and red spring colouring is seen
here. In summer the leaves turn to
green, in autumn to shades of orange
and red.

Acer palmatum 'Dissectum Atropurpureum'
CUT-LEAF PURPLE MAPLE
The light, spreading structure of a 30-
year-old informal upright, 65cm (26in)
high, shows the elegance of this cultivar.
In autumn the finely-cut leaves change
from purple to bright orange.

Acer palmatum 'Ukon'
UKON MAPLE
The trees have been planted as a
group for six years from young
grafted plants and are each now 15
years old. The overall height is
75cm (30in) and the curved trunks
have been carefully arranged to
allow some crossing, creating a
natural, uncontrived appearance.

Foliage *Lime green palmate
leaves give a refreshing
appearance to the group
in summer.*

Container *A brown
unglazed Japanese Tokoname
shallow oval provides a
discreet base for the group.*

Arundinaria
BAMBOO

Arundinaria nitida

Leaf shown half life size

Bamboos originate in the Far East, particularly China and Japan, and are readily recognized throughout the world. The strong, graceful canes bear grass-like leaves that rustle and nod with the slightest breeze, giving an oriental feel to any garden. Bamboos have been botanically classified and reclassified many times and are commonly sold in garden centres under incorrect names. The species most often used for bonsai are varieties of *Arundinaria, Phyllostachys* and *Sasa*. The "sacred bamboo" commonly used is not a bamboo at all but *Nandina domestica*, a shrub related to *Berberis*. Bamboos are usually grown as bonsai either in a group planting to represent a bamboo grove, or as accent or accessory plants complementing other bonsai species.

BONSAI STYLES

Multiple-trunk is recommended. Single-trunk style is sometimes used for varieties with strong, interesting stems, but as individual stems only live for five to six years, replacement shoots must be allowed to grow if the plant is to live on. Usually grown as small to medium bonsai.

CULTIVATION

Position Partial shade. Protect from frost.

Watering Water daily at least, more often for plants grown in shallow pots or on slabs. Bamboos are moisture-loving but should not be allowed to stand in water, and the soil must be free-draining.

Feeding Every two weeks through spring and summer, preferably using a high-nitrogen feed such as lawn fertilizer.

Repotting About once every two years, in late spring. Use basic soil mix on slabs and in shallow containers, a free-draining mix in deeper pots.

Pruning Cut down dwarf forms to ground level in early spring. Larger forms are sometimes controlled by systematic peeling of leaf sheaths, but this is not essential.

Propagation By division of rhizomes in early spring.

Foliage *Fresh green leaves are borne on arching stems.*

Arundinaria nitida
BAMBOO
A six-year-old plant grown in multiple-trunk style has an overall height of 25cm (10in).

Structure *To renew the stems, the canes are cut down to ground level every second year in spring.*

Container *Green glazed Japanese Tokoname "drum" pot.*

Nandina domestica
SACRED or HEAVENLY BAMBOO
This bonsai is comparable to the *Arundinaria* in style and size, but the bamboo is planted with rock to create a sense of landscape.

Foliage *The delicate compound leaves turn to brilliant scarlet in autumn before leaf fall.*

Foliage *Fresh green leaves form a textured mass at the apex of the design, spreading into a more open pattern below.*

Container *A blue glazed Japanese Tokoname oval forms a striking complement to the fine structure of the bonsai.*

Phyllostachys aurea
BUDDHA'S BELLY BAMBOO
These groups are smaller, at 20cm (8in) in height, again grown to form multiple stems and planted for a landscape effect.

Structure *Curious swellings above each stem joint give rise to the plant's common name.*

Containers *Green glazed oval and unglazed brown pot with glazed water section. Both are Japanese Tokoname ware.*

Betula nana
DWARF BIRCH

Betula nana

Leaf shown life size

The dwarf birch is native to the northern temperate areas. It is also commonly called the Arctic birch, surviving in the extreme conditions that occur from Scotland up to the Arctic circle, even growing in mountainous areas close to glaciers where the trees are only clear of snow and ice for three months of the year. When grown as a garden tree it can become very straggly and unkempt, but when clipped it makes an attractive, compact shape. For bonsai cultivation, tight pruning is required to maintain compact foliage masses. Although the dwarf birch does not develop the white trunk that is the great attraction of the silver birch, it more than compensates with its shiny dark copper-coloured trunk and delicate twigs which provide a particularly decorative effect in winter. The tiny leaves turn a rich gold in autumn. This is an excellent subject for the smaller bonsai sizes and extremely useful in saikei plantings.

BONSAI STYLES

Informal upright, slanting, broom, root-over-rock, clasped-to-rock, twin-trunk, clump, straight line, sinuous, group, saikei. Suitable for extra-small and small sizes.

CULTIVATION

☼ **Position** Full sun or partial shade. Some frost protection is needed in winter to avoid twig die-back.

♦ **Watering** Daily throughout the growing season, sparingly in winter, but do not allow the soil to dry out.

▨ **Feeding** Do not feed until one month after leaves have opened, then feed every two weeks throughout the growing season.

▬ **Repotting** Every second year, in early spring before bud burst. Use basic soil mix.

✄ **Pruning** New shoots should be constantly trimmed back to one or two leaves to create compact foliage masses. Trim out crossing branches and tidy up the shape in winter while the tree is leafless.

✍ **Propagation** From softwood cuttings in spring and summer. Cuttings root very easily.

Betula nana
DWARF BIRCH
These 12-year-old trees, grown from cuttings, form an attractively compact group with an overall height of 35cm (14in).

Structure *The group consists of 21 trees, the varied angles of the trunks fanning out the mass of delicate twigs and glossy foliage. These are planted on a slab of natural rock.*

Foliage *The tiny, glossy green, serrated leaves take on beautiful orange hues in autumn.*

Betula pendula
SILVER BIRCH

Betula pendula

Leaf shown half life size

Natives of the temperate and cold areas of the northern hemisphere, the birches constitute one of the toughest and most tolerant groups of deciduous trees, generally the first to establish themselves on waste ground and often the last trees seen growing at the tree line at high elevations. The elegant silver birch is the species most frequently grown as bonsai, featuring the pale trunk, graceful twigs and golden autumn foliage colour. Young trees have shiny copper-brown trunks that may take many years of growth in a pot before forming the silvery-white bark with its dark lines and cracks. But two to three years in the open ground can achieve the same result.

Betula pendula
SILVER BIRCH
This elegant informal upright, 75cm (30in) high, is 35 years old. It is a collected tree that has been trained as bonsai for 20 years.

BONSAI STYLES

Informal upright, twin-trunk, group. Suitable for small to extra-large sizes.

CULTIVATION

☼ **Position** Full sun or partial shade. Provide protection from severe frosts to avoid twig die-back.

💧 **Watering** Daily throughout the growing season. In winter, supply enough water to keep the soil from drying out.

▦ **Feeding** Do not feed until one month after leaves open, then feed every two weeks until late summer.

▬ **Repotting** In early spring before bud burst, every second year until the tree is aged about 10 years, then as necessary according to root development. Use free-draining soil mix.

✂ **Pruning** Trim new shoots back to two or three leaves in spring and at successive flushes of growth. Remove large leaves throughout the growing season. Birches bleed profusely, so use of a wound sealant is advised.

🌱 **Propagation** From seed sown in winter or spring.

Foliage *Attractively serrated leaves turn from green to rich shades of yellow and orange in autumn.*

Structure *The overall impression is of a strong, erect tree, but the gentle curving and twisting of the trunk adds to the visual interest.*

Container *A German semi-matt glazed rectangle with rounded corners by Petra Engelke provides horizontal balance for the curving tree trunk.*

Caragana arborescens
CHINESE PEA TREE

Caragana arborescens

Leaf shown half life size

Caragana species, members of the *Leguminosae* or pea family, originate in central Asia. They are very adaptable, tough trees, capable of growing in poor soil and in freezing, windswept conditions where few other plants would survive. As bonsai they are, strangely, equally tolerant of very high temperatures and are frequently grown as indoor trees without any apparent ill effect. The Chinese pea tree, which comes from the wastes of Siberia, is a popular deciduous subject for bonsai, delicate and graceful despite its tough character. *C. sinica* (*C. chamlagu*), the Mongolian redshrub, often appears as imported specimens originating from China and Taiwan. The leaves are more glossy and leathery than those of *C. arborescens*, and tend to be semi-evergreen in a mild climate or in indoor conditions. Bonsai growers must beware of the slender, sharp spines on the twigs of these plants.

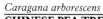

Caragana arborescens
CHINESE PEA TREE
This small informal upright, shown here at life size, is four years old.

BONSAI STYLES

Suitable for all styles except formal upright, and for all sizes.

CULTIVATION

☼ **Position** Full sun outdoors: if grown indoors, place in the lightest position possible. Outdoor plants are unlikely to need winter protection; plants accustomed to indoor culture will become less hardy and should be protected from severe frost.

💧 **Watering** Daily or every two days throughout the growing season. Keep the soil relatively dry during winter.

🖼 **Feeding** Every two to three weeks throughout the growing season.

▥ **Repotting** Every second year in winter or early spring, before bud burst. Use free-draining soil mix.

✂ **Pruning** Hard branch pruning can be done in winter in young developing trees. Total branch removal is effective, as new shoots will sprout from the trunks to give much more compact growth. Summer pruning consists of shortening new shoots as they develop. Take care when wiring to avoid impaling your fingers on the spines.

✔ **Propagation** From stratified seed sown in spring. From softwood cuttings in summer.

Structure *Grown from seed to 90cm (36in) high, then shortened to 8cm (3in) and potted, the tree has been in bonsai training for one year.*

Foliage *Delicately symmetrical compound leaves turn from fresh green to yellow in autumn.*

Container *A cream glazed Japanese Tokoname round pot enhances the proportions of the small tree.*

Carmona microphylla (Ehretia buxifolia)
FUKIEN TEA

This large evergreen shrub is one of the most convincingly "tree-like" tropical species and it is suitable for indoor bonsai cultivation in temperate climates. Most bonsai specimens originate from southern China. The plant's small leaves and compact habit make it possible to shape a bonsai simply by clipping, without any need for wiring. White flowers are carried among the shiny dark green leaves in spring and early summer, followed by berries which ripen from green to red. *Ehretia buxifolia* is the correct botanical name, but bonsai enthusiasts worldwide have been familiar with the plant for many years by the synonym *Carmona microphylla*, or by the common name Fukien tea, hence its listing here under these names.

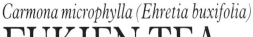

Carmona microphylla

Leaf shown half life size

Carmona microphylla
FUKIEN TEA
This specimen is a Chinese-styled twin-trunk 30 years old and 87cm (35in) high.

Foliage *Glossy green box-like leaves fully clothe the branches.*

BONSAI STYLES
Suitable for all styles and all sizes.

CULTIVATION
☼ **Position** Good light, but shade from hot summer sun. This tree needs a warm location, in the range 15-24°C (60-75°F) throughout the year.

💧 **Watering** Keep soil continuously moist throughout the growing season. Water sparingly in winter but make sure the soil does not dry out.

▦ **Feeding** Once every two weeks from early spring to early autumn. In winter, feed every four to six weeks.

▦ **Repotting** Every second year, in early spring at the start of the growing season. Use basic soil mix.

✂ **Pruning** Trim new growth back to two or three leaves as soon as six to eight leaves have formed. Woody branches can be wired at any time.

✍ **Propagation** From seed, sown in greenhouse conditions at any time. From softwood cuttings in spring or summer.

Container *A green glazed Chinese rectangle complements the tree's colouring and silhouette.*

Structure *A low branch styled as a twin trunk emphasizes the dramatic line of the powerful main trunk and links to the small secondary trunk on the right.*

Carpinus
HORNBEAM

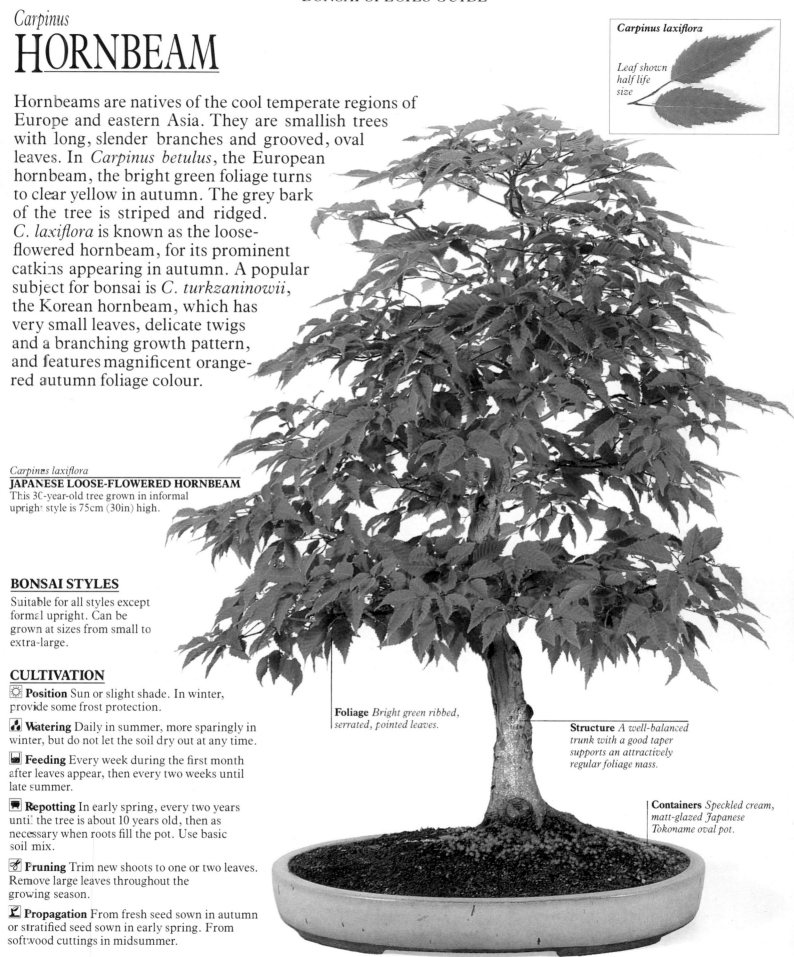

Carpinus laxiflora
Leaf shown half life size

Hornbeams are natives of the cool temperate regions of Europe and eastern Asia. They are smallish trees with long, slender branches and grooved, oval leaves. In *Carpinus betulus*, the European hornbeam, the bright green foliage turns to clear yellow in autumn. The grey bark of the tree is striped and ridged. *C. laxiflora* is known as the loose-flowered hornbeam, for its prominent catkins appearing in autumn. A popular subject for bonsai is *C. turkzaninowii*, the Korean hornbeam, which has very small leaves, delicate twigs and a branching growth pattern, and features magnificent orange-red autumn foliage colour.

Carpinus laxiflora
JAPANESE LOOSE-FLOWERED HORNBEAM
This 30-year-old tree grown in informal upright style is 75cm (30in) high.

BONSAI STYLES

Suitable for all styles except formal upright. Can be grown at sizes from small to extra-large.

CULTIVATION

☼ **Position** Sun or slight shade. In winter, provide some frost protection.

💧 **Watering** Daily in summer, more sparingly in winter, but do not let the soil dry out at any time.

▦ **Feeding** Every week during the first month after leaves appear, then every two weeks until late summer.

▧ **Repotting** In early spring, every two years until the tree is about 10 years old, then as necessary when roots fill the pot. Use basic soil mix.

✂ **Pruning** Trim new shoots to one or two leaves. Remove large leaves throughout the growing season.

⚹ **Propagation** From fresh seed sown in autumn or stratified seed sown in early spring. From softwood cuttings in midsummer.

Foliage *Bright green ribbed, serrated, pointed leaves.*

Structure *A well-balanced trunk with a good taper supports an attractively regular foliage mass.*

Containers *Speckled cream, matt-glazed Japanese Tokoname oval pot.*

Cedrus
CEDAR

Cedrus is a small genus of only four species of evergreen conifers. They are handsome and impressive, tall trees and all are suited to bonsai cultivation. *Cedrus atlantica*, the Atlas cedar, originates from the Atlas mountains of Algeria and Morocco. It has green foliage and dark grey bark: *C.a. glauca* (blue cedar) is an attractive form with blue-grey foliage and paler grey bark. The Cyprus cedar, *C. brevifolia*, bears clusters of short, dark green needles while *C. deodara*, the Deodar or Indian cedar, is distinguishable from other species by its larger needles and drooping leader. *C. libani*, the cedar of Lebanon, is a dramatic and unmistakable tree, with dark green foliage and spreading branches held horizontally.

Cedrus atlantica
ATLAS CEDAR
This extremely fine group planting of 20-year-old trees stands 105cm (42in) high.

BONSAI STYLES

Formal and informal upright, twin-trunk, group. *C. brevifolia* can be grown at extra-small to large sizes, other species medium to extra-large.

CULTIVATION

☼ **Position** Full sun throughout the year, but protect from extremes of temperature, especially young plants.

💧 **Watering** Daily during the growing season, less frequently in winter. Allow moisture to be absorbed between waterings, as cedars dislike wet soil.

▨ **Feeding** Every two weeks throughout the growing season.

▣ **Repotting** Every three to five years in spring, in free-draining soil mix. *C.a. glauca* is sensitive to root disturbance and may shed the previous season's needles at repotting (extra humidity at this time can help to avoid this) but new buds soon burst forth.

✂ **Pruning** Pinch back new shoots in spring and in successive flushes of growth. Do not cut the needles as this causes browning of needle tips.

🌱 **Propagation** From seed sown in spring. From softwood cuttings in spring or hardwood cuttings in autumn. By grafting in late summer: grafting is the usual method for *C. brevifolia* and *C. a. glauca*.

Cedrus atlantica

Leaf shown half life size

Foliage *Compact clusters of fresh green, small needles.*

Structure *The elegance of the group comes from the tall, straight trunks, spaced openly but subtly bonded by the network of branches.*

Container *A brown unglazed Japanese Tokoname oval forms a natural-looking low base for the perspective effect of the group.*

Celastrus orbiculatus
ORIENTAL BITTERSWEET

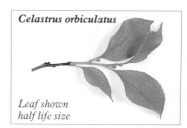

Celastrus orbiculatus

*Leaf shown
half life size*

This vigorous deciduous climbing shrub, a native of China and Japan, is grown mainly for the beauty of its fruits. These are woody green capsules that split open to reveal a golden yellow lining and three brilliant red seeds, remaining on the tree for much of the winter. Bittersweet's mid green leaves are oval and toothed. Both leaves and fruits are relatively small, which makes this plant especially suitable for bonsai.

Celastrus orbiculatus
ORIENTAL BITTERSWEET
This eight-year-old tree grown in root-over-rock style is 20cm (8in) in height.

BONSAI STYLES

Informal upright, slanting, semicascade, cascade, root-over-rock, clasped-to-rock, twin-trunk, clump, straight line, sinuous. Suitable for small to medium sizes.

CULTIVATION

Position Good light with plenty of sun, which encourages autumn fruiting. Small bonsai require some winter protection.

Watering Daily throughout the growing season, and supply a generous amount of water. Water less frequently in winter, but keep soil moist at all times.

Feeding Twice monthly during the growing season.

Repotting In early spring, annually or every second year, depending on root development. Use basic soil mix.

Pruning Bittersweet is a strong-growing plant which needs thorough pruning. When the inconspicuous green flowers have appeared in spring, trim back new shoots to one or two leaves. Trim again to two or three leaves in late autumn. Wire in summer – branches are supple and easily wired.

Propagation From softwood cuttings in summer. By layering or air layering in spring or summer.

Foliage *Bright green oval leaves turn yellow in autumn.*

Structure *The heavy roots of this species create a dramatic effect gripping the heavily textured Japanese Ibigawa rock.*

Container *A speckled cream, semi-matt Japanese Tokoname oval gives depth to the base of the design.*

Chaenomeles
FLOWERING QUINCE

These natives of China and Japan make some of the most beautiful and easily cultivated of early spring-flowering bonsai. The flowers – white, pink, orange or red – are produced on bare branches. *C. japonica*, Maul's flowering quince, bears brilliant red flowers. The highly desirable dwarf form *C.j.* 'Chojubai' has the unique characteristic of producing its smaller red or white flowers year round. The white-flowered *C. speciosa* 'Nivalis' can be particularly recommended for bonsai, and the many cultivars of *C.* × *superba*, of which 'Etna', with rich vermilion flowers, and 'Pink Lady', a clear rose pink, are among the best.

Chaenomeles japonica 'Chojubai'

Leaf shown half life size

BONSAI STYLES

Suitable for all styles except formal upright and broom. Can be grown at extra-small to medium sizes.

Flowers *Scarlet spring flowers are first borne on bare branches in early spring and reappear through the year among the bright green leaves.*

CULTIVATION

☼ **Position** Full sun. Provide frost protection during colder months.

Watering Daily throughout the growing season, and mist-spray foliage except when in flower or fruit. Water sparingly in winter but do not allow soil to dry out.

Feeding Every two weeks from the end of flowering until leaves fall.

Repotting Every year or two years in mid autumn; alternatively, with care, in early spring before bud burst. Use basic soil mix.

Pruning For maximum flowering, allow new shoots to elongate untrimmed through summer, then trim back to two nodes of current season's growth in mid autumn. Remove any basal shoots.

Propagation From seed in early spring; germination is rapid. From softwood cuttings in midsummer or hardwood cuttings in winter. By selecting hardwood cuttings to make a preformed trunk, it is possible to produce a bonsai in one year. By division, particularly the dwarfer forms. Grafting is often used to propagate named hybrids.

Chaenomeles japonica 'Chojubai'
DWARF JAPANESE FLOWERING QUINCE
This specimen, 38cm (15in) high at 12 years old, was grown from a cutting and trained in sinuous style.

Structure *Exploiting the shrubby habit of this species, low branches were layered along the soil surface to develop the effect of several trunks.*

Container *A German oval container with subtle glazing by Petra Engelke complements the broad spread of the sinuous style.*

Chaenomeles sinensis (Pseudocydonia sinensis)
CHINESE QUINCE

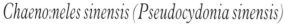

Chaenomeles sinensis

Leaf shown half life size

The Chinese quince is a distinctive tree indigenous to China and Korea. It has an attractive, flaky bark and carries a mass of glossy green leaves that turn through shades of gold, orange, red and purple in autumn. Small pink flowers appear in spring, followed by large, fragrant yellow fruits in autumn. The winter display is particularly striking in this species, with the decorative effect of bark and fruits seen against a strong pattern of writhing branches. This is a tree that has had many different identities. It is now correctly classified as *Pseudocydonia sinensis*, but is included here under its more commonly used pseudonym for direct comparison with the Japanese quince, *Chaenomeles speciosa*.

Chaenomeles sinensis
CHINESE QUINCE
This twin-trunk bonsai is 25 years old and 90cm (36in) high.

Foliage *The fresh green of the thick, glossy, oval leaves gives way to a varied range of warm tints in autumn.*

BONSAI STYLES

Informal upright, twin-trunk, group. Suitable for medium to large sizes.

CULTIVATION

☼ **Position** Full sun. Protect from frost in winter.

💧 **Watering** Daily during the growing season, sparingly in winter but keep soil moist. Take particular care to give plenty of water as fruit is swelling, to avoid fruit-drop.

▦ **Feeding** Every two to three weeks throughout the growing season.

▬ **Repotting** Root prune and repot in autumn, about every two years. Use basic soil mix.

✂ **Pruning** Heavy branch pruning is done in autumn at root pruning time. In summer, trim back new shoots to two or three leaves. Wire new shoots while still flexible, as older branches can be brittle.

✍ **Propagation** From stratified seed sown in early spring. From softwood cuttings in summer.

Container *A blue glazed Japanese Tokoname oval provides colour contrast.*

Structure *A well-balanced twin-trunk design shows off the colourful flaky bark characteristic of this species.*

Chamaecyparis
FALSE CYPRESS

These long-lived, resilient evergreens are natives of North America and Japan. Their shape is generally columnar or conical, and they have flat, fan-shaped branches with scale-like leaves. *Chamaecyparis obtusa*, the Hinoki cypress, is the species most widely used for bonsai cultivation. Its blunt-ended, deep green leaves are lined with blue around the underside edges. There are two dwarf cultivars excellent for bonsai — *C.o.* 'Nana Gracilis' is most commonly available in Europe but the Japanese dwarf form 'Yatsubusa'is preferable, being more compact, with a neater habit of growth.

Chamaecyparis obtusa 'Yatsubusa'
DWARF HINOKI CYPRESS
Consisting of 10-year-old trees grown from cuttings, this group stands 30cm (12in) high.

Chamaecyparis obtusa 'Yatsubusa'

Leaf shown life size

BONSAI STYLES

Suitable for all styles except broom, and for all sizes.

CULTIVATION

☼ **Position** Good light, but protect from full sun in summer to avoid leaf scorch. Protect foliage from drying winds in cold conditions, particularly when soil is frozen.

Watering Water daily and give foliage a daily mist-spray from late spring to early autumn. Do not let the soil dry out at any time.

Feeding Every two weeks from early spring to mid autumn.

Repotting For young trees, every second year in early to mid spring. Repot specimens over 10 years old when roots fill the bottom of the pot. Use basic soil mix.

Pruning Pinch out the tops of foliage sprays throughout the growing season.

Propagation From cuttings rooted in sharp sand in summer or autumn. By grafting in late summer.

Foliage *Fine-textured dark green leaves give density to the silhouette.*

Structure *The arrangement of the five-tree planting on the low ceramic base creates a natural impression of open landscape.*

Container *A free-form pottery slab by German designer Petra Engelke creates an interesting irregular contour around the base of the design.*

Cotoneaster
COTONEASTER

Cotoneaster horizontalis

Leaf shown life size

These popular garden shrubs include prostrate, spreading and upright varieties, both evergreen and deciduous. The small-scale leaves, flowers and fruits make cotoneasters highly suitable for bonsai cultivation and they can be grown in a variety of styles. Of the deciduous species, *Cotoneaster horizontalis* is widely grown as bonsai. It has dark green, shiny leaves, pink flowers and orange-red berries. The bright berries of *C. adpressus praecox* make a fine complement to the scarlet colouring of the foliage in autumn. A number of the evergreen species make excellent bonsai, including *C. microphyllus* which has slender leaves, white flowers and large red berries, and the more compact *C. conspicuus decorus*, which bears fragrant masses of white flowers in spring. *C. 'Skogholm'* is an attractive dwarf form with small leaves but large fruits, and the tiny *C. congestus* can be recommended for very small bonsai.

BONSAI STYLES

Informal upright, slanting, semicascade, cascade, root-over-rock, clasped-to-rock, twin-trunk, clump. Suitable for extra-small to medium sizes.

CULTIVATION

☼ **Position** Full sun. Provide some frost protection in winter.

💧 **Watering** Daily throughout the growing season. In winter, water sufficiently to prevent soil from drying out, particularly for evergreen varieties.

▦ **Feeding** Every two weeks until flowering and thereafter monthly until late summer.

▬ **Repotting** Annually in early spring until the tree is 10 years old, then as necessary when roots fill the pot. Use basic soil mix.

✂ **Pruning** Cut back old branches in early spring. Constant scissor-trimming of new shoots throughout the growing season quickly results in denser twig growth.

✔ **Propagation** From stratified seed sown in spring. From softwood cuttings in summer or hardwood cuttings in autumn or winter.

Fruit *The bright red fruits form the main display in autumn as the leaves gradually fall.*

Structure *Wiring has created a balanced silhouette and angular movement in the trunk and branches.*

Cotoneaster horizontalis
ROCKSPRAY COTONEASTER
This informal upright is 8 years old and 25cm (10in) high.

Container *A blue glazed Japanese Tokoname "cloud" pot is chosen for dramatic contrast with the bright reds of autumn leaves and fruit.*

Flowers *Small star-like, white flowers are clustered over the glossy green foliage in spring.*

Structure *After a period in open ground allowing the shrub to make prolific growth, the shape of the bonsai was created by pruning.*

Cotoneaster conspicuus decorus
COTONEASTER
Trained in informal upright style, this bonsai is 10 years old and 20cm (8in) high.

Container *Grey unglazed Japanese Tokoname round pot with rope design around the top rim.*

Cotoneaster 'Skogholm'
COTONEASTER
'Skogholm' is a useful dwarf cotoneaster. This 8-year-old semicascade, grown from a cutting, is only 12cm (5in) high. The small glossy evergreen leaves and brilliant scarlet berries are complemented by a pale blue, matt-glazed semicascade pot.

Crassula arborescens
JADE TREE

In temperate regions, this unusual small evergreen succulent is grown as a houseplant, but it also makes an interesting tree-like indoor bonsai. A native of South Africa, where the tree can reach 3m (10ft) in height, it has thick branches and smooth, rounded, fleshy leaves. The leaves of *Crassula arborescens*, the species most commonly grown as bonsai, are a striking jade green, developing a red tinge if grown in a sunny position. Pale pink flowers appear in winter or early spring.

Crassula arborescens

Leaf shown half life size

Foliage *Generously clustered, succulent leaves are a brilliant green, strongly edged with red if the bonsai is grown in full sun.*

BONSAI STYLES
Informal upright, twin-trunk, clump. Suitable for medium to large sizes.

CULTIVATION
☼ **Position** Provide a well-lit position throughout the year. The plant does well in direct sunlight and prefers a warm location, but in winter will tolerate temperatures down to 10°C (50°F).

💧 **Watering** Water moderately in summer — the plant needs little moisture. In winter give just enough water to prevent wrinkling of leaves — in cool conditions, this means watering about every three to four weeks.

▣ **Feeding** Once a month from late spring to early autumn.

▣ **Repotting** Every second year in spring, in free-draining soil mix.

✂ **Pruning** In spring, pinch back the tips of new shoots as soon as they reach the required length. Prune branches as necessary during the growing season. Remove leaves from the trunk and the bases of old, lower branches to create a tree-like effect.

✎ **Propagation** From cuttings at any time. A branch or even a single leaf roots easily in a sandy, well-drained soil mixture.

Structure *Stout, fleshy stems give a tree-like appearance to a species that can also be grown as a succulent houseplant.*

Crassula arborescens
JADE TREE
Grown as indoor bonsai in clump style, this tree is 20 years old and 70cm (28in) high.

Container *A traditional glazed Chinese round pot emphasizes the convergence of trunks at the base of the tree.*

Crataegus
HAWTHORN

These small deciduous trees, seen in the wild across North America, Asia and western Europe, are often used as hedging plants because of their dense growth and prickly branches. The small leaves make them particularly suitable for bonsai, and in spring the trees are covered with masses of white, pink or red flowers which give way to clusters of orange or red autumn berries. The white flowers of the common hawthorn, *Crataegus monogyna*, are strongly fragrant. *C. oxyacantha* is less common as a native species but has given rise to many notable hybrids, of which 'Paul's Scarlet', with double scarlet flowers, is a particularly beautiful example. The Japanese hawthorn, *C. cuneata*, is an attractive species bearing white flowers and large rosehip-type berries.

Crataegus oxyacantha 'Paul's Scarlet'

Leaf shown half life size

Flowers *The double, bright red flowers of this particularly prolific cultivar make a spectacular display in spring.*

Foliage *The attractive irregularly shaped leaves are very hardy and tolerant.*

BONSAI STYLES

Suitable for all styles except formal upright and broom, and for all sizes.

CULTIVATION

☼ **Position** Full sun. Hawthorn is quite resistant to windy conditions. Small bonsai sizes need frost protection in winter.

Watering Water generously once a day throughout the growing season. Reduce watering in winter but do not allow soil to dry out. Plants are susceptible to mildew and need regular spraying.

Feeding Twice monthly during the growing season.

Repotting Annually in early spring or early autumn, in basic soil mix.

Pruning Pinch out terminal shoots to two or three leaves in spring. Reshape by branch pruning, after flowering or in late autumn after leaf fall.

Propagation For species, from seed stratified in winter and sown in spring. From softwood cuttings in summer. Grafting in late winter or early spring is the usual method for *C.o.* 'Paul's Scarlet'.

Structure *The grafted tree was field-grown for five years to develop the trunk and has since been trained as bonsai for four years.*

Crataegus oxyacantha 'Paul's Scarlet'
DOUBLE RED FLOWERING HAWTHORN
This informal upright is 65cm (26in) high at 12 years of age.

Container *Grey unglazed Japanese Tokoname oval pot.*

Roots *Exposed roots form a strong, visually interesting anchorage.*

Cryptomeria japonica

JAPANESE CEDAR

Cryptomeria japonica is the single species of this genus, but it has given rise to many cultivars. In Japan, this tall, straight-trunked tree is grown for timber, but in Europe and North America it is cultivated as an ornamental tree. The growth pattern tends to a regular conical shape. The colouring is striking, with red-brown bark that peels away in strips and pointed needle-like foliage of a bright blue-green. There is a dwarf Japanese cultivar often selected for bonsai, *C.j.* 'Yatsubusa', which has a naturally narrow conical form and tightly compact foliage growth.

Cryptomeria japonica 'Yatsubusa'
Leaf shown life size

Cryptomeria japonica 'Yatsubusa'
DWARF JAPANESE CEDAR
The trees in this group are between 10 and 15 years old and have been growing together in this design for 4 years. The overall height is 25cm (10in).

Structure *The design has two distinct parts, the trees in the background group being smaller and more slender to increase the sense of perspective.*

BONSAI STYLES

Formal upright, clasped-to-rock, twin-trunk, clump, group. Dwarf forms are particularly good for rock-planting and saikei. *C. japonica* is suitable for medium to extra-large sizes, dwarf forms for extra-small to medium sizes.

CULTIVATION

☼ **Position** Provide a light position, but protect from full sun in summer. Frost protection in winter is advisable. Leaf colour may change in cold, frosty conditions from fresh green to olive green, brown or almost purple, but the bright colouring is quickly recovered in warmer weather.

💧 **Watering** Water generously once a day and mist-spray foliage daily during the summer months. Water sparingly in winter but protect foliage from drying winds.

▦ **Feeding** Every two weeks from spring to late autumn.

▥ **Repotting** Initially every two years, in mid spring. For older trees, about every five years according to root development. Use basic soil mix.

✂ **Pruning** Throughout the growing season, pinch out new growth when it is about 1.2cm (½in) long.

⚘ **Propagation** From softwood cuttings in summer.

Foliage *Fine-textured evergreen foliage follows the trunk line closely. In autumn the colour turns to a rich bronze.*

Container *The group is planted on a slab of Cornish slate, providing a natural landscape setting for the trees.*

Elaeagnus multiflora
ELAEAGNUS

The Elaeagnus family is widespread, native to Asia and North America but long cultivated in other countries. Species can be deciduous or evergreen, and generally are fast-growing, wind-resistant shrubs or small trees, seeming to do well in poor soil. They are often planted as windbreaks and shelter belts, particularly in exposed locations and near the sea. *Elaeagnus multiflora* is a good deciduous bonsai subject, with leaves that are green above and silver on the undersides. The small fragrant flowers are produced in spring, followed by small oblong, blood-red fruits in summer. *E. pungens*, the thorny elaeagnus, is an evergreen species, the foliage having shiny green upper surfaces and prominent brown speckles on the white undersides. Its flowers appear in autumn.

Elaeagnus multiflora

Leaf shown half life size

Elaeagnus multiflora
ELAEAGNUS
This specimen, trained from a young graft, is 10 years old and 20cm (8in) high.

Foliage *Leathery bright green leaves are silvery-white on the undersides, some also finely speckled with brown.*

Structure *The twig growth has a naturally upward direction and the tree has not been wired, but has been styled by pruning.*

Container *A blue glazed Japanese Tokoname "cloud" pot provides a strong complement to the mass of bright foliage colour.*

BONSAI STYLES
Informal upright, slanting, semicascade, cascade. Suitable for small to large sizes.

CULTIVATION

 **Position** Sun or shade. Give some frost protection in winter.

Watering Daily throughout the growing season, sparingly in winter but do not allow soil to dry out.

Feeding Every two weeks throughout summer.

Repotting Every second year in early spring, in basic soil mix.

Pruning Major structural pruning should be done in winter. Summer pruning consists of shortening new shoots as they develop.

Propagation From softwood cuttings in summer.

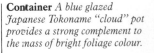

Euonymus
EUONYMUS

Euonymus alatus

Leaf shown life size

This very varied genus contains both evergreen and deciduous shrubs and small trees, found on all continents except Africa and South America. Deciduous species provide brilliant autumn colour in the foliage and fruits. The finest display belongs to *Euonymus alatus*, the winged spindle tree. The leaves turn a fascinating purple-pink, small orange fruits are carried on the undersides of the branches, and the ridged bark has interesting corky "wings". Two other species make particularly attractive bonsai — *E. europaeus*, the European spindle tree, which bears striking scarlet seed capsules, and *E. sieboldianus*, the Japanese spindle, with pale green flowers, pinkish-white fruits and red seeds.

BONSAI STYLES

Suitable for all styles except broom, and for all sizes.

CULTIVATION

☼ **Position** Full light with some sun. Small bonsai sizes require frost protection in winter.

💧 **Watering** Water daily in summer, less frequently in winter but do not allow soil to dry out. Mist-spray leaves during the growing season.

▦ **Feeding** Every two weeks from late spring to late summer.

▦ **Repotting** Annually in early spring until the tree is 10 years old, then every two years, or as required when roots fill the pot. Use basic soil mix.

✂ **Pruning** Trim new growth back to two or three leaves in spring. Repeat trimming two or three times during the growing season. Prune old branches in autumn or early spring.

✐ **Propagation** From softwood cuttings in summer or hardwood cuttings in autumn. By layering in spring or summer.

Foliage *Green compound leaves take on red tints in autumn.*

Euonymus alatus
WINGED SPINDLE
Trees grown from cuttings, aged from three to five years, form a group 20cm (8in) high.

Bark *Corky wing-like growths, giving rise to the common name, form an irregularly toothed outline to each trunk.*

Structure *Slender, angled trunks and crossing branches create a natural effect in this nine-tree planting, trained as a group for one year.*

Container *A white glazed Japanese Tokoname oval sets off the pattern of dark trunks and bright leaf colour.*

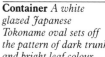

Fagus crenata
JAPANESE WHITE BEECH

The beeches are handsome, hardy deciduous trees native to the northern hemisphere. The Japanese white beech differs from the European species (see facing page) in having smaller, narrower and more pointed foliage and a slender, pale trunk. It is accepted practice to scrub the trunk with water and an old toothbrush, but sometimes a lime-sulphur solution is used as a winter spray to kill pests and this has the useful side effect of bleaching the bark, sometimes making the trunk appear almost stark white. Beeches are often seen in bonsai as forest plantings, recreating the serene mood of a beech wood in nature. The rich russet colouring of the autumn foliage is a special feature of these trees, and in the Japanese beech the dead leaves remain on the tree right through the winter, until new buds extend in spring.

Fagus crenata

Leaf shown half life size

BONSAI STYLES

Formal and informal upright, slanting, twin-trunk, clump, group. Because of the leaf size, medium to extra large-sizes are preferable.

CULTIVATION

☼ **Position** Full sun, except in summer when partial shade is required. Protect young foliage from wind.

💧 **Watering** Daily throughout the growing season. Avoid water on the leaves on sunny days as the foliage scorches easily. Water sparingly in winter but do not allow soil to dry out.

▪ **Feeding** Do not feed for the first month after leaves appear, then feed every two weeks until late summer.

▪ **Repotting** In spring, every second year until the tree is about 10 years old, thereafter as required when roots fill the pot. Use basic soil mix.

✂ **Pruning** In spring, pinch back growing tips to two sets of leaves. Remove only large leaves through the growing season; total leaf-cutting is inadvisable.

🗲 **Propagation** From fresh seed sown in autumn or stratified seed sown in spring.

Fagus crenata
JAPANESE WHITE BEECH
Trees aged 15 years are grown in group style with an overall height of 75cm (30in).

Foliage *Ribbed oval leaves turn from fresh green to russet brown in autumn and are retained through winter.*

Structure *The group is composed of three smaller groups of closely planted trunks.*

Container *Brown unglazed Japanese Tokoname shallow oval pot.*

Bark *With maturity, the bark colour lightens almost to white, forming an effective contrast with the warm autumn leaf colour.*

Fagus sylvatica
EUROPEAN BEECH

Fagus sylvatica is the native European beech, widely grown for timber, as hedging and for ornament. Beeches are slow-growing trees and a single large-trunked bonsai specimen is a long-term project. This is a practical reason why beeches are often grown as forest plantings, as these gain an air of maturity with trees only a few years old. But the time spent on cultivating an individual specimen is rewarded by the majestic form of the European beech, with its graceful pattern of spreading branches carrying a mass of foliage that turns from a fresh light green in spring through darker green in summer to the warm autumnal shades of russet and gold. There are also purple, weeping and cut-leaf forms of *F. sylvatica* that are best grown as single specimens.

Fagus sylvatica

Leaf shown half life size

Foliage *Silky-textured, serrated oval leaves are green in summer and turn golden in autumn.*

Structure *The silhouette shows the typically upright, spreading growth of the beech.*

BONSAI STYLES
Formal and informal upright, slanting, twin-trunk, clump, group. The relatively large leaves are best suited to medium to extra-large bonsai sizes.

CULTIVATION
☼ **Position** Full sun, but shade from strong sun in summer. Provide protection from wind for young foliage.

💧 **Watering** Daily throughout the growing season. Do not let water fall on the leaves in bright sun, as this causes leaf scorch. Water sparingly in winter, but make sure the soil stays moist.

▣ **Feeding** Do not feed for one month after leaves appear, then feed every two weeks until late summer.

▣ **Repotting** Every second year in spring, until the tree is about 10 years old, then as necessary according to root development. Use basic soil mix.

✄ **Pruning** Pinch back growing tips to two sets of leaves in spring. Large leaves can be removed at any time during the growing season, but total leaf-cutting is inadvisable.

✓ **Propagation** From fresh seed sown in autumn or stratified seed sown in spring.

Container *A "Goma" unglazed Japanese Tokoname oval, warm-toned to complement spring and summer leaf colour and enhance the rich autumn colouring.*

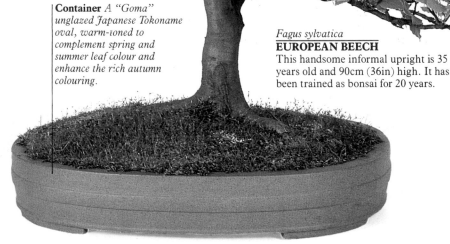

Fagus sylvatica
EUROPEAN BEECH
This handsome informal upright is 35 years old and 90cm (36in) high. It has been trained as bonsai for 20 years.

Ficus
FIG

Ficus retusa

Leaf shown
half life
size

The figs constitute a large tree family with many hundreds of species showing a variety of characteristics. Most are natives of the jungles of south-east Asia and are therefore classed as tropical. Many people are familiar with *Ficus elastica*, the rubber plant commonly grown as a houseplant, but for bonsai the smaller-leaved forms are most effective. *Ficus benjamina*, the graceful weeping fig and *F. retusa*, an erect branching plant, are the two most commonly seen bonsai species in Europe and North America. In the warmer climates of Australia a much wider range of figs can be grown, including *F. macrophylla*, the Moreton Bay fig, *F. rubiginosa*, the Port Jackson fig and *F. platypoda*.

Ficus retusa
FIG
This vigorous specimen grown in informal upright style is 25 years old and 75cm (30in) high.

BONSAI STYLES

Can be grown in all styles and at all sizes, but small-leaved forms are best cultivated as small-scale bonsai. Banyan types such as *F. retusa* have such marvellous aerial roots that these are often featured, sometimes in clasped-to-rock style.

CULTIVATION

☼ **Position** Tolerates low light levels but requires warm conditions, with temperature no lower than 15°C (60°F). Protect from draughts and try to avoid fluctuations in temperature and soil moisture.

💧 **Watering** Water generously during the growing season but moderate the supply in winter, particularly if the plant is grown in low light (as with indoor bonsai grown in a normally lit living room). Check the soil daily and make sure it remains continuously moist. Mist-spraying is beneficial, as the plant needs high humidity.

▣ **Feeding** Every two weeks throughout the growing season.

▣ **Repotting** Every second year in spring, in basic soil mix.

✂ **Pruning** Trim new shoots back to two or three leaves throughout the growing season, except where extension growth is needed. Strong plants respond well to total leaf-cutting in summer. All cuts will ooze latex sap, so larger branch pruning is best carried out in winter and wounds treated with a cut paste or similar. Wiring can be done at any time, but remove wire quickly if there are signs of it biting into the stems, as they mark easily.

✍ **Propagation** From softwood cuttings in summer. By air layering in spring.

Foliage *Glossy evergreen leaves are densely massed on divided branches.*

Structure *The powerful trunk supports an interesting arrangement of branches at varying angles.*

Roots *Heavy aerial roots form a complex network swathing the base of the trunk.*

Container *A green glazed Chinese "cloud" pot gives balance to the design.*

Fuchsia
FUCHSIA

These plants have a fascination for many people, with fuchsia societies existing all around the world whose members propagate and grow the thousands of different fuchsia types. A common method of fuchsia growing is as a "standard", whereby the stem is tied to a cane and side shoots rubbed off until a trunk-like stem is formed, on which new shoots are trimmed and pinched back to form a pendulous head. Bonsai fuchsias are similarly trained to form tree-like shapes. As natives of Central and South America, fuchsias are sub-tropical plants although many varieties can withstand a slight degree of frost. The best choices for bonsai are those with small leaves and flowers, such as *Fuchsia microphylla*, *F. × bacillaris* and the cultivars 'Tom Thumb' and 'Lady Thumb'.

Fuchsia microphylla

Leaf shown life size

Fuchsia microphylla
DWARF FUCHSIA
This is an 8-year-old specimen only 15cm (6in) high, grown from a cutting in root-over-rock style. This species is grown as bonsai for its attractive structure rather than for flower display.

BONSAI STYLES
Informal upright, slanting, semicascade, cascade, root-over-rock. Suitable for extra-small to medium sizes.

CULTIVATION
☼ **Position** Fuchsias grown indoors need a bright position. When grown outdoors, the minimum temperature must be 7°C (45°F).

Watering Daily throughout the growing season. In winter, keep the soil barely moist or allow it to dry out between waterings, but keep up humidity by mist-spraying.

Feeding Every two weeks throughout the growing season.

Repotting Annually in early spring, in basic soil mix.

Pruning Constantly pinch out new shoots throughout the growing season. Branch pruning can be carried out in winter.

Propagation From softwood cuttings in spring or summer.

Foliage *Tiny leaves and fine, delicate twigs contribute to an impressively tree-like image even on this small scale.*

Structure *Interesting shapes and textures in the trunk and roots are effectively displayed by the styling on rock.*

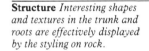

Container *Brown unglazed Japanese Tokoname shallow oval pot.*

MAIDENHAIR TREE
Gingko biloba

The gingko, one of the few deciduous conifers, is the only remaining member of a family of trees common in prehistoric times. Long thought to be extinct in the wild, it was rediscovered in Chekiang province, eastern China, in the seventeenth century and has since been grown as an ornamental tree all over the world. In Japan it is associated with sacred sites and is often found growing near Buddhist temples. It is commonly planted as a "street" tree in the Far East, being tolerant of pollution and almost pest-free. The young tree has an open branch structure that with age gives way to a dense columnar shape. It is most effective as bonsai when this natural formation is recreated by pruning to achieve a "flame-shaped" or columnar silhouette.

Gingko biloba

Leaf shown half life size

Foliage *Large attractively shaped leaves take on this pale yellow tone in autumn.*

Gingko biloba
MAIDENHAIR TREE
This 20-year-old tree grown in formal upright style stands 75cm (30in) high.

Structure *The young tree was planted out for several years to build a heavy trunk; it has since been pot-grown for 12 years.*

Container *Brown unglazed Japanese Tokoname ware.*

BONSAI STYLES
Informal upright, clump. Due to leaf size and coarseness of twigs, medium to extra-large sizes are preferred.

CULTIVATION
☼ **Position** Full sun, except for very young specimens which need some shade. Protect from frost in winter, particularly the roots, which have very high moisture content.

🌢 **Watering** Daily throughout the growing season; give plenty of water to moisten the soil thoroughly. Keep soil relatively dry throughout winter as roots are easily frost-damaged if too wet.

▦ **Feeding** Twice monthly from spring until midsummer.

▰ **Repotting** In early spring, annually until the tree is 10 years old. Thereafter, repot every second year, then every third year for aged specimens. Use basic soil mix.

✂ **Pruning** Prune new growth twice during the growing season, in spring and autumn. Trim shoots back to two or three leaves, with topmost leaf on the outside. Cut back branches after leaf fall. When styling, avoid large cuts visible from the front, as cuts do not callus and grow over as in other deciduous trees. Avoid wiring if possible, as the soft bark marks very easily.

✍ **Propagation** From seed stratified in autumn and sown in early spring. From hardwood cuttings in autumn. By air layering in spring.

Gleditsia triacanthos
HONEYLOCUST

Gleditsia triacanthos

Leaf shown life size

The honeylocust is native to the central and eastern United States of America. In nature it is a large, elegant tree with delicate frond-like leaves that turn a beautiful pale yellow in autumn. The branches bear distinctive three-pointed thorns. The tree is a member of the pea family *(Leguminosae)* and its seeds are encased in long brown, flattened seed pods. The honeylocust has been found to be ideal for city planting as it is highly tolerant of atmospheric pollution, an attribute equally useful for bonsai cultivation in town gardens.

Gleditsia triacanthos
HONEYLOCUST
This six-year-old tree, 25cm (10in) in height, is styled as an informal upright.

Foliage *Fresh green compound leaves give a delicate appearance to the bonsai, although the tree has a strong, tolerant constitution.*

Structure *The trunk was thickened by growing in open ground for four years. The tree has been potted for only a few months and its shape will undergo further refinement.*

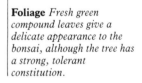

Container *German "Schilf" glazed round pot by Petra Engelke balancing the height and radial spread of the bonsai.*

BONSAI STYLES

Informal upright, slanting, semicascade, cascade, twin-trunk. Suitable for small to medium sizes.

CULTIVATION

☼ **Position** Full sun. Provide some frost protection in winter to avoid twig die-back.

Watering Daily throughout the growing season, sparingly in winter to keep soil evenly moist.

Feeding Every two weeks throughout the growing season.

Repotting Every second year in spring, in basic soil mix.

Pruning In winter, branches can be pruned back hard or totally removed back to the trunk. New shoots will readily appear from old wood in spring. Summer pruning consists of shortening new shoots as they grow.

Propagation From seed sown in spring. From softwood cuttings in summer.

Ilex crenata
JAPANESE EVERGREEN HOLLY

Ilex crenata 'Convexa'

Leaf shown life size

The hollies are long-lived trees and shrubs found throughout the northern hemisphere. The common European holly, *Ilex aquifolium*, is familiar for its glossy, prickly leaves, but it does not make a good bonsai subject as the leaves are thick and coarse and it forms stout green shoots rather than a fine, woody twig structure. The Japanese evergreen holly, *I. crenata*, is a much better choice for bonsai, having small leaves and finer twig growth. Both *I. crenata* and *I. serrata* (see facing page) are commonly called Japanese holly, but they are not at all similar in appearance and it is necessary to specify that one is evergreen and the other deciduous. *I. crenata* is a slow-growing evergreen shrub with smooth, box-like leaves and insignificant white flowers that are followed, on female plants, by shiny black berries. Two varieties are also useful for bonsai, *I. c.* 'Convexa', a more compact form with glossy, convex leaves, and *I. c.* 'Stokes', a dwarf compact form with tiny leaves.

BONSAI STYLES

Suitable for all styles except broom, and for extra-small to large sizes. Interesting roots sometimes develop which may be featured in the bonsai design.

Ilex crenata 'Convexa'
JAPANESE EVERGREEN HOLLY
Styled as informal upright, this tree is 15 years old and 20cm (8in.) high.

Foliage *Small, glossy evergreen leaves provide bright colour interest.*

Roots *Heavy, twisted roots exposed above the soil add to the textural complexity of the design.*

Structure *The long, low branch extending from the main angle of the trunk contributes to an asymmetrical triangular silhouette.*

Container *German green glazed round pot with subtly varied colouring by Petra Engelke.*

CULTIVATION

 **Position** Indifferent to sun or shade. Very shade-tolerant and therefore sometimes used for indoor culture where low light levels would be a problem for other plants. Outdoor bonsai need frost protection for the roots in winter, and foliage should be sheltered from freezing winds.

Watering Water frequently, as soon as the soil dries out. Mist-spray foliage daily in summer, but not when in full sun.

Feeding Every two weeks throughout the growing season.

Repotting Every second year, in basic soil mix.

Pruning Early formative pruning can be almost like topiary, with constant clipping to form compact growth. Subsequent training to refine the structure consists of removing surplus branches and shortening new shoots back to two or three leaves. Take care if wiring is necessary, as stems are brittle.

Propagation From softwood cuttings in spring or summer, which must be taken from female plants to produce fruiting specimens.

Ilex serrata (I. sieboldii)

JAPANESE DECIDUOUS HOLLY

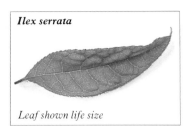

Ilex serrata

Leaf shown life size

A native of Japan, *Ilex serrata* is a beautiful bonsai subject. The thin, serrated leaves are closer in appearance to a cherry or apple leaf than to the glossy, spiny evergreen foliage of the common holly (*I. aquifolium*). It makes a fine sight in autumn and winter, when the light grey bark contrasts well with the bright red berries. Autumn leaf colour ranges through shades from yellow to purple. To obtain berries a female form must be grown, but a male is needed for pollination. This should be grown nearby, but need not be bonsai – the male form can be cultivated as a garden shrub or full-size pot-grown specimen.

I.s. 'Leucocarpa' is a white-berried form sometimes used for bonsai in Japan, and in recent years a yellow-berried variety has become available. Another good choice for bonsai is the dwarf form *I.s.* 'Subtilis' ('Koshobai'), a miniature highly suited to the smallest bonsai sizes. This is a hermaphrodite, and so does not need a male plant for pollination, and acts as a pollinator.

Foliage *Delicate oval deciduous leaves turn from light green to shades of red and purple in autumn.*

Ilex serrata
JAPANESE DECIDUOUS HOLLY
This 15-year-old informal upright is 45cm (18in) high.

Structure *The split and divided trunk, attractively aged, supports an open branch structure of interest in winter when it carries the bright berries.*

Container *A blue glazed Japanese Tokoname "cloud" pot provides balance and contrast in the design.*

BONSAI STYLES

Suitable for all styles and all sizes.

CULTIVATION

Position Sun or shade. A sunny position is best for good autumn colour and early ripening of berries. Provide some frost protection in winter.

Watering Daily through summer. Keep the soil moist through autumn and winter or the fruit will drop.

Feeding Every two weeks throughout the growing season.

Repotting Annually in early spring, or every second year for specimens aged about 10 years or more. Use basic soil mix.

Pruning Remove all unwanted new shoots in early summer while they are still tender. Trim other shoots back to two or three leaves.

Propagation From stratified seed sown in early spring (but most seedlings will be male and plants will not bear fruit). From softwood cuttings in spring or summer. By air layering in spring.

Jasminum nudiflorum
WINTER JASMINE

Jasminum nudiflorum

Leaf shown half life size

The bright yellow flowers of winter jasmine are a cheerful and welcome sight in the depths of winter, whether the plant is grown as bonsai or in its more familiar role as a climbing shrub. The flowers are borne on bare wood and the single star-shaped blossoms stand out well against the arching green branches. In spring and summer, the stems are covered with narrow, dark green leaves and the scale of both leaves and flowers makes this charming deciduous shrub especially suitable for bonsai cultivation.

BONSAI STYLES

Informal upright, slanting, semicascade, root-over-rock, clasped-to-rock, twin-trunk, clump. Suitable for extra-small to medium sizes.

CULTIVATION

Position Sunny, but shaded from full sun in summer. Protect from hard frosts in winter.

Watering Daily in summer. Through winter, supply enough water to prevent soil from drying out.

Feeding Two or three times a month from the end of flowering until late summer.

Repotting Annually, at any time of year if treated carefully, but preferably in autumn. Use basic soil mix.

Pruning The winter jasmine flowers on the previous year's wood. New shoots should be pruned back to one set of leaves in late spring and branches can be pruned again to three or four sets of leaves in autumn.

Propagation From softwood cuttings in summer, or hardwood cuttings in autumn or winter. By air layering in summer.

Flowers *Sunshine yellow flowers appear on bare branches in winter, soon to be followed by tiny dark green leaves.*

Structure *The configuration of trunk and branches has been styled by pruning; no wiring was necessary.*

Jasminum nudiflorum
WINTER JASMINE
This shrubby plant is given an effectively tree-like appearance in an informal upright bonsai 10 years old and 17cm (7in) high.

Container *A blue glazed Japanese Tokoname oval creates a striking colour contrast with the flowers.*

Juniperus × media 'Blaauw'
CHINESE JUNIPER

Juniperus × media is recognized as a naturally occurring hybrid, a cross between *J. chinensis* and *J. sabina*, indigenous to north-east Asia. Many popular garden varieties of these hybrids are in cultivation with widely varying appearance and habits. The foliage tends to have a mixture of juvenile needle-like leaves and adult scale-like leaves. This combination on one plant makes it difficult to design an effective bonsai, so generally varieties or clones with predominantly one or the other type are preferred. *J. × m.* 'Blaauw' is a strong-growing conifer in which the main stems splay out upward from the centre to create a fan-shaped silhouette of fine-textured scale-like foliage in an attractive shade of bluish grey-green. The bark is shaggy, purple-brown in colour, and has the advantage for bonsai of giving an appearance of age while still young.

BONSAI STYLES
Suitable for all styles except broom, and for all sizes.

CULTIVATION

☼ **Position** The foliage can scorch in hot sun, so partial shade is advisable during summer months, otherwise place in full light. Shelter from hard frosts to prevent discoloration and damage to foliage.

💧 **Watering** Daily through summer, and mist-spray foliage. Water less frequently in winter, but keep soil moist.

▦ **Feeding** Every two weeks from the beginning of the growing season until mid autumn.

▤ **Repotting** Every second year for young trees. Trees aged 10 years or more can be repotted up to every five years, according to root development which should be inspected annually. With care, can be repotted at any time of year, but early spring is preferable. Use free-draining soil mix.

✎ **Pruning** Maintain a compact shape by finger-pruning, but do not pinch back too hard at any one time as this encourages a flush of juvenile needle-like growth. Wiring can be done at any time.

⚘ **Propagation** From softwood cuttings at any time.

Juniperus × media 'Blaauw'

Leaf shown half life size

Foliage *Fine scale-like evergreen foliage provides rich texture in the design.*

Juniperus × media 'Blaauw'
CHINESE JUNIPER
The many fine characteristics of this 20-year-old tree are well displayed in root-connected triple-trunk style at 85cm (34in) high.

Structure *The three-trunk style was created from a multi-trunk young tree, pruned and wired to give horizontal branch spread. It has been grown as bonsai for four years.*

Container *Grey unglazed Japanese Tokoname rectangle with indented corners.*

Juniperus rigida
NEEDLE JUNIPER

This graceful small evergreen tree is a native of Japan, where it is very popular for bonsai cultivation. It has fine, needle-like leaves borne on arching branches with drooping tips. Female trees produce berries which ripen from green to purplish-black over two years, but for fruiting to occur, male and female trees must be grown together during the flowering season in early spring. Another attractive needle juniper for bonsai is *Juniperus communis*, a plant widely distributed across Europe, North America and Asia. Its needles are banded with white on the upper surfaces and have pale undersides. There are many different cultivated varieties including prostrate and columnar forms.

Juniperus rigida
NEEDLE JUNIPER
This 30-year-old tree, styled as informal upright, stands 51cm (20in) high.

BONSAI STYLES

Suitable for all styles except broom, and for all sizes.

CULTIVATION

☼ **Position** Full sun. Give some frost protection in winter, as severe frost may turn the needles brown.

❀ **Watering** Daily through summer, and mist-spray foliage. Water sparingly during winter months but keep soil moist.

▪ **Feeding** Every two weeks from the beginning of spring to early autumn.

▤ **Repotting** At any time during the growing season, but preferably early to mid spring. Repot young specimens every two years, trees aged 10 years or more up to every five years, as necessary according to root development. Use free-draining soil mix.

✂ **Pruning** Pinch out the tops of new growth throughout the growing season. Lower and inner branches may die back without adequate sun and air, so prune the tree to allow light to penetrate. Best time for wiring is autumn to winter.

✍ **Propagation** From stratified seed sown in spring. From softwood cuttings in summer.

Juniperus rigida

Leaf shown life size

Fruit *Purplish-black, ripe berries provide decorative contrast to the spiky needles. Shown in spring, this is the previous season's crop.*

Structure *Wiring is used to create an open spread of branches and redistribute the foliage masses.*

Foliage *Clusters of short, prickly needles clothe the full length of each branch.*

Trunk *The tree was grown in open ground for several years, then pruned back severely and the trunk heavily sculpted to form the driftwood effect.*

Container *Terracotta-coloured unglazed Japanese Tokoname "drum" pot with glazed green rivet design, reflecting the colour contrast of bark and foliage.*

Juniperus sargentii
CHINESE or SARGENT'S JUNIPER

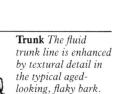

Juniperus sargentii

Leaf shown life size

This juniper is a native of Japan where it forms a semi-prostrate shrub in rocky areas in the mountains and by the sea. It has bright green adult scale-like foliage and an attractive red-brown, shaggy bark. The trunk and branches are highly flexible and can be bent and shaped without damage. Many fine examples of bonsai using this material are to be seen in Japan, some with a history of several generations. Some of the finest specimens have been styled from collected trees from mountainous regions and are enhanced by the incorporation into the design of existing dead wood which can be carved, bleached and treated against decay to give a very aged, rugged look to the bonsai. The foliage pads naturally create gentle, rolling curves forming a cloud-like silhouette.

Foliage *The fine-textured foliage has been repeatedly finger-pruned to create cloud-like masses.*

BONSAI STYLES

Suitable for all styles except broom, and for all sizes.

CULTIVATION

☼ **Position** Some shade is required from hot summer sun, otherwise place in full light. Shelter from hard frosts, which discolour foliage to a bronze colour until renewed in spring.

Watering Daily throughout the growing season, and mist-spray foliage in summer. Keep soil moist in winter as freezing winds can dry out the foliage.

Feeding Every two weeks from the beginning of the growing season until mid autumn.

Repotting Every second year for young specimens. Trees aged over 10 years can be repotted up to every five years, according to root development. With care, trees can be repotted at any time of year, but early spring is preferable. Use free-draining soil mix.

Pruning Finger-prune tips of new growth as they extend throughout the growing season. Do not prune too hard, or juvenile needle-like growth will be encouraged. Wiring can be done at any time.

Propagation From softwood cuttings at any time.

Juniperus sargentii
CHINESE or SARGENT'S JUNIPER
This 25-year-old tree styled as informal upright gives an impression of massive height at an actual size of 75cm (30in).

Structure *Wiring has been used to develop the informal shape, a solid structure on which to display the neat pads of foliage.*

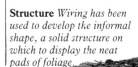

Container *A red-brown Japanese Tokoname oval selected to highlight the natural warm tones of the bark colours.*

Trunk *The fluid trunk line is enhanced by textural detail in the typical aged-looking, flaky bark.*

Lagerstroemia indica
CRAPE MYRTLE

The crape myrtle is a sub-tropical tree-like shrub native to China, Japan and Korea. It has long been popular as an ornamental plant in countries around the Mediterranean and in the southern states of the USA. One reason for its popularity is the generous display of showy flowers, in shades from white through pink to mauve, which appear in late summer. This is a short-lived flourish, however, and in bonsai cultivation an equal attraction is the decorative bark, which peels away in strips resulting in a grey trunk patterned with areas of pink and brown. This can be appreciated year round and is seen at its best in winter, when most other flowering bonsai are lacking in interest.

Lagerstroemia indica

Leaf shown half life size

Lagerstroemia indica
CRAPE MYRTLE
This specimen is 20 years old and 50cm (20in) high, grown in root-over-rock style.

Foliage *A spreading canopy of bright green leaves balances the depth created in the design by the rock planting.*

BONSAI STYLES

Informal upright, slanting, semicascade, root-over-rock. Suitable for medium to extra-large sizes.

CULTIVATION

☼ **Position** In temperate climates, can be grown outdoors in summer. Must be kept cool but frost-free in winter, to allow leaf-drop and dormancy. A combination of warm temperatures and low light levels results in sappy, elongated growths, so maintain cool conditions through winter and early spring when daylight hours are short.

💧 **Watering** Daily from spring through autumn. Water sparingly during winter dormancy, but check soil regularly and do not allow it to dry out completely.

▦ **Feeding** Every two weeks throughout the growing season.

▥ **Repotting** Annually in early spring, in basic soil mix.

✄ **Pruning** Let new shoots extend until late spring, then cut back to two or three leaves on each shoot. Do not prune further until autumn, as flowers appear on new shoots that develop after the late spring pruning.

✍ **Propagation** From seed sown in spring. From softwood cuttings in summer.

Bark *Colourful mottled patches develop with age.*

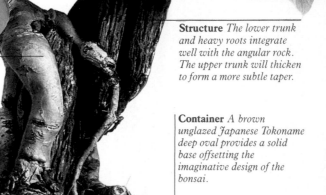

Structure *The lower trunk and heavy roots integrate well with the angular rock. The upper trunk will thicken to form a more subtle taper.*

Container *A brown unglazed Japanese Tokoname deep oval provides a solid base offsetting the imaginative design of the bonsai.*

Larix decidua
EUROPEAN LARCH

Larches are among the few deciduous conifers and they are found in the mountainous and cooler regions of the northern hemisphere. Their natural habit is a slender, upright, conical silhouette with gracefully drooping branches and foliage. The bright green needle-like leaves grow in clusters and turn to a golden colour in autumn before they are shed. Larches are highly recommended as first bonsai for beginners, being tough, adaptable trees suited to a wide range of styles and sizes. *Larix decidua*, the European larch, is an elegant tree native to central and southern Europe. It has a greyish bark, forming interesting cracks and ridges in older specimens, and pale straw-coloured twigs.

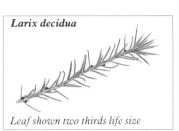

Larix decidua

Leaf shown two thirds life size

BONSAI STYLES

Suitable for all styles except broom, and for all sizes.

CULTIVATION

☼ **Position** Full sun. In locations with warm and humid conditions, larches do not grow so well as in situations more like their native conditions; the needles grow longer and are reflexed as compared to the short, compact needle clusters which form in cooler, drier climates. Small bonsai sizes need frost protection in winter.

💧 **Watering** Daily throughout the growing season. Water sparingly in winter but do not allow soil to dry out.

▦ **Feeding** Every two weeks throughout the growing season.

▤ **Repotting** Larches produce strong roots and resent being pot-bound; roots should be inspected every year and annual root pruning may be necessary. Repot in early spring, before buds show green, in basic soil mix.

✂ **Pruning** During the growing season, pinch back new shoots from side branches and trunk. Branch and twig refinement, pruning to shape and/or wiring are best carried out in winter when the tree is bare of foliage.

✐ **Propagation** From seed sown in late spring. From cuttings from leading shoots in late summer or early autumn. By layering in late spring or early summer.

Foliage *Small, fine, needle-like deciduous leaves turn to straw-yellow shades in autumn before dropping.*

Structure *Straight, gently tapering trunk supports an even spread of horizontal branches.*

Bark *The aged appearance has developed naturally over the 24 years of the tree's life.*

Larix decidua
EUROPEAN LARCH
This impressive 24-year-old tree, grown from seed and styled as a formal upright, is 30cm (12in) high.

Container *A red-brown unglazed Japanese Tokoname oval subtly enhances the tree's range of seasonal colours.*

Larix kaempferi (L. leptolepis)
JAPANESE LARCH

As indicated by the common name, *Larix kaempferi* is a native of Japan, although it is widely planted in other areas of the world. In Great Britain it is favoured as a forestry tree, as it grows more strongly and quickly than the European species, an attribute also useful in bonsai specimens. Like all larches it has a graceful conical shape, with drooping branches and branchlets. The new twigs are red-orange darkening to almost purple by winter time, and this colouring is what mainly differentiates the Japanese from the European larch. These two species are the larches most commonly grown in Europe, although there is also a hybrid between them, *L. × eurolepis* (Dunkeld larch) which is popular in Scotland. In North America *L. laricina*, the tamarack, is widespread, particularly in the northern states of the USA and in Canada.

Larix kaempferi

Leaf shown life size

Larix kaempferi
JAPANESE LARCH
This graceful tree in slanting style is 65cm (26in) high and 20 years old, and has been trained as bonsai for 10 years.

BONSAI STYLES

Suitable for all styles except broom, and for all sizes.

CULTIVATION

⚙ **Position** Full sun. In warm and humid locations, larches grow needles that are long and reflexed, as compared to the short, compact needle clusters exhibited in cooler, drier climates more like their native conditions. Small bonsai sizes require protection from frost.

💧 **Watering** Daily throughout the growing season. In winter, water less frequently, but do not let the soil dry out.

▦ **Feeding** Every two weeks throughout the growing season.

▣ **Repotting** Like all larches, this species is strong-rooted and resents being pot-bound. Inspect roots every year; annual root pruning may be necessary. Repot in early spring, before buds show green, in basic soil mix.

✀ **Pruning** Pinch back new shoots from side branches and trunk throughout the growing season. Branch and twig refinement, pruning to shape and/or wiring are best carried out when branches are bare in winter.

⚑ **Propagation** From seed sown in late spring. From cuttings from leading shoots in late summer or early autumn. By layering in late spring or early summer.

Foliage *Short needles are distributed evenly in dense clusters. In autumn the colour turns to an attractive pale yellow.*

Structure *Several years in open ground before potting allowed the trunk to thicken and a strong root buttress to develop.*

Container *The width of the unglazed Japanese Tokoname oval balances the spread of the tree's lower branches.*

Lonicera
HONEYSUCKLE

Honeysuckle species are widely distributed throughout the northern hemisphere. There are deciduous and evergreen forms, shrubby and climbing plants, many with fragrant blossoms. All are worth trying as bonsai and provided a substantial trunk can be obtained, the softer growth can be successfully trained to shape. The dwarf shrubby honeysuckle *Lonicera nitida* is excellent for bonsai. Its tiny evergreen leaves make it suitable for even the smallest bonsai. It responds very well to clipping and shaping, which transforms its somewhat lax habit into tightly formed, dense pads of foliage.

Lonicera nitida
Leaf shown life size

Lonicera nitida
DWARF HONEYSUCKLE
This interesting informal upright is 25 years old and 65cm (26in) in height.

Foliage *Tiny, densely packed evergreen leaves form attractive foliage pads.*

Structure *A clean, tapering trunk line has been created by pruning and training an old hedging plant, grown as bonsai for five years.*

Container *English glazed oval with curving sides, with subtle colour variation and crackle-glaze effect.*

BONSAI STYLES

Suitable for all styles except broom, and for all sizes. Dwarf forms are particularly well suited to small sizes.

CULTIVATION

Position Full sun, with partial shade in summer. Frost protection is advisable for small bonsai and those grown in shallow pots or on slabs.

Watering Daily throughout the growing season. Less water is needed in winter, but take care not to let the soil dry out, especially for evergreen species.

Feeding Every two weeks in the summer.

Repotting In late spring, about every second year, in basic soil mix.

Pruning In early stages of development, plants can be treated almost in the manner of topiary — constant clipping is vital to encourage dense growth. Thereafter, more detailed work with fine scissors is necessary to refine the design. Old trunks can be carved in winter and wiring is best done in late spring or early summer.

Propagation From softwood or hardwood cuttings in spring or summer. By layering or air layering in summer.

Malus
CRAB APPLE

These charming shrubs and small trees are popular for their spring blossom and colourful autumn fruit. The variety most often seen as bonsai is *Malus cerasifera*, the Nagasaki crab apple, because of its prolific flowering and fruiting. The flowers are pink in bud, opening to white; these give way to a generous display of cherry-like red fruits. *M. halliana*, Hall's crab apple, has attractive pink flowers and glossy green foliage, but the purple fruits are small and sparse. *M.* 'Golden Hornet' bears a generous crop of yellow fruits retained long after leaf fall. Of the many varieties suited to bonsai *M.* 'Red Jade' is a lovely weeping form, *M.* 'Profusion' is a purple-leaved form with wine red flowers and deep red fruits.

Malus cerasifera

Leaf shown half life size

Foliage *The fresh green of late spring forms a perfect foil for the flower colours.*

Flowers *Tight pink buds unfold into fragrant, white-petalled blossoms with prominent stamens.*

BONSAI STYLES

Informal upright, slanting, semicascade, twin-trunk, clump. Suitable for all sizes: for small bonsai, select varieties with smallest fruits.

CULTIVATION

☼ **Position** Full light or sun throughout the year. *Malus* can withstand very cold winters, but some frost protection is advisable for roots of bonsai in shallow containers.

💧 **Watering** Daily throughout the growing season. Give plenty of water when the plant is fruiting or the apples will shrivel and drop. The plants are susceptible to mildew — regular spraying is necessary.

🔲 **Feeding** Every week until flowering. Stop feeding as fruit forms and do not resume until fruits are well developed: otherwise, the feed may trigger leafy growth at the expense of a good crop of fruits.

▦ **Repotting** Annually in early spring before bud burst. Use basic soil mix.

✂ **Pruning** In spring, finger-prune new shoots to one or two leaves. Trim long shoots in autumn.

🌱 **Propagation** Most commonly by grafting. From seed sown in late autumn. By layering in spring or early summer.

Malus cerasifera
NAGASAKI CRAB APPLE
This beautiful example of an informal upright is 12 years old and 30cm (12in) high.

Container *A relatively deep unglazed Japanese Tokoname pot allows the reservoir of moisture needed to encourage fruiting.*

Structure *A rugged trunk was formed from a graft grown for several years in open ground. The shape of the bonsai was created by pruning.*

Malus halliana
HALL'S CRAB APPLE
A small informal upright, 6 years old and only 12cm (5in) high, shows a charming arrangement of neat oval leaves, tinted purple on the undersides, and deep pink buds that open to brighter pink flowers. Natural lichens give the bark an aged appearance.

Fruit *Bright red berries take over as the main focus of interest in autumn, as the leaves take on red tints and gradually drop away.*

Structure *A mass of twiggy branches was retained after pruning to maximize flower and fruit production.*

Malus cerasifera
NAGASAKI CRAB APPLE
The autumn display of *M. cerasifera* is shown in an informal upright 25 years old and 85cm (34in) high. Comparison with the bonsai in full blossom (opposite) shows the range of seasonal attractions in this species.

Container *The depth allows enough moisture to be retained between waterings to swell the crop of berries.*

Morus
MULBERRY

Morus alba

Leaf shown one third life size

Mulberries originate in Asia and have long been cultivated in China for the mulberry leaves which are the staple diet of the silkworm. It was also for the purpose of providing food for silkworms that the trees were introduced to Europe during the time of the Roman empire, but they have since become a familiar ornamental feature of parks and gardens. In nature, mulberries are small to medium-sized trees, forming gnarled, picturesque shapes. The heavy trunk, rugged bark and toothed leaves form an interesting combination of shape and texture in a bonsai specimen. The flowers are fairly insignificant, but are soon followed by small edible fruits which ripen from white to reddish-pink.

Morus alba
WHITE MULBERRY
An impressive effect of age is achieved in this informal upright, 30 years old and 50cm (20in) high.

Foliage *Bright green serrated leaves form a decorative mass.*

BONSAI STYLES

Informal upright, slanting, semicascade, cascade, root-over-rock, twin-trunk, clump. Suitable for all sizes.

CULTIVATION

☼ **Position** Full sun. Some frost protection in winter is recommended.

💧 **Watering** Daily throughout the growing season. Water less frequently in winter but keep soil moist at all times, the tree is moisture-loving.

Feeding Apply fertilizer every two weeks from spring to summer. Change to a high-potash feed in late summer to autumn.

Repotting About every two years, in early spring, in free-draining soil mix.

Pruning Trim new growth back to two leaves. Remove large leaves as they appear. Prune heavy branches in late winter or early spring before bud burst.

Propagation From stratified seed sown in spring. From cuttings in spring. By layering or air layering in summer.

Structure *A powerful root spread anchors the movement through the excellently tapered trunk, which also has great textural interest.*

Container *A grey unglazed Japanese Tokoname oval forms a strong base for the heavy trunk of the bonsai.*

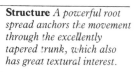

Murraya paniculata

JASMINE ORANGE

The combination of graceful, delicate leaves and a pale satin-like trunk makes *Murraya paniculata* a popular subject for bonsai in southern China and India, where it is indigenous. The common name jasmine orange derives from the strongly and sweetly scented, bell-shaped white flowers, similar to those of jasmine, and the small brightly coloured berries, resembling tiny oranges, that form in midsummer. Another common name sometimes used is the satinwood tree, referring to the texture of the trunk. This tropical evergreen shrub needs warm growing conditions and in temperate climates is only suitable for growing as indoor bonsai.

Murraya paniculata

Leaf shown one quarter life size

Foliage *The small leaflets of the evergreen pinnate foliage give a delicate appearance to the bonsai.*

BONSAI STYLES

Informal upright, slanting, semicascade, cascade, twin-trunk, clump, group. Suitable for all sizes.

CULTIVATION

☼ **Position** The tree needs plenty of light and warmth, but should be shaded from hot summer sun. In winter, maintain a minimum temperature of 17°C (63°F).

💧 **Watering** Daily throughout the growing season, less frequently in winter. Maintain a regular watering routine to keep soil lightly moist, but not soaked, as *Murraya* requires humid conditions.

▣ **Feeding** Every two weeks between mid spring and early autumn. In winter, feed every four to six weeks.

▤ **Repotting** Every second year in spring, in basic soil mix.

✂ **Pruning** Prune at any time during the growing season. Trim new shoots back to two leaves when five or six leaves have been produced.

✦ **Propagation** From seed sown in autumn. From softwood cuttings in spring or summer.

Murraya paniculata
JASMINE ORANGE
This 20-year-old tree is 85cm (34in) high and styled as an informal upright.

Bark *Pale, smooth bark is a feature of this species, sometimes called the satinwood tree.*

Structure *Strong roots flowing into ridges and hollows at the base of the trunk emphasize the upright line and clean taper above.*

Container *A green glazed Chinese incurved round pot matches the elegance of the tree.*

Picea SPRUCE

Spruces are quick-growing evergreen conifers, native to the northern hemisphere. *Picea glehnii*, the Sakhalin spruce, is the preferred species for bonsai in Japan, but plant health regulations prevent its export. The northern European species *P. abies*, the common or Norway spruce, is familiar in Great Britain as the traditional Christmas tree, with its conical shape, shiny, dark green needles and red-brown bark. *P. a.* 'Little Gem' is a dwarf form highly suitable for rock-planting and for small bonsai. This is almost indistinguishable from *P. glehnii* 'Yatsubusa', the dwarf spruce commonly used for the same purpose in Japan. Another dwarf form well suited to bonsai is *P. glauca* 'Albertiana conica', a cultivar of the Alberta spruce native to the Canadian Rocky Mountains. This is also conical in shape and is often featured in group plantings.

Picea abies 'Little Gem'

Leaf shown life size

BONSAI STYLES

Suitable for all styles except broom. Dwarf cultivars are best suited to small sizes, other species can be grown at medium to large sizes.

CULTIVATION

☼ **Position** Full sun. Small bonsai require frost protection in winter.

◑ **Watering** Water daily throughout summer and mist-spray foliage. Water sparingly in winter but do not let soil dry out.

▦ **Feeding** Every two weeks from early spring to mid autumn.

▬ **Repotting** Every second year in early to mid spring, before bud break, or in autumn. Trees over 10 years of age may be repotted about every five years. Use free-draining soil mix.

✄ **Pruning** Throughout spring and summer, pinch out new growth when shoots are about 2.5cm (1in) long. With the soft part of your fingertips, pull off about one-third. Prune branches and wire between late autumn and winter.

✍ **Propagation** From stratified seed sown in winter or early spring. From cuttings of current season's growth in late autumn or early spring.

Foliage *Tree-like silhouettes have been created by thinning out the tight green "buns" of small needles.*

Structure *The striking shape of the rock is emphasized by arranging the trunk lines of the small trees to lead the eye through the design.*

Picea abies 'Little Gem'
DWARF SPRUCE
Tiny 10-year-old trees planted on rock form a dramatic landscape effect. The tallest tree is 8cm (3in) high.

Container *A green-grey Japanese Tokoname "suiban" (water tray) contains the pool surrounding a rugged piece of Ibigawa rock.*

Pinus mugo
MOUNTAIN PINE

Pinus mugo

Leaf shown life size

The mountain pine is native to the mountains of central Europe. It is very tough and able to withstand harsh conditions, forming a scrubby, semi-prostrate twisted tree in a poor situation but capable of becoming a dense, bushy large shrub or small tree in more favourable situations. Rugged old specimens have been collected from the mountains of Switzerland and Austria with the potential to become superb bonsai in years to come. The variable nature of the mountain pine has given rise to many dwarf and slow-growing clones in cultivation. Two of the more popular named clones are 'Gnom', which forms a small, tight, globular mound of dark green, short needles, and 'Mops', a similar but slower-growing and more dwarf form.

BONSAI STYLES

Suitable for all styles except broom, and for all sizes. Dwarf forms are best suited to smaller bonsai sizes and are particularly effective in clasped-to-rock style.

CULTIVATION

Position Full sun. Protect from severe winter frosts and freezing winds.

Watering Daily in summer, except when soil is already moist. Pines do not like wet or waterlogged conditions. Mist-spray foliage in summer. Water sparingly in winter but do not let soil dry out.

Feeding Every three to four weeks from spring to early winter.

Repotting In early or mid spring, or in late summer, every two to five years depending on age and root development, as determined by regular inspection. Use free-draining soil mix.

Pruning When the candle-like new shoots appear, twist or pinch off any that become overgrown. Remove long primary shoots throughout the growing season. Thin or remove old or crowded twigs and foliage in autumn or winter. This is a very flexible tree for wiring.

Propagation In mid to late winter fresh seed soaked in water overnight and exposed to frost after sowing germinates easily. Grafting is the usual propagation method for dwarf forms.

Foliage Firm, upright needles growing in pairs give a vigorous character to the bonsai.

Structure The stout trunk was developed by 14 years in open ground. The bonsai has been shaped in only five years by pruning and wiring.

Pinus mugo
MOUNTAIN PINE
The tree is 21 years old and 62cm (25in) high, grown in slanting style.

Container A grey unglazed Japanese Tokoname rectangle has the visual effect of balancing the slanted trunk.

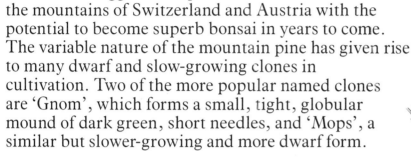

Pinus parviflora (P. pentaphylla)
JAPANESE WHITE PINE

Pinus parviflora

Leaf shown half life size

Pinus parviflora grows as a conical, medium-sized tree when young but develops a flat-topped, irregular appearance with age. A native of Japan, it is popular there for garden planting and bonsai cultivation. The botanical name translates as "small-flowered pine" and in spring small flower clusters appear which, if fertilized, form cones that may remain on the tree for some years. Usually they are removed, both to prevent waste of the tree's energy in setting seed and to preserve the design, as the cones can destroy the visual effect of the limited scale of a bonsai specimen. Many cultivars exist and those most frequently seen are dwarf forms, such as *P. p.* 'Kokonoe' and *P. p.* 'Nasamasume'.

BONSAI STYLES
Suitable for all styles except broom, and all sizes. Dwarf forms are particularly suited to smaller sizes and to clasped-to-rock style.

CULTIVATION
Position Full sun. Some frost protection is advisable in severe winters, and protection from drying, cold winds.

Watering Daily in summer, except when soil is already moist. Pines are more susceptible to deterioration from too much water than from too little. Mist-spray foliage in summer. In winter, reduce watering but do not let soil dry out.

Feeding Every three to four weeks from spring to early winter.

Repotting In early to mid spring, every two to five years depending on age and root development, as determined by regular inspection. Use free-draining soil mix.

Pruning When the candle-like shoots appear in spring, pinch out one-third to half of the new growth. Every second year, prune branch tips in late summer. Remove old needles in late summer or early autumn to allow winter light into the tree.

Propagation In winter, soak fresh seed in water overnight, discard seeds that float and use those that have sunk for sowing. Place outside and expose to frosts, but protect from birds and rodents. Germination is reliable if seed is fresh. *P. parviflora* is commonly grown by grafting onto the stronger rootstock of *P. thunbergii* and this is carried out in late winter or early spring.

Pinus parviflora
JAPANESE WHITE PINE
This strong and well-balanced informal upright is 50 years old and stands 75cm (30in) high.

Structure *Grafted on a lower trunk of Japanese black pine* (P. thunbergii) *to provide rugged bark and strong roots, the tree was field-grown for some years to thicken the trunk.*

Foliage *The needles grow in bunches of five and have white stripes on the undersides, giving the tree its common name.*

Container *A grey unglazed Japanese Tokoname rectangle complements the symmetrical silhouette of the tree.*

Pinus parviflora 'Kokonoe'
DWARF JAPANESE WHITE PINE
This dwarf form is a good choice for
smaller bonsai sizes because of the close-
growing tiny needles. In this 12-year-old
informal upright under training, several
seasons' growth will be needed to fill out
the foliage masses fully. The bonsai is
35cm (14in) high.

Structure *The small trees
have had some wire training,
to integrate the design by
encouraging them to follow
the lines of the rock.*

Pinus parviflora 'Miyajima'
DWARF JAPANESE WHITE PINE
The dwarf cultivars are ideally suited to
growing on rock, as in this detailed
planting. The 4-year-old trees are only
8cm (3in) high.

Container *The bonsai
material is planted on
Ibigawa rock displayed in a
grey-green unglazed Japanese
Tokoname "suiban" (water
tray).*

Pinus sylvestris
SCOTS PINE

Pinus sylvestris 'Beuvronensis'

Leaf shown half life size

The Scots pine is a native of western and northern Europe. An old specimen in nature has a distinctive outline, with horizontal spreading branches and a flattened top. The blue-green needles are shorter than those of most pines and are carried in pairs. The upper trunk and branches have flaking orange bark. Young trees have relatively uninteresting conical growth, which is perhaps why this species has been comparatively neglected for bonsai cultivation in favour of Japanese pines. In Britain, however, it has recently been promoted as excellent bonsai material and increasingly fine specimens are being developed. The Scots pine has given rise to many dwarf cultivars and selected clones. One of the most popular is *Pinus sylvestris* 'Beuvronensis', originating from France, a true miniature retaining the gracefulness of the full-sized tree. *P. s.* 'Watereri', better described as a slow-growing rather than a dwarf form, has striking blue-green needles and is easily trained.

Foliage *Compact, small needle clusters make this a good subject for bonsai.*

BONSAI STYLES

Suitable for all styles except broom. Particularly good as literati, which is the natural style of a mature Scots pine. Can be grown at all sizes, but dwarf forms, with shorter needles, are best for smaller sizes.

CULTIVATION

☼ **Position** Full sun. Provide protection from frosts and cold winter winds.

💧 **Watering** Like all pines, the Scots pine dislikes wet soil. Check daily but water only when the soil is drying out, moderately through the growing season and more sparingly in winter.

▦ **Feeding** Every three to four weeks from spring to early winter.

▪ **Repotting** In early to mid spring, every two to five years depending on age and root development, as determined by regular inspection. Use free-draining soil mix.

▪ **Pruning** Pinch off overgrown shoots just as needles begin to appear. Remove long primary shoots throughout the growing season. On other smaller shoots, remove one-third to half of the new candle. Prune branch tips every second year. In late summer or early winter, remove old needles and overcrowded twigs to allow winter light into the tree.

✎ **Propagation** In winter, soak fresh seed in water overnight, discard seeds that float and use those that have sunk for sowing. Place outside and expose to frosts, but protect from birds and rodents. Germination is rapid if seed is fresh. For cultivars, propagation is by grafting in late winter or early spring.

Branches *The tree has been in bonsai training for one year and the branches are extensively wired to redirect previously upward growth.*

Trunk *Literati style takes advantage of a naturally graceful trunk line.*

Pinus sylvestris 'Beuvronensis'
DWARF SCOTS PINE
This specimen, 28 years old and 99cm (39in) high, is grown in literati style.

Container *Brown unglazed Japanese Tokoname in curved round pot.*

Pinus thunbergii
JAPANESE BLACK PINE

Pinus thunbergii

Leaf shown half life size

Like the white pine, *Pinus parviflora* (see page 142), this striking ornamental tree is a native of Japan. Pines are among the classics of bonsai, and the Japanese black and white pines are the most popular species. *P. thunbergii* is commonly grown in parks and gardens where, even in full-size trees, pruning and grooming are carried out in the same way as for bonsai specimens. The tree bears long, thick, dark green needles grouped in pairs and held stiffly upright. The trunk develops a craggy bark. These characteristics combine to give a strong, aggressive appearance as compared to the softer effect of the white pine. The black pine is very tolerant of poor conditions, surviving in nature on impoverished, stony soil, and because of this root tolerance and the rough bark, it is the usual rootstock on which the white pine is grafted.

BONSAI STYLES

Suitable for all styles except broom, and particularly well suited to literati, which emphasizes the rugged bark on the trunk. Can be grown at all sizes, but dwarf forms with shorter needles are available for rock plantings.

CULTIVATION

☼ **Position** Full sun. Provide protection from frosts and freezing winter winds.

♦ **Watering** The black pine is very drought-resistant but appreciates plenty of water provided that the soil is quick-draining. Check daily, but water only when soil shows signs of dryness. In winter, water very sparingly.

▦ **Feeding** Every three to four weeks from spring to early winter.

▬ **Repotting** In early to mid spring every two to five years, depending on age and root development, as determined by regular inspection. Use free-draining soil mix.

✄ **Pruning** Pinch off overgrown shoots just as needles begin to appear. Remove long primary shoots throughout the growing season. On other smaller shoots, remove one-third to half of the new candle. Prune branch tips every second year. In late summer or early autumn, remove old needles and overcrowded shoots to allow winter light into the tree.

✿ **Propagation** In winter, soak fresh seeds overnight, discard seeds that float and use those that have sunk for sowing. Place outside and expose to frost, but protect from birds and rodents. Germination is reliable if seed is fresh.

Foliage *The forceful, upright growth of the bright green needles contributes to the tree's strong character.*

Structure *Literati styling emphasizes the sense of movement in the trunk line and draws attention to the attractively rugged bark.*

Pinus thunbergii
JAPANESE BLACK PINE
This literati-style pine is 35 years old and 70cm (28in.) high.

Container *English red-brown unglazed incurved round pot by Gordon Duffet complements the balance of the tree's design.*

Prunus mume
JAPANESE FLOWERING APRICOT

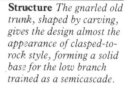

Prunus mume

Leaf shown half life size

The large *Prunus* family consists of trees and shrubs grown for their stoned fruits – apricots, cherries, peaches, plums – and a wide range of ornamental species grown for the beauty of their flowers. They are found in temperate regions throughout the northern hemisphere, although the greatest variety occurs in Japan and the Far East. *Prunus mume*, said to have originated in China and Korea, has been extensively cultivated over generations in Japan for its beautiful fragrant blossoms, which burst out on the bare branches in late winter. A small bonsai displayed indoors when in flower fills the whole room with its scent. Many cultivars are available in Japan, of which very few are seen in the West. *P. spinosa*, the blackthorn or sloe, is a common hedgerow plant in Europe but as bonsai it has a delicacy similar to that of *P. mume* and makes an excellent alternative.

BONSAI STYLES

Suitable for all styles except formal upright or broom, and for all sizes.

Flowers *Fragrant pink and white blossoms are borne on bare branches in late winter.*

Prunus mume
JAPANESE FLOWERING APRICOT
This 30-year-old tree, 40cm (16in) in height, has an unusually dramatic design combining aspects of semicascade and clasped-to-rock styles.

Structure *The gnarled old trunk, shaped by carving, gives the design almost the appearance of clasped-to-rock style, forming a solid base for the low branch trained as a semicascade.*

CULTIVATION

☼ **Position** Full sun. Protect from frost in winter to avoid twig die-back and damage to flowers.

💧 **Watering** Daily throughout the growing season. Water sparingly in winter, but keep the soil continuously moist from the time when flower buds start to swell, to avoid bud and flower drop.

▦ **Feeding** Heavy summer feeding results in more flowers for the winter. The amount of feed required depends upon the type of soil and watering supplied. Feed at least every two weeks throughout summer: this can be increased in amount and frequency.

▨ **Repotting** Annually in late winter, as soon as flowering has ceased. Use basic soil mix.

✂ **Pruning** Trim back hard after flowers have fallen. Allow rampant growth in summer and trim back resulting shoots in autumn.

✎ **Propagation** From hardwood cuttings in late winter. By layering in summer. By grafting in winter or spring.

Container *English brown unglazed rectangle by Gordon Duffet provides clean lines offsetting the complex textures of the bonsai.*

Flowers *Fragrant red flowers appear before the leaf buds form.*

Structure *To fatten the trunk of the grafted plant, it was grown in the ground for several years. The branches are brittle and need careful wiring to avoid cracking.*

Prunus mume
JAPANESE FLOWERING APRICOT
A slender tree styled as an informal upright has a very different mood from that of the carved specimen (opposite). This tree is 30 years old and 75cm (30in) high.

Prunus spinosa
SLOE
The sloe is better appreciated in bonsai than it is in nature, for its fine twigs and small leaves, and delicate white spring flowers. It is similar in character to *P. mume* and can be grown as an alternative where it is more readily available. This example, 10 years old and 53cm (21in) high, has been styled over one year by carving and pruning.

Container *Brown unglazed Japanese Tokoname round pot.*

Prunus serrulata
FLOWERING CHERRY

Prunus serrulata
Kiku-shidare Sakura

Leaf shown half life size

The wild cherries of the Far East have been cultivated and hybridized for generations in Japan, to such an extent that there now exist hundreds of flowering cherries with single, semi-double or double blossoms, from white through shades of pink to a deep red-pink. The exact origins of these hybrids are not always clear, but they are among the loveliest flowering trees in cultivation. The problem is that all the beauty is expended within only one or two weeks in spring, and thereafter the trees appear relatively uninspiring, although there is some interest in the autumn foliage colour. Typically, the twigs and leaves of flowering cherries are too coarse to give a refined image in bonsai. An exception to this is *Prunus subhirtella* 'Autumnalis', which has delicate twigs, small leaves that colour well in autumn, and flushes of white or pale pink, semi-double flowers appearing on bare wood throughout the winter whenever there is a frost-free period. Of the larger hybrids, some are well worth growing, despite their coarseness, for the brief glory of the flowers. One of the most reliable is *P.serrulata* 'Kanzan', bearing large double, dark pink flowers that usually conceal the branches completely.

BONSAI STYLES

Suitable for all styles except broom, and for all sizes.

CULTIVATION

☼ **Position** Full sun. Provide some frost protection in winter. It is advisable to protect flower buds as they begin to swell in late winter to early spring, as birds can strip a bonsai tree of buds in minutes.

💧 **Watering** Daily throughout the growing season. Avoid dropping water onto open flowers as this spoils the petals; try also to shield them from heavy rain. Water sparingly in winter but do not allow soil to dry out.

Feeding Every two weeks after flowering has finished until late summer.

Repotting Annually, in late spring before bud burst or in late autumn. Use basic soil mix.

Pruning Trim back after flowering. Prune back tips of new shoots as they grow in summer. Prune branches in winter where required.

Propagation By grafting in early spring.

Structure *The clean line of the single trunk provides the simplest structure for showing off the heavy flower clusters.*

Flowers *Double pink flowers appear in early spring before the leaves.*

Prunus serrulata 'Kiku-shidare Sakura'
JAPANESE FLOWERING CHERRY
This young tree, grown by air layering, is only 10cm (4in) high but the semicascade style shows the spectacular effect of the flowering cherry as bonsai.

Container *A biscuit-coloured glazed Japanese Tokoname square pot provides the weight and depth needed to balance the angle of the semicascade.*

Punica granatum
POMEGRANATE

This deciduous broad-leaved tree is grown for its flowers and fruit. It is a native of Asia and the Mediterranean regions, growing best in a warm climate. The flowers, which appear in summer, are usually bright scarlet but there are also white, pink and yellow forms, single and double. The round, leathery fruits are yellow, flushed with red, and contain black seeds surrounded by juicy, edible pulp. They rarely form when the plant is grown in cool temperate climates, unless the summer months are exceptionally hot.

BONSAI STYLES

Suitable for all styles except formal upright and broom. Can be grown at sizes from small to extra-large, but dwarf forms are recommended for extra-small and small sizes.

CULTIVATION

☼ **Position** Full sun. As a native of Mediterranean climates, the pomegranate is not fully hardy and needs protection from low temperatures and frost.

💧 **Watering** Water daily through the growing season, providing a generous supply of moisture after flowering to help fruits to swell. Keep the soil moist in winter.

▦ **Feeding** Every week from the start of the growing season until flowering begins.

▭ **Repotting** About every second year in early spring. For trees about 10 years of age or more, repotting may be less frequent according to root development. Use basic soil mix.

✂ **Pruning** Trim back new growth to two sets of leaves when three to four sets have developed. Do not trim shorter, round-tipped shoots that will carry flowers. Thin out unwanted bushy growth throughout the growing season.

✔ **Propagation** From stratified seed sown in spring. From softwood cuttings in midsummer.

Punica granatum

Leaf shown half life size

Foliage *Glossy bright green leaves carried on reddish leaf stalks form an attractive display throughout the growing season.*

Punica granatum
POMEGRANATE
This handsome specimen is 30 years old and 53cm (21in) high, grown in informal upright style.

Structure *The beautiful twisted trunk, supporting an elegant spread of slender branches, was thickened during several years' growth in open ground.*

Container *A blue glazed Japanese Tokoname "cloud" pot adds to the colour interest in the design.*

Pyracantha angustifolia

Leaf shown half life size

Pyracantha
PYRACANTHA or FIRETHORN

Pyracanthas are familiar garden shrubs grown for their clusters of small white flowers in summer and, especially, for the masses of brilliant yellow, orange or scarlet berries carried on the spreading, spiny stems in autumn. These features, and the glossy green, oval leaves, make the plants equally decorative when grown as bonsai. Pyracanthas are tolerant and easy to train, so ideal for beginners. Although of shrubby habit, a pyracantha can be successfully cultivated as a single-trunk specimen. *Pyracantha angustifolia*, *P. coccinea* and their many hybrids and cultivars are most frequently seen as bonsai. *P.c.* 'Teton', a particularly fine dwarf, compact form with rich green, small leaves and yellow-orange berries, is highly recommended for the smallest bonsai sizes.

BONSAI STYLES

Informal upright, slanting, semicascade, cascade, root-over-rock, clasped-to-rock, twin-trunk, clump. Suitable for all except extra-large sizes.

CULTIVATION

Position Full light or partial shade. Provide some protection in winter: prolonged exposure to frost or freezing winds can cause damage or winter kill. Some tropical bonsai pyracanthas are now being imported to temperate regions and need winter protection.

Watering Daily throughout the growing season. Take care to keep soil moist even in winter, as cold winds can dry the foliage.

Feeding Feed well every week until flowering. Start feeding again when fruit has developed, and continue every two weeks until mid autumn.

Repotting Every two years in early spring, in basic soil mix.

Pruning In late spring, shorten new shoots on established branches to two sets of leaves. Prune older wood in early spring or late summer. Remove large leaves throughout the growing season. Take care when wiring, as old woody branches are brittle.

Propagation From seed sown in autumn or winter. From cuttings of current season's growth at any time of year. By layering or air layering, spring to early summer.

Foliage *Bright green oval leaves act as a foil for the decorative spring flowers and autumn fruit.*

Structure *The young plant was pot-grown and wired to shape while still young and supple.*

Pyracantha angustifolia
PYRACANTHA or FIRETHORN
This specimen grown in semicascade style is eight years old and 25cm (10in) high.

Fruit *This is an orange berried form carrying a generous crop of fruit: cultivars with yellow or red berries are also available.*

Container *The grey-brown unglazed Japanese Tokoname semicascade pot has sufficient height to leave free the full sweep of the lower branch.*

Quercus robur
ENGLISH OAK

Quercus robur

Leaf shown half life size

This broad-leaved deciduous tree is the more common of the two native British oaks, and is also found through Europe, in south-west Asia and in North Africa. The English oak is extremely long-lived, up to 800 years or more in some cases. With age, it develops a massive trunk, supporting thick, splayed branches and a very broad crown. This solidity of structure is equally evident in bonsai specimens. The other main attraction is the gentle progression of the foliage colour, from a beautiful light green in spring, darkening through the growing season and then turning to a rich bronze-gold in autumn.

Foliage *The typical lobed, bright green leaves have reduced in size as a result of careful pruning and cultivation.*

BONSAI STYLES

Informal upright, slanting, broom, twin-trunk, clump, straight line, sinuous and group. Suitable for medium to extra-large sizes.

CULTIVATION

☼ **Position** Full sun. Provide frost protection in winter.

💧 **Watering** Daily throughout the growing season, sparingly in winter but keep soil continuously moist. The oak is susceptible to mildew and needs regular spraying.

▪ **Feeding** Every two weeks from summer through autumn.

▪ **Repotting** In early spring before buds open, annually for young trees, every two to three years for specimens over 10 years of age. Use basic soil mix.

✂ **Pruning** Trim new shoots back to one or two pairs of leaves.

⚘ **Propagation** From seed – sow fresh acorns in autumn; protect from rodents and 100 per cent germination can be expected in spring. By air layering in summer.

Structure *The combination of thick trunk, heavy root buttress and rugged branches creates the impression of a majestic oak in nature.*

Quercus robur
ENGLISH OAK
This impressive award-winning specimen in informal upright style is 60 years old and 70cm (28in) high. It has been trained as bonsai for only five years.

Container *Grey unglazed Japanese Tokoname rectangle with rounded corners.*

Rhododendron
AZALEA

The genus *Rhododendron* is one of the largest, encompassing the most spectacular of all the flowering shrubs. There are many hundreds of species giving rise to thousands of cultivars, which for reference are usually grouped into rhododendron species or hybrids, and deciduous or evergreen hybrid azaleas: there is no botanical difference between rhododendrons and azaleas. Many of the species are indigenous to Japan and the Japanese have been propagating and hybridizing these plants since the seventeenth century. The evergreen Satsuki azaleas are the group most commonly seen as bonsai; many Japanese enthusiasts grow these exclusively. Unlike most rhododendrons and azaleas which bloom in late spring, Satsukis flower in midsummer. The Kurume azaleas, mainly originating from *Rhododendron kiusianum*, are the second most popular group for bonsai.

Rhododendron indicum 'Kaho'

Leaf shown life size

BONSAI STYLES

Suitable for all styles except broom, and for all sizes, although small-leaved and small-flowered varieties are preferred for the smaller bonsai sizes.

CULTIVATION

Position Partial shade. Protect from frost in winter, and from heavy rain while in flower.

Watering Water at least once a day throughout the growing season to keep soil continuously moist, and mist-spray foliage. Use only lime-free (soft) water: rainwater is ideal. Reduce watering in winter, but do not allow soil to dry out at any time. The fine, fibrous roots soon become desiccated in dry soil.

Feeding In spring, feed every two weeks until flowering. When flowering has ended, feed once a month until early autumn. Use only a type of fertilizer recommended for acid-loving plants.

Repotting As soon as flowers have withered, annually or as necessary when roots fill the pot. Use lime-free soil mix: all rhododendrons must be grown in acid soil.

Pruning After flowering ceases, remove all new shoots, then prune secondary shoots more lightly until midsummer. It is important to remove dead flowers carefully as soon as they have faded.

Propagation From softwood cuttings in early summer. By air layering in early summer.

Foliage *Evergreen oval leaves are almost totally obscured by the flowers in midsummer.*

Flowers *The individual blooms are comparatively large for bonsai, but the effect depends on the massed display of so many flowers.*

Rhododendron indicum 'Kaho'
SATSUKI AZALEA 'KAHO'
Seen in the spectacular phase of full flower, this is an informal upright 25 years old and 50cm (20in) high.

Structure *A low, spreading silhouette is supported on a sturdy trunk.*

Container *Grey unglazed Japanese Tokoname oval pot.*

Rhododendron obtusum
JAPANESE KURUME AZALEA
The range of visual interest offered by Kurume azaleas is well represented in this multiple-trunk specimen 30 years old and 40cm (16in) high.

Flowers *Brilliant pink flowers are heavily massed on the branches, obscuring the sparser foliage growth.*

Structure *The stump of a discarded garden shrub was allowed to grow freely for two years, the new growth then pruned and wired after potting.*

Container *A grey unglazed Japanese Tokoname oval forms a smooth, compact base drawing attention to the bonsai's complex root structure.*

Rhododendron indicum 'Hakurei'
SATSUKI AZALEA 'HAKUREI'
In this 20-year-old azalea, 25cm (10in) high and with a spread of 90cm (36in), the cascade style perfectly displays the delicacy of the creamy flower buds, white star-like flowers and slender evergreen leaves.

Sageretia theezans
SAGERETIA

Sageretias are tender shrubs native to central and southern Asia and to the warmer areas of North America. *Sageretia theezans*, from southern China, is the species usually seen as bonsai. Needing warm conditions, it is grown as indoor bonsai in cooler temperate climates. It has slender branches, sometimes thorny, and small, shiny evergreen leaves. Small white flowers that appear in summer are followed by blue berries. The rough brown bark scales off in patches to create a very interesting trunk, similar in effect to the trunks of plane trees or ageing trident maples.

Sageretia theezans

Leaf shown half life size

Sageretia theezans
SAGERETIA
The attractive foliage and bark of this 35-year-old tree, grown in slanting style at 63cm (25in) high, explain the popularity of this species as an indoor bonsai subject.

Foliage *Rounded masses of glossy mid-green, oval leaves have been formed by regular clipping.*

Structure *The heavy, aged trunks were developed by many years of growing in open ground.*

Bark *Peeling bark provides a varied colour range along the beautifully textured trunks.*

Container *A blue glazed Chinese rectangle contributes subtle interest to the design in both its colour and shape.*

BONSAI STYLES
Suitable for all styles and sizes.

CULTIVATION

☼ **Position** Sageretia needs a temperature range of 12-18°C (54-65°F) through winter and 18-24°C (65-75°F) in summer with high humidity. If grown indoors, it should be given a position well lit throughout the year but must be shaded from hot summer sun to avoid scorching.

💧 **Watering** Water daily in summer and make sure the soil does not dry out even in winter. For indoor bonsai, check the soil condition daily. It is critical to maintain a humid atmosphere around the plant.

Feeding Every two weeks in summer, monthly in winter.

Repotting Every second year, in spring, in basic soil mix.

Pruning During the growing season, prune new shoots back to one or two pairs of leaves.

Propagation Softwood cuttings root easily through spring and summer.

Salix
WILLOW

Salix babylonica

Leaf shown one quarter life size

This large genus of deciduous shrubs and small trees is found throughout the northern hemisphere in cool and temperate regions. Willows are noted for their graceful and unusual shapes, which may be weeping, twisted or upright, for their attractive spring catkins and for the varied colours of bark and foliage. Many are vigorous growers. One of the best species for bonsai cultivation is *Salix babylonica*, the weeping willow. This beautiful tree, a native of China, is often planted by water in parks and gardens; it is well suited to watery sites, which help to show off the elegant curtain of thin, pliable branches clothed with narrow leaves, because willows are moisture-loving plants. There are a number of small leaved varieties and a golden form available.

BONSAI STYLES

Informal upright, slanting, semicascade, cascade, root-over-rock, twin-trunk, saikei. Suitable for medium to extra-large sizes.

CULTIVATION

☼ **Position** A sunny position is preferable, but provide some shade from hot summer sun. Protect from severe winter frost to avoid twig die-back.

Watering Water daily throughout the growing season, more often in hot weather as necessary. This is one of the few bonsai that will benefit from standing in a shallow tray of water in midsummer. Reduce watering in winter but do not allow the soil to dry out at any time.

Feeding Every two weeks from early spring until late summer.

Repotting This is a fast-growing tree that may need repotting twice a year, in early spring and midsummer. Use basic soil mix.

Pruning In early spring, prune back the previous year's shoots to one or two buds.

Propagation From softwood or hardwood cuttings at any time. Even wrist-thick branches will root easily in moist sand.

Foliage *Fine strap-like, fresh green leaves are borne on cascading golden shoots.*

Structure *Branches are cut back twice a year to encourage delicate shoots and a refined weeping habit.*

Salix babylonica
WEEPING WILLOW
This graceful species provides an opportunity for atmospheric design, here demonstrated by a pair grown in slanting style over water. The trees are 15 years old, the larger one 35cm (14in) high.

Container *Brown unglazed Japanese Tokoname "Saikei style" container with glazed reservoir.*

Sequoiadendron giganteum

WELLINGTONIA

The Wellingtonia, or "big tree" of California is a real bonsai challenge. The famous specimen known as General Sherman, which stands in its native state, has the distinction of being accepted as the world's largest living thing, with a height of 81 metres (272 ft) and girth of 24 metres (79 ft). The oldest authenticated age of a felled specimen is about 3200 years. As bonsai it is fast-growing and needs constant attention while young, with routine weekly finger-pruning throughout the growing season. The habit of growth is upright and wiring is essential to form a good shape, although the tree tends to resume upward growth once freed from the wires. But this monumental evergreen conifer holds a fascination similar to that of the majestic English oak, and there will always be bonsai growers willing to accept its challenge.

Sequoiadendron giganteum
WELLINGTONIA
This 20-year-old specimen, styled as a formal upright, stands 90cm (36in) high.

BONSAI STYLES

Formal upright, twin-trunk, group. Suitable for medium to extra-large sizes.

CULTIVATION

☼ **Position** Partial shade in summer. Provide some frost protection in winter, and also protection from freezing winds.

💧 **Watering** Water well every day throughout the growing season. The foliage benefits from watering or spraying in summer. In winter, water sparingly and protect leaves from drying winds.

▦ **Feeding** Every two weeks from spring to autumn.

▥ **Repotting** Every two years, in basic soil mix.

✂ **Pruning** Pinch out new growths continually, and remove totally any downward growths stemming from strong upward growth.

✍ **Propagation** From seed sown in winter or early spring. From softwood cuttings in spring and summer.

Sequoiadendron giganteum

Leaf shown two thirds life size

Foliage *Evergreen scale-like foliage falls into a graceful conical outline.*

Structure *The tall, straight trunk and evenly spreading branches are a perfect recreation of the way that the tree grows in nature.*

Container *A brown unglazed Japanese Tokoname rectangle.*

Serissa foetida
TREE OF A THOUSAND STARS

This evergreen shrub is a native of Japan, China and India. The bark and roots have an unpleasant (fetid) smell which gives the plant its botanical name, while the masses of star-like flowers give rise to the common name. The smooth green leaves are small, and the white flowers appear in summer. There are single and double white-flowered forms, a purple-flowering and a variegated-leaved form. As a sub-tropical plant, this is suitable for indoor cultivation as bonsai in temperate climates.

Serissa foetida 'Variegata'

Leaf shown life size

Foliage *Small oval leaves show an attractive contrast in the dark green and pale yellow variegation.*

BONSAI STYLES

Suitable for all styles except formal upright and broom. Can be grown at extra-small to medium sizes.

CULTIVATION

☼ **Position** This species tolerates hot conditions and should be given a sunny location. In winter, maintain a minimum temperature of 12°C (54°F) and protect from draughts of cold air.

💧 **Watering** Daily during the growing season. Mist-spray foliage daily, except when the tree is in flower, as dampness discolours the petals. Maintain a high humidity level. Keep soil relatively dry during winter months when daylight hours are short.

▥ **Feeding** Every two weeks through the growing season, monthly in winter.

▥ **Repotting** Every second year in early spring, in basic soil mix.

✂ **Pruning** Trim new shoots back to one or two pairs of leaves after repotting.

Ⴔ **Propagation** Softwood cuttings root easily in spring or summer.

Serissa foetida 'Variegata'
TREE OF A THOUSAND STARS
This charming tree in informal upright style is six years old and 15cm (6in) high.

Structure *An interesting natural growth pattern has been exploited, the tree being trained only by clipping to create a pleasing shape and encourage prolific flowering.*

Container *Brown glazed Japanese Tokoname rectangular pot.*

Sorbus aucuparia
ROWAN or MOUNTAIN ASH

Sorbus aucuparia

Leaf shown one third life size

This popular garden tree is perhaps the best known of the *Sorbus* family, which includes a number of very decorative deciduous trees and shrubs. The slender, upright shape and graceful pinnate leaves of the small rowan trees are highly attractive in bonsai specimens. *Sorbus aucuparia* makes a charming display throughout the growing season, with clusters of small, creamy-white flowers in spring and the fresh green leaf colour of spring and summer. It becomes a spectacular sight in autumn, with the foliage developing brilliant gold and orange tints that create a striking setting for the bright red berries.

Foliage *The serrated leaflets of the tree's compound leaves adapt well to the scale of bonsai.*

Structure *An elegant contrast comes from the fine twigs branching out from a sturdy trunk, developed through six years of growing in open ground.*

BONSAI STYLES

Suitable for all styles except formal upright and broom, and for all sizes.

CULTIVATION

☼ **Position** Full sun. No winter protection should be necessary, as the tree is particularly hardy and frost-resistant.

◕ **Watering** Daily throughout the growing season, sparingly in winter, but do not allow soil to dry out.

▦ **Feeding** Every two weeks throughout the growing season.

▬ **Repotting** Annually or every second year in early spring, before bud burst. Use basic soil mix.

✂ **Pruning** Constantly cut back new growth to one or two leaves, except where extension growth is required to develop the overall shape.

✌ **Propagation** From stratified seed sown in late winter or early spring. Named cultivars can be grafted onto common stock.

Sorbus aucuparia
ROWAN or MOUNTAIN ASH
This is an eight-year-old tree, 25cm (10in) in height, styled as an informal upright.

Container *A grey unglazed Japanese Tokoname "drum" pot balances the sturdy trunk and spreading crown of the bonsai.*

Stewartia monodelpha
STEWARTIA

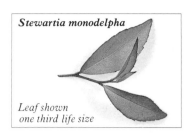

Stewartia monodelpha

Leaf shown one third life size

The Stewartia, indigenous to Japan, has been increasingly used for bonsai in recent years. The beautiful shiny copper bark and neat, delicate twig pattern are sufficient reason to grow this tree, but if a better reason was needed it arrives in the form of spectacular autumn foliage tints of scarlet and purple. *Stewartia* is a small genus of lime-hating deciduous shrubs and trees closely related to camellias. The dwarf compact form *Stewartia monodelpha* is one of the two species commonly preferred for bonsai cultivation, the other being *S. pseudocamellia*. Because of the specially attractive trunk and bark, bonsai specimens feature well in winter when they are without leaves.

BONSAI STYLES

Formal upright, group. Suitable for small to medium sizes.

CULTIVATION

☼ **Position** Partial shade during summer. Allow full sun in autumn to enhance foliage colour. Provide frost protection in winter.

💧 **Watering** Daily throughout the growing season. Use only lime-free (soft) water: rain water is ideal. Reduce watering in winter but keep soil evenly moist at all times: in common with other thin-leaved ericaceous plants, stewartias resent drying out and leaves shrivel readily with lack of moisture.

▦ **Feeding** Every two weeks throughout the growing season, using only ericaceous fertilizer.

▤ **Repotting** Every second year in early spring, in lime-free soil mix.

✂ **Pruning** Constantly trim back new shoots to one or two leaves except where extension growth is required to develop the overall shape. Take care if wiring, as the bark is soft and easily marked.

✍ **Propagation** From seed sown in winter or spring. From softwood cuttings in summer.

Stewartia monodelpha
STEWARTIA
This group planting has an overall height of 50cm (20in). The trees are 10 years old and have been grown together as a group for two years.

Foliage *Fresh green leaves turn to brilliant red and purple shades in autumn.*

Structure *The multiple slender trunks and fine twigs feature well in winter when the coppery bark is fully revealed after leaf fall.*

Container *A handmade unglazed, irregular ceramic slab by German designer Petra Engelke forms the base for the group.*

Tamarix
TAMARISK

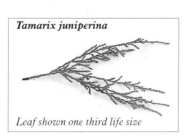

Tamarix juniperina

Leaf shown one third life size

This unusual deciduous shrub has a fragile, feathery appearance which belies its toughness. Tamarisks are particularly resistant to wind, especially salt-laden wind, so are often planted as hedges and windbreaks in coastal areas. With their delicate leaves and flowers, they make admirable bonsai. The small green, scale-like leaves are arranged along slender, frond-like branches which shimmer with the slightest breeze. Clusters of small purplish- or brownish-pink flowers appear in large quantities through spring and summer. Tamarisks are found in the wild from western Europe to China, but most cultivated varieties come from the Mediterranean and need protection from hard frosts.

Tamarix juniperina
TAMARISK
A dramatic effect is achieved in this carved informal upright, 40 years old and 85cm (34in) high.

Foliage *Delicate feathery foliage grows naturally upward and has to be wired to create this weeping effect.*

BONSAI STYLES

Informal upright, slanting, semicascade, cascade, root-over-rock, clasped-to-rock, twin-trunk, clump. Suitable for small to large sizes.

CULTIVATION

Position Full light, but shade from hot summer sun. Provide protection from hard frost in winter.

Watering Check soil condition daily and supply enough water to keep it slightly moist at all times.

Feeding Every two weeks throughout the growing season.

Repotting In mid spring, annually or every second year according to root development. Use free-draining soil mix.

Pruning Current season's growth should be cut back hard in autumn. New soft spring growth will grow upward – this must be brought down by gentle wiring or by using a fine net or plastic mesh to hold down the shoots for a few weeks until they set into weeping form.

Propagation From softwood cuttings in summer, or hardwood cuttings in winter. By layering in late spring or early summer.

Structure *An old sawn-off stump was the original material for the bonsai, carefully carved and styled to develop the striking form and colour of the design.*

Container *A brown glazed Japanese Tokoname incurved round pot closely encircles the broad base of the aged trunk.*

Taxus baccata
ENGLISH YEW

Taxus baccata

Leaf shown half life size

One of the finest of the evergreen conifers, the yew is both slow-growing and very long-lived. The English yew has interesting historical associations, dating back to the medieval period when the longbow was an essential weapon. Every parish in England was required to provide a quota of bow staves and these were made from yew because of the flexibility of the wood, a characteristic that also makes the yew easy to shape as bonsai. The leaves and berries of the yew are very poisonous and it was necessary to grow the trees out of reach of grazing animals. They were therefore commonly planted in churchyards, often the only area fenced off from the common grazing land, and this traditional association survives today. The English yew is an attractive species with short, dark green needle-like foliage, neatly arranged on wide, spreading branches, and grey-brown bark which may peel off in strips to reveal a reddish underlayer.

BONSAI STYLES

Suitable for all styles except broom, and all sizes.

CULTIVATION

 **Position** Tolerates some sun, but a partially shaded position is preferred and the tree will even grow in dense shade.

Watering Daily throughout the growing season, and mist-spray foliage. Water sparingly in winter but do not allow soil to dry out.

Feeding Twice monthly throughout the growing season.

Repotting Every third or fourth year in spring, in free-draining soil mix.

Pruning Pinch out new growth during the growing season to encourage branching. If fruit is required, do not trim new shoots until after the small green flowers have appeared in spring. Prune branches in autumn. Wiring can be done at any time with due care, although autumn is preferable.

Propagation From cuttings of current season's growth taken in autumn and given winter protection; these should be rooted by spring. By layering or air layering in summer.

Foliage *Dark green leaves have a flattened needle-like appearance. The foliage masses will be further trained and refined to fill out the design.*

Structure *A good trunk line is emphasized by the arrangement of branches, which contrasts leafy twigs with starkly cut jins.*

Taxus baccata
ENGLISH YEW
Trained from ordinary nursery stock, this informal upright is 20 years old and 45cm (18in) high.

Container *A brown unglazed Japanese Tokoname oval complements the line and colour of the dark trunk.*

Taxus cuspidata
JAPANESE YEW

A native of Japan, *Taxus cuspidata* is a small to medium-sized tree similar in silhouette to the English yew *T. baccata*, but its needle-like foliage is dark green on the upper surfaces and cream underneath. The wood is flexible and can be easily bent and wired. It is also fine-grained and carves well for detailed treatment of jins or driftwood areas in a design. If the deep pink fruits of the Japanese yew are required, a female tree must be grown near a male form for pollination. There is a dwarf form, *T.c.* 'Nana' which is much more compact and a better choice for the smaller bonsai sizes.

Taxus cuspidata

Leaf shown half life size

Taxus cuspidata
JAPANESE YEW
This 20-year-old tree, 30cm (12in) high, is grown as an informal upright with a generous spread of fine branches.

Foliage *Flattened needle-like, evergreen leaves are deliberately kept sparse to focus attention on the lines of trunk and branches.*

Structure *The trunk was heavily wired to create the strong curves and thickened after shaping by a period of growth in open ground.*

Container *A brown unglazed Japanese Tokoname incurved round pot provides visual weight anchoring the fluid movement in the design.*

BONSAI STYLES

Suitable for all styles except broom, and for all sizes.

CULTIVATION

☼ **Position** Tolerates some sun, but prefers a position with at least partial shade and will even grow in dense shade.

💧 **Watering** Daily throughout the growing season, and mist-spray foliage. Reduce watering in winter but keep soil evenly moist.

▦ **Feeding** Twice monthly throughout the growing season.

▣ **Repotting** Every third or fourth year, in spring, in free-draining soil mix.

✂ **Pruning** Throughout the growing season pinch out new growth to encourage branching. If fruit is required, do not trim new shoots until after the small green flowers have appeared in spring. Prune branches in autumn. Wiring can be done at any time with due care, although autumn is preferable.

✍ **Propagation** From cuttings taken in autumn and given winter protection; these should be rooted by spring. By layering or air layering in summer.

Tsuga heterophylla

WESTERN HEMLOCK

Tsuga heterophylla

Leaf shown two thirds life size

The hemlocks are a family of evergreen conifers native to North America, China and Japan. They are typically tall trees of elegant pyramidal shape, with spreading branches that droop downward at the tips, creating a cascade effect. *Tsuga heterophylla*, the western hemlock native to the western part of North America, is often planted as an ornamental specimen. It has a narrow, conical shape and slightly drooping branches. The short, soft needle-like leaves are a glossy dark green when mature, but young foliage is a beautiful light green.

Tsuga heterophylla
WESTERN HEMLOCK
This is a six-year-old tree, trained as an informal upright for two years and now 23cm (9in) high.

Foliage *The delicate needle-like leaves are a pleasantly fresh, soft green.*

BONSAI STYLES

Suitable for all styles except broom, and for small to extra-large sizes.

CULTIVATION

Position Partial shade. The tree is very hardy but needs protection from freezing winds that will dry out the foliage.

Watering Daily throughout the growing season. Mist-spray foliage daily in summer. Reduce watering in winter, but do not allow soil to dry out.

Feeding Twice a month throughout the growing season.

Repotting In spring, every second year for young trees, every three to four years for trees aged about 10 years or more. Use free-draining soil mix.

Pruning Throughout the growing season, pinch off new shoots just before they harden, leaving only a few needles. Wiring can be done at any time, but preferably not in spring, to avoid damage to new shoots.

Propagation From seed sown in winter or early spring. From softwood cuttings in summer and autumn.

Structure *Detailed wiring has been applied to the branches to create an open, spreading effect.*

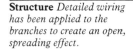

Container *Brown unglazed Japanese Tokoname shallow oval pot.*

Ulmus parvifolia
CHINESE ELM

Ulmus parvifolia

Leaf shown life size

This native of China, Korea, Taiwan and Japan is perhaps the best and most popular species of elm for bonsai. It is a small tree of good rounded shape with persistent leaves that are reluctant to drop in winter. In fact, although the Chinese elm is normally deciduous, in warmer climates the leaves do not drop; in California, for example, the plant is evergreen. The leaves are very small, as indicated by the botanical name *parvifolia* (small-leaved) and the twigs are also very fine, which makes this one of the few species effective in the broom style of bonsai cultivation. Long, stout, flexible roots are also a feature, making this tree particularly suitable for clasped-to-rock style. *Ulmus parvifolia* 'Variegata' is a popular variegated form.

BONSAI STYLES

Suitable for all styles and all sizes.

CULTIVATION

☼ **Position** Full light and sun. Provide frost protection for the roots as these are highly susceptible to damage.

💧 **Watering** Daily throughout the growing season, more frequently if necessary in very hot weather. Water more sparingly in winter, but do not allow the soil to dry out between waterings at any time.

▦ **Feeding** When leaf buds have opened in spring, feed once a week during the first month, then every two weeks until late summer.

▨ **Repotting** Annually in early spring until about 10 years of age, then as necessary according to root development, which should be inspected annually. Use free-draining soil mix.

✂ **Pruning** In spring, trim back new shoots to one or two sets of leaves. All elms respond well to leaf-cutting in midsummer, but this is not usually necessary for small-leaved forms such as *U. parvifolia*.

✍ **Propagation** From softwood or hardwood cuttings in early summer. Root cuttings taken in winter do exceptionally well.

Foliage *Small serrated, oval leaves and delicate twig growth provide year-round interest.*

Ulmus parvifolia
CHINESE ELM
This 10-year-old tree stands 17cm (7in) high and is grown in root-over-rock style.

Structure *The tree rises naturally above the rock, with the triangular silhouette well balanced on the slight curve of the bare trunk.*

Roots *The Chinese elm produces heavy roots, well suited to this style. In this design they bind tightly over Ibigawa rock.*

Container *A grey unglazed Japanese Tokoname oval provides an open setting for the root-over-rock design.*

Ulmus procera
ENGLISH ELM

The English elm in nature has been ravaged by Dutch elm disease in recent years and is no longer the common sight it once was. Bonsai elms, however, appear to be at little risk, possibly because there is little bark for the disease-carrying beetle to thrive on and also because an easily applied, normal spraying routine will keep the problem at bay. It is far easier to treat a small pot-grown specimen with systemic insecticide and fungicide than a full-sized tree growing in open ground. In nature the tree forms a distinctive shape, like an inverted figure eight. It is an ideal bonsai subject as the leaves reduce dramatically when the tree is grown in a pot, especially if leaf-cutting is carried out in midsummer. The special features are bright yellow autumn foliage colour and attractive bark, grey-brown in colour and developing fissures with age.

BONSAI STYLES
Suitable for all styles and all sizes.

CULTIVATION

☼ **Position** Full light and sun. Small bonsai sizes require frost protection in winter.

💧 **Watering** Daily throughout the growing season, more frequently if necessary in very hot weather. Reduce watering in winter but do not allow the soil to dry out.

🗔 **Feeding** Once leaf buds have opened in spring, feed once a week during the first month, then every two weeks until late summer.

▣ **Repotting** Annually in early spring. For trees aged 10 years or more, root development should be inspected annually and repotting carried out when roots fill the pot. Use free-draining soil mix.

✍ **Pruning** In spring, trim back new shoots to one or two sets of leaves. The English elm responds well to leaf-cutting in midsummer.

🗹 **Propagation** From softwood or hardwood cuttings in early summer. Root cuttings taken in winter do exceptionally well. Propagation from suckers of the English elm is also possible.

Ulmus procera

Leaf shown half life size

Foliage *Small serrated leaves well-suited to the scale of the bonsai turn from mid green to clear yellow in autumn.*

Structure *Training has reproduced the typical silhouette of the English elm in nature, the tall, straight trunk forming the central axis of the design.*

Ulmus procera
ENGLISH ELM
This elm was collected from the wild and has been trained in formal upright style. The tree is 30 years old and 105cm (42in) high.

Container *Light green glazed Japanese Tokoname oval pot.*

Wisteria
WISTERIA

A climbing wisteria covering a house or garden wall is a truly spectacular sight when in full flower, and the lavish display of fragrant racemes is equally attractive in bonsai specimens. The flowers are so large that a bonsai is usually styled to create the impression of a weeping tree, with the flower formations simulating drooping branches. The hanging clusters of pea-type flowers – in blue, mauve or white – appear in late spring or early summer against the background of fresh green foliage. Two species are mainly used for bonsai, the Japanese wisteria, *Wisteria floribunda*, and the Chinese wisteria, *W. sinensis*. Chinese wisteria has shorter and more strongly scented flower racemes than those of the Japanese species, and it is the more vigorous grower of the two.

Wisteria floribunda

Leaf shown one fifth life size

Flowers *The graceful flower racemes are treated as "branches" in the design, forming a graceful weeping effect.*

Structure *The grafted trunk has been grown sufficiently tall to accommodate the cascade of flowers.*

Wisteria floribunda
JAPANESE WISTERIA
This specimen is 12 years old and 35cm (14in) high, styled as an informal upright.

Container *Grey-brown unglazed Japanese Tokoname deep oval pot.*

BONSAI STYLES
Informal upright, slanting, semicascade, cascade, root-over-rock. Suitable for medium to extra-large sizes.

CULTIVATION
☼ **Position** Full light with plenty of sun. Protect from frost in winter if temperatures fall below –5°C (23°F).

💧 **Watering** Daily throughout the growing season. During the hottest months of summer, keep the container in a shallow dish of water so roots can soak up moisture through the drainage holes. Reduce watering in winter, but make sure soil remains continuously moist.

▦ **Feeding** After flowering has ceased, feed once a week until midsummer. Begin feeding again in early autumn, once a week until late autumn.

▣ **Repotting** Every third year, as soon as flowering is over. Use basic soil mix.

✂ **Pruning** Wisteria needs pruning several times a year, beginning in spring immediately after flowering. Prune again in early summer, midsummer and autumn, each time reducing new shoots to two or three sets of leaves.

🗲 **Propagation** From hardwood cuttings in late winter or early spring. By layering or air layering in summer. By grafting in early spring. Propagation from seed is easy but less effective than other methods, as plants grown from seed take many years to come to flower.

Zelkova serrata
JAPANESE ELM

The Japanese elm belongs to a genus of fine deciduous trees native to Japan, China and the Caucasus, and closely related to the species of *Ulmus* which constitute the native European elms. It is a strong grower, with a short, straight trunk dividing into long erect branches. This is a classic tree for the broom style, developing a dense mass of delicately formed twigs. It is one of the best bonsai for winter display, when it is bare of leaves, but exposure of the intriguing twig structure is preceded by the special attraction of the autumn foliage colour, ranging through shades of yellow, orange, bronze and crimson. An impressive effect is also achieved in multiple-trunk styling, due to the tree's density and fineness of the twigs.

BONSAI STYLES
Suitable for all styles except literati, and particularly suited to the broom and group styles. Can be grown at all sizes.

CULTIVATION
☼ **Position** Full sun for most of the year, but shade slightly from hot summer sun. Provide some frost protection to avoid twig die-back.

Watering Daily throughout summer, moderately at other times, but do not allow the soil to dry out between waterings.

Feeding Once leaf buds have opened in spring, feed every week for the first month, then every two weeks through summer.

Repotting Annually in early spring until about ten years old. Thereafter, as necessary according to root development. Use basic soil mix.

Pruning Trim new shoots back to one or two sets of leaves. Remove large leaves throughout the growing season. Strong, established trees can be leaf-cut in midsummer.

Propagation From seed sown in late winter or early spring. From cuttings in summer. By air layering in summer.

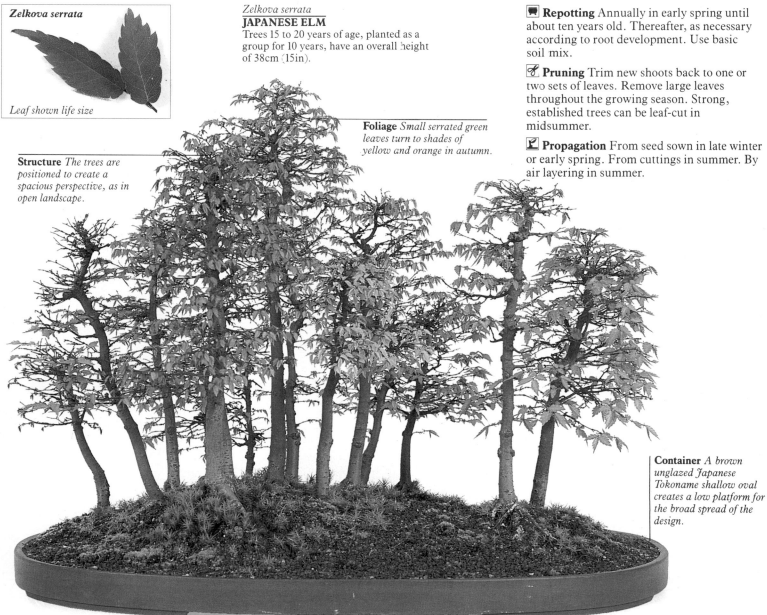

Zelkova serrata

Leaf shown life size

Zelkova serrata
JAPANESE ELM
Trees 15 to 20 years of age, planted as a group for 10 years, have an overall height of 38cm (15in).

Foliage *Small serrated green leaves turn to shades of yellow and orange in autumn.*

Structure *The trees are positioned to create a spacious perspective, as in open landscape.*

Container *A brown unglazed Japanese Tokoname shallow oval creates a low platform for the broad spread of the design.*

CHAPTER FOUR

ROUTINE MAINTENANCE

Horticultural skill is only one aspect of bonsai growing, but it is the essential basis of a healthy life for the tree that allows its potential as bonsai to be fulfilled. This chapter provides detailed information on day-to-day care of bonsai relating directly to the advice on cultivation for each type of tree or shrub as given in the Bonsai Species Guide (pages 90 to 167) and the Compendium of Trees and Shrubs for Bonsai (pages 190 to 217). This information covers positioning the bonsai, watering and feeding, techniques of root pruning, repotting and maintenance pruning, and protecting the bonsai against pests and diseases.

POSITION

There are three main elements to consider when you decide how to position bonsai. Your choice of location should provide the best conditions for healthy growth of the trees, with regard to sun or shade, humidity levels, and local climate. It should also allow you a good viewpoint– although you may not be cultivating the bonsai for formal display, you should be able to appreciate them fully as you water and groom them day to day. It naturally follows that you also need to choose the best position for working with the bonsai.

Recommendations for positioning individual species are given in the Species Guide (pages 90-167) under the heading Cultivation. The following considerations may also help you in siting your bonsai, but the exact location necessarily depends both on local conditions and the species of trees that you are cultivating. If you are a newcomer to bonsai, or have recently moved your trees to a new locale, the best course is to contact the local bonsai society for advice.

Local climate
Most bonsai traditionally are hardy trees and as such are required to be grown outdoors in the fresh air, being brought inside only for display over a day or two, if at all. However, although you can grow the same trees as bonsai as you might plant for full-size specimens in the garden, the bonsai are likely to need more care. When they are growing in pots, the roots are more subject to becoming too hot or frosted, dried out or waterlogged, depending on weather conditions, whereas the roots of a tree growing in the ground are better protected.

A useful generalization on positioning bonsai is to avoid extremes. Bonsai growers in England are fortunate in having a climate that is not naturally extreme and most trees can happily stay outside through summer and winter. However, in some parts of the world where the sun becomes extremely hot – such as California, South Africa and parts of Australia – it is vital to provide shade for most bonsai and, similarly, in areas with severe winters – as in Canada, the north-east coast of the USA and Scandinavia – it is necessary to provide effective frost protection.

Viewing and working with bonsai
Bonsai are best appreciated at eye level, so they look best if displayed on raised stands or shelves. Eye level is, of course, subjective: if a bonsai is viewed from a standing position, it would need to be on a shelf 1.2-1.5m (4-5 ft) high, but if normally viewed from a sitting position, then about 1m (3ft) would be adequate.

With trees grown at eye level, however, day-to-day maintenance becomes difficult, so often a compromise is made and the bonsai are displayed somewhat lower – at table-top height for convenience in routine tasks.

Winter care
Some sort of winter protection is necessary for certain trees. This varies from species to species (refer to the Species Guide for individual requirements) and according to the severity of winter conditions in your area.

Be careful not to over-protect the trees – certainly, do not bring them indoors in winter into heated rooms, as this will break their dormancy and trigger new sappy growth. Trees must be shielded against frost and wind, but they need to remain under maximum light. An adequately ventilated glasshouse or cold-frame is a good possibility. It even helps to place the bonsai under the display bench, particularly if it is possible to devise a clear plastic "curtain" that can be dropped down in extremes of weather. Trees with delicate twigs may particularly need this type of protection. Evergreen foliage is also vulnerable to damage from freezing winds.

The roots are the part of the plant most at risk, particularly on fleshy-rooted trees such as gingko, Chinese elm and trident maples. Often it is enough just to give some attention to insulating the pot and root area. This can be done by plunging the pot into the ground or, better still, sinking it into a prepared bed of pine needles or similar "insulating material". Pine needles are ideal for this purpose, as they provide good protection but also adequate drainage, so they will not become waterlogged or rotted.

Tropical and sub-tropical trees should be maintained at higher temperatures in heated glasshouses, according to the requirements of each species.

Indoor bonsai
The above information relates to traditional bonsai subjects, temperate trees such as pines, maples, elms and so on, grown outdoors. However, in recent years bonsai growers in temperate climates have developed a wider interest in growing tropical and sub-tropical bonsai indoors. This is a much more difficult task, as there is a giant difference in environment between outdoor conditions in places such as Taiwan and the Philippines where the trees originate and the type of warmth, light and humidity occurring in the conditions of the average suburban living room. An ordinary room can perhaps offer adequate warmth, but not the light or humidity levels required for strong growth.

Most, if not all tropical and sub-tropical bonsai are developed out of doors in their native climate and are exported to temperate countries, where they are maintained in glasshouses with controlled temperature and humidity before going on sale. The individual bonsai grower then has the sometimes impossible task of acclimatizing the bonsai to a dark living room.

The most successful "indoor" material seems to be grown in a glasshouse or conservatory and is only displayed indoors for a few days at a time. Observation suggests that it is very difficult to maintain an indoor subject in good health in a normal living room for more than a year. No doubt with the increasing popularity of "indoor" bonsai, more experience will be gained over the next few years.

WATERING AND FEEDING

The routines that you establish for watering and feeding your bonsai do not only relate to how "thirsty" the trees are and the conditions in particular seasons of the year. The amount of water and nutrients that you must supply also depends on the quality of the potting soil. The more moisture-retentive the soil mixture, the less water and feed required, and vice versa.

Watering routine

This is the most important single factor in successful cultivation of bonsai. More bonsai die from inadequate watering than from any other cause. Bonsai in a poor soil mixture, with no fertilizer supplied during the growing season, do not grow as well or as strongly as they might but they will not die because of these conditions. Without enough water, however, the trees will rapidly suffer irreversible damage.

Because of the comparatively shallow pots used for bonsai, the trees' root systems dry out at a much faster rate than they would if they were in the ground. Usually, daily watering is required throughout spring, summer and autumn. In winter, if the bonsai remain outside exposed to rain and snow, very little watering is required as the trees have a much lower requirement for moisture during the period of dormancy. However, with bonsai under protection, in an unheated greenhouse or cold frame, you must take care that they do not dry out.

Tropical and sub-tropical bonsai grown indoors need special care with winter watering as, unlike temperate trees, they continue to grow, albeit more slowly than in summer, and need to be kept moist.

Supplying water

Watering is best done from above, using a watering can, or hosepipe, fitted with a very fine rose. Specialized watering cans and hose sprinklers are available for bonsai use. The watering can must have a long neck to provide sufficient "head" of water for the spray. The hose sprinkler has a removable head that enables the fine holes of the rose to be cleaned.

The best time to water the bonsai is in the evening after the sun has gone down. This means that moisture remains in the soil and is available to the roots overnight and well into the morning, whereas if watering is done in the morning, the soil could dry out completely within a few hours. Another reason to avoid watering during the day is that any droplets of water that get onto the tree's leaves can act as a lens for the sun's rays, encouraging leaf scorch.

Feeding

Bonsai that are not fed may survive, but will not thrive. There is a choice between solid or liquid fertilizer. Solid fertilizer is available in grades from powder, to granules, to small blocks or cakes. Granules are the best choice, as they take three to four weeks to break down and each time it rains or the bonsai are watered, a little more fertilizer is dissolved. It is easy to see the granules on the soil surface and so to tell when a further application is needed.

Liquid fertilizer is quick-acting, but it is more difficult to tell how much has been absorbed. Heavy rainful immediately after a liquid feed may wash all the nutrients through the soil before the roots can absorb any. The same is true of solid fertilizer in powder form.

A method commonly used by Japanese growers is to apply fish meal or rape seed in the form of small cakes or blocks, which slowly break down in the same way as fertilizer granules. This has the disadvantage of being unsightly, and can act as a breeding ground for maggots.

The availability of brand-name products will vary in different areas, but there are general points to remember when choosing the fertilizer. A general, balanced fertilizer is most often used from spring through to autumn and many growers achieve good results with this alone. However, it is generally accepted that in autumn the fertilizer should be changed to a type low in nitrogen and high in phosphorus and potassium, as the growth of the trees slows towards the dormant period.

All fertilizers should show their analysis listed on the packaging as a ratio of the three main elements: nitrogen (N), phosphorus (P) and potassium (K). These are given in the order NPK: a typical autumn feed would be in the ratio 0:10:10. Follow the manufacturer's directions on dosage. There is no point in applying a specialized product but deliberately interfering with its efficiency.

Make sure you choose a fertilizer formulated for use with ericaceous plants if you are applying it to *Enkianthus*, *Rhododendron* cultivars (azaleas), *Stewartia* and other lime-hating plants.

Soil mixtures

Different trees require different types of soil. Suitable soil mixtures for individual species are given in the Species Guide under the Cultivation heading. The ingredients of the three types of soil mix recommended there are listed on page 174 with the instructions on repotting bonsai.

The basic requirements for a potting soil are that it should have good drainage, to prevent roots rotting in waterlogged soil, but should retain enough moisture to supply the roots adequately. The soil should have a sufficiently loose and open texture to allow oxygen to circulate. Different elements can supply these characteristics to a potting soil. With experience, you may learn to create your own suitable soil mixtures. Always remember to take into account the composition and texture of the soil when watering and feeding, particularly to make sure that it does not either drain too quickly or hold water and become too damp, as either a too-wet or too-dry soil will cause root damage.

ROOT PRUNING AND REPOTTING

After a period of growth varying from one to five years, depending on the size and age of the bonsai, the roots fill the container and the tree becomes "pot-bound". With an ordinary pot-plant in this condition, the solution is to pot it on into a larger container, giving a greater area of soil in which the roots can make further growth. The aim of repotting a bonsai is the same, but the method is different. The bonsai pot is part of the overall design and has been specially selected to complement the tree, so it is important to preserve the relationship between tree and container. In the process of repotting, the tree is put back into the same container, but first the roots are cut back to make space for fresh potting soil that allows free growth to resume.

The purpose of root pruning

Root pruning does not have the effect of dwarfing or stunting the tree, as is often thought. In fact, it allows the tree to grow more strongly because new feeder roots can develop in the soil. A number of new fibrous roots grow out from each cut root, gradually increasing the mass of feeder roots that keep the tree healthy and well nourished.

To determine whether root pruning is necessary, you can examine the rootball by easing the tree from the pot and tilting it to check the underside of the soil. You can check your trees annually, but it may not be necessary to carry out the full process of root pruning and repotting every year. Root pruning is necessary when you find that the rootball consists of long circling roots forming a dense mass coiled into the shape of the pot base. If the roots are still contained within the soil, you can simply return the tree to the pot for another year.

The rate of root growth varies between species and with the age of the tree. Each entry in the Species Guide (pages 90-167) contains guidelines for repotting individual species.

ROOT PRUNING A JAPANESE LARCH

The technique of root pruning is demonstrated on a Japanese larch (*Larix kaempferi*). Larches are very vigorous growers and usually require root pruning every year. They resent being pot-bound far more than other trees and in this case annual root pruning and repotting should be regarded as essential. The usual time for root pruning and repotting is in spring, but larches are very hardy trees and the process can be carried out in mid to late winter, at any time that the soil is not frozen. The repotted tree can be returned to an open position and it is not usually necessary to provide frost protection.

The process of root pruning consists of first disentangling the mass of circling roots, then trimming back the long roots with shears. When these longer roots have been cut away, you should also trim the roots on the underside of the rootball, to maintain a flat root system that settles easily back into the pot. On an established bonsai, it is possible to encourage a radial root system and discourage circling root formation by making wedge-shaped cuts into the rootball, angled towards the trunk base. This also ensures renewal of young, vigorous fibrous roots close to the trunk.

In a mature bonsai, the shape and spread of the surface roots that show above the soil are an important aspect of the design, so you should be careful not to damage this area of the root mass while pruning the roots and making the wedge-shaped cuts.

The general aim of root pruning is to shorten the roots by about one third. This allows space in the pot to add enough fresh potting soil to ensure healthy growth, yet still leaves enough of the original rootball to avoid weakening or stressing the tree.

Inspecting the rootball
Cut the anchorage wires and tilt the tree from the pot. Circling roots indicate that root pruning and repotting are necessary.

1 Comb out the roots with a metal root hook, working radially from the trunk base. Avoid damage to radial roots that will be displayed on the surface.

2 When the root mass is disentangled, the length of the circling roots can be seen clearly. You can cut away all of this length in the root pruning.

3 After trimming the long roots, cut wedge-shaped pieces out of the rootball to encourage more fibrous root-growth close to the trunk.

REPOTTING

Although it is not necessary to change the pot during repotting for horticultural reasons, it can provide an opportunity to change the container if you feel it does not suit the design as well as you expected. In this example, the larch has been growing in an oval pot with a rounded profile. It was decided that a plainer grey unglazed oval pot would create a dignified effect more appropriate to the tree, so this was the one prepared for repotting.

Usually when repotting you will be replacing the tree in its original container, and this should be cleaned after the tree is removed. The first step is to use a stiff brush to brush out the remaining potting soil. Often this is enough, but if the pot needs to be cleaned more thoroughly, you can simply scrub it out with clean water and a little washing-up liquid.

Soil mixtures

The basic requirements for a potting soil for bonsai are that it should provide adequate drainage so that roots do not become waterlogged, but should also have good moisture retention that allows the roots to take in the water they need. A loose, open-textured soil aids moisture retention and provides ventilation, allowing oxygen to circulate so that the roots can "breathe".

Three types of soil mix are recommended to cover the requirements of the plants listed in the Species Guide. The mixtures are composed as follows:

- Basic soil mix:
One part loam; two parts sphagnum moss peat; two parts granite grit
- Free-draining soil mix:
One part loam; one part sphagnum moss peat; three parts granite grit
- Lime-free (ericaceous) soil mix:
One part loam; three parts sphagnum moss peat; one part granite grit

These are mixtures that will work well for the recommended trees and shrubs. The recipes do not contain any fertilizer, which can be added as required once the plant is established. Nutrients can scorch new roots initially and you should not feed a repotted bonsai for two or three weeks after the initial new growth has begun in spring (see also page 172).

REPLANTING THE TREE

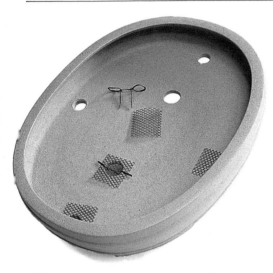

1 Prepare the pot by covering the drainage holes with plastic mesh, held in place with twists of wire, to prevent the potting mixture from washing out through the holes (see also page 53).

2 Insert the anchorage wire into the pot. Push it down through a drainage hole, pass it under the pot and up through another hole on the opposite side, leaving long ends of wire that will secure the tree.

3 Bend the long ends of the anchorage wire over the sides of the pot rim. Using the prepared soil mixture appropriate to the tree, spread an even layer of potting soil across the base of the container.

4 Place the tree on the fresh layer of soil, carefully positioned to give the correct front view. Bring the anchorage wires up and over the rootball and secure them by twisting with pliers.

5 Add more soil mixture and carefully work it into the root mass with a chopstick, pushing it down to fill the cut sections. Continue adding soil until the pot is filled to just below the rim.

6 When the soil is fully worked into the roots, water the tree thoroughly. To complete the repotting, lay moist moss over the soil surface and firm it down with a trowel.

Before repotting
You must inspect the rootball to see if the tree needs repotting. There are no signs other than the density of the root mass.

After repotting
Usually you will see no difference in the bonsai before and after repotting, although in this case the pot has been changed to improve the overall design. Root pruning and repotting gives the larch another year of healthy growth. For other species, it may be two or more years before you need to carry out the whole procedure again.

MAINTENANCE PRUNING

When you have mastered the necessary horticultural skills to keep a bonsai alive – positioning, watering, feeding and repotting the tree will grow healthily and strongly, and it will need to be shaped and groomed as it grows. These processes maintain the existing form but provide the opportunity to adjust, improve and refine the shape of the tree.

Pinching back (finger-pruning) and trimming of terminal growth results in secondary growth further back on the twig or branch, increasing the bushiness and fullness of the foliage masses. This enhances the effect of the tree's maturity. If this grooming is not done, the most vigorous shoots will grow thick and strong. It is always the upper

branches of a tree that grow most vigorously, so neglecting to groom the top branches will result in top-heavy growth, with the lower branches withering and dying. The upper shoots must be trimmed early enough to prevent unsightly thickening, but the lower branches can be allowed to extend somewhat before pruning until they develop the required thicknesses.

This combination of techniques results in a tree with delicate twigs at the apex and strong lower branches. The process can also be used effectively to fatten up trunks on developing bonsai. To do so, the maintenance pruning must be accompanied by adequate watering and feeding routines.

FINGER PRUNING OF CONIFERS

Grooming of conifers such as junipers, spruces, cedars, larches and cryptomerias is usually done with the fingertips. If the foliage is cut across with scissors, the tips of the cut shoots turn brown and the bonsai is temporarily disfigured. If you use the soft pads

of your fingertips to pinch out the shoots as shown opposite, there is no damage.

Conifer foliage falls into two distinct categories – needle-like and scale-like. Trees with needle-like foliage include junipers, larches, cedars, spruces and cryptomerias; those with scale-like foliage include cypresses

and some junipers. There are junipers that have exclusively one or the other type of foliage, but some varieties have needles when young and develop scale-like leaves as they mature, and the terms "juvenile" and "adult" foliage are often used respectively in describing these characteristics.

Before finger pruning
This example of Juniperus squamata 'Meyeri' *has grown unrestricted for two months after initial bonsai shaping. The overall shape is becoming masked by surplus foliage.*

After finger pruning
Finger pruning over the whole of the tree has clarified the original lines of the design and restored a balanced shape. The process is repeated over the life of the bonsai, increasing the branching of the twigs and density of the foliage.

FINGER PRUNING NEEDLE-LIKE FOLIAGE

1 Hold the branch carefully between the finger and thumb of one hand. With the other hand, grasp the leading shoot gently but firmly between the pads of your forefinger and thumb.

2 Pull the shoot straight towards you in one quick movement. It should break away cleanly, parting from the branch without any damage to the remaining foliage.

3 Pinch out the shoots all over the apex of the tree in the same way. Finger prune the lower branches as necessary. This leaves the tree with a cleaner, more refined and compact silhouette.

FINGER PRUNING SCALE-LIKE FOLIAGE

1 Hold the branch between the fingers and thumb of one hand. Grip the leading shoot between forefinger and thumb of the other hand, at an angle that will allow you to make a twisting motion as you pull the shoot.

2 Twist the shoot and pull it free of the plant at the same time. As with the straight action applied to the needle-like foliage, this breaks the shoot cleanly without damage to the remaining foliage.

3 Repeat the finger pruning all over the tree to tidy the shape. You can see here how the contours of the apex have been refined by comparison with the more ragged shape in the first picture of this sequence.

SCISSOR TRIMMING

The important point to remember when grooming bonsai is that scissors are used to cut stems, not the foliage. Any kind of leaf that is cut through will look untidy and turn brown at the edges. You can use your fingernails to pinch out very soft, immature stems and pine "candles" – the extending pine buds – if they have not yet hardened. But you will need to use scissors to cut off tougher stems and candles to avoid tearing the tissues.

Like finger pruning, scissor trimming is carried out throughout the growing season to refine the shape of the tree and encourage bushier growth, as shown right by the example of a Chinese elm (*Ulmus parvifolia*) before and after scissor trimming.

Before trimming

After trimming

1 To trim the stem of a deciduous tree, hold the top of the shoot and cut through the stem immediately above a leaf.

2 You can simply discard the cut shoot, or use it as material for propagating a new plant if appropriate (see page 186).

3 Cut off all long shoots extending from the silhouette of the tree to leave a clean, compact shape.

SCISSOR TRIMMING PINE CANDLES

1 Place the fine, sharp scissor points at the base of candle, taking care not to trap or cut any of the surrounding needles.

2 Make sure that you cut through the candle base in a single, clean cut, leaving no ragged tissues.

3 Candle-cutting refines the shape of the tree, and new buds will develop at the base of each cut.

LEAF-CUTTING

With some species, you can remove all the leaves in summer to force a second crop. This effectively gives two years' growth in one, as new leaves develop from buds that have formed for the next year. These leaves tend to be smaller and their autumn colour brighter. The timing of leaf-cutting is critical – too soon and the buds will not have formed; too late, the new leaf crop may not harden off before autumn and there will not be time for buds to form to replace those that have opened.

Suitable species are those that have the habit of continuous or successive flushes of growth, such as birches, elms and maples. The Japanese maple *Acer palmatum* 'Deshojo' (below) when leaf-cut gives a second crop of its brilliant red spring foliage.

Before leaf-cutting

After leaf-cutting

1 Start at the apex of the tree and remove the leaves systematically, working from the top downwards.

2 Cut immediately behind the base of the leaf, leaving the leaf-stalk (petiole) on the branch.

3 Leave the leaf-stalks to preserve moisture for the dormant buds at their bases. The stalks will drop off before the buds open.

PESTS AND DISEASES

Most bonsai are hardy trees or shrubs not particularly susceptible to pests and diseases, but if a problem occurs it is important that you can recognize it in order to apply an effective remedy. The pictures on these pages identify the most common pests and diseases.

Routine spraying with a systemic insecticide and fungicide is a useful preventive measure. A systemic treatment gets into the sap stream of the plant and enables it to counter-attack the problem over a period of two to three weeks. A routine monthly spray from early spring through summer is ninety per cent effective. Spray when the leaves are in bud or after they have fully opened, not while buds are unfurling as the spray action may damage the soft new leaves. Make sure that the brands of insecticide and fungicide that you use are compatible and follow the manufacturer's instructions on dosage.

BLACKFLY

These tiny creates are aphids, one of the most common pests to attack garden plants, shrubs and trees. The damage is caused by the aphids invading stems, leaves and fruit to suck the sap. They can also carry disease from one plant to another. You can easily see the tiny black insects on the stems or leaves of the plant, or you may notice that leaves and new shoots are curled and distorted. Aphids are persistent pests and you must ensure that your treatment completely eradicates them over a period of time.

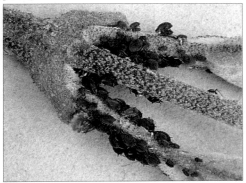

Blackfly

GREENFLY

The many types of aphid are mostly named by colour – blackfly, greenfly, whitefly. Another common type that you see is woolly aphid, which resembles tiny cotton balls. Thin-leaved deciduous trees are most suceptible to aphid attack; the woolly aphid is a common pest of pines and crab apples. The insects cluster on young shoots and the undersides of leaves and you may notice the sticky"honeydew"that they secrete. Systemic insecticide acts as prevention or cure. Damaged shoots can be pruned out.

Greenfly

CUCKOO SPIT

The evidence of infestation by cuckoo-spit insects that you will readily see on the plant is globules of white froth on leaves and shoots. The larvae of the insects live inside the spit-like masses and, like aphids, suck the sap of the plant. Similar damage is caused, with leaves becoming wilted and shoots misshapen. Insecticide treatment is required to kill the larvae. The unsightly patches of "spit" can be removed by spraying with clean water or gently wiping leaves and stems with a damp cloth.

Cuckoo spit (above left)

Larva of the cuckoo-spit insect (above right)

SCALE INSECT

There are various types of these sap-sucking insects. They do not move around on the stems but remain in one place and develop a hard, shell-like protective coating. Signs of damage to the plant are wilted leaves and the sticky honeydew coating leaves and shoots. On inspection, you will see that the insects appear as tiny white, red or brown nodules, making stems and leaves appear blistered. As with all sap-sucking insects, systemic insecticide is the most effective treatment.

Scale insect

ORBITAL MITE

These are tiny red or black "pinhead" insects that feed on algae growing on the tree bark. You may see them clustered on the undersides of branches or hiding in crevices in the bark. It appears that orbital mites are harmless to the tree and do not affect its overall growth rate and vigour or do damage to external features such as bark or leaves. They are, however, an unsightly pest, but you can easily brush them off the bark using an old toothbrush.

Orbital mite

LEAF MINER

These are fly larvae that hatch from eggs laid on the underside of leaves by the adult insects. They feed on the leaves, taking the soft, interior tissues. The leaf miners appear as blister-like shapes on the leaves. The damage they cause shows as white markings on the leaf surfaces and deterioration of the tissues. If you find this problem in a bonsai, pick off the damaged leaves and spray the tree regularly with systemic insecticide following the manufacturer's instructions.

Damage caused by leaf miner

CATERPILLARS

Caterpillars can be very destructive to leaves and young stems. They feed on the foliage, making holes in the leaves and even stripping them completely. Some types also cause damage to tree bark and roots. Caterpillars are the larvae of butterflies and moths – these adult creatures are quite harmless to plants – and they hatch out in spring, so they can begin immediately to feed on young foliage. Systemic insecticide treatment makes the sap poisonous, gradually killing off the invaders as they feed. Because the damage caterpillars cause is so unsightly, especially to small bonsai, routine preventive treatment is best to avoid having to take drastic steps to cure the problem when it occurs. Damaged leaves can be removed to improve the tree's appearance.

Caterpillar (above)

Caterpillar damage to leaf (right)

VINE WEEVIL

Adult beetles feed on leaves, giving them notched, irregular edges. The larvae of vine weevils attack roots, affecting the plant's ability to make healthy new growth. Control of the larvae is difficult, as they can stay in the soil for up to six months, and root infestation may not become apparent until repotting. Soaking the pot in a solution containing gamma-HCH, an ingredient of some insecticides, is recommended. It is best to get advice on a suitable product as required.

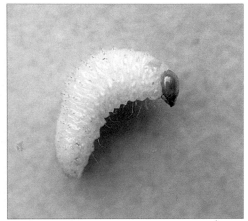

Vine weevil larva (above)

Vine weevil leaf damage

Adult vine weevil (right)

PEACH LEAF CURL

This disease mainly affects *Prunus* species. Early signs are blisters on the leaves, reddish at first, then turning white as they enlarge. The leaves become misshapen, curled and discoloured, and will eventually fall. This is not just a cosmetic problem, as peach leaf curl also weakens the tree. The fungus can survive on the tree after leaves have fallen, even over the winter, hence the need for thorough preventive treatment with a systemic fungicide. If the disease does occur, you must remove and destroy the affected leaves.

Peach leaf curl

SLUGS AND SNAILS

Foliage, shoots and roots are susceptible to damage from slugs and snails. You may not see the creatures feeding, but their presence is evident from large holes appearing in leaves. They can quickly strip leaves from a small plant. There are various proprietary brands of poisonous slug bait, in pellet or cream form, that can be left near the plant to attract slugs or snails. Liquid slug-killers that can be watered into the soil are less suitable for bonsai where there is such a small amount of soil in the container.

Garden slug

MILDEW

Oak, hawthorn and crab apples are particularly susceptible to mildew. Damp, poorly ventilated conditions allow it to thrive. It is seen as white, powdery patches on foliage and stems. These are fungal spores that extract sap from the tree and cause loss of vigour. If untreated, the mildew turns from brown to black as it creates a breeding ground for new spores to form. Treatment with systemic fungicide cannot remove existing mildew, but it does stop the problem from spreading, hence the importance of routine preventive treatment against this disease.

Mildew

CHAPTER FIVE

PROPAGATION TECHNIQUES

Propagating your own original stock for bonsai provides you with a wide choice of material and the most complete method of acquiring suitable specimens for bonsai training. The basic techniques of propagating new material from seed and cuttings or by layering or grafting are explained here with step-by-step examples. Suitable methods of propagation for individual species and cultivars are recommended in the Bonsai Species Guide (pages 90 to 167) and the Compendium of Trees and Shrubs for Bonsai (pages 190 to 217) and can be cross-referred to the more detailed information in this chapter.

SOWING SEED

Seed sowing, although time-consuming, is a way of producing many seedlings suitable for eventual training into bonsai. The choice of words is important here, as this is not a process of "growing bonsai" from seed, but of cultivating material for that may prove suitable for bonsai use.

Many people around the world are attracted by the "bonsai kits" sometimes offered for sale in garden centres and from mail-order catalogues. The kit usually contains merely a few seeds and some soil. This is a very expensive and unreliable way to buy seed and, as should be clear from the information in the previous chapters about selecting and training material for bonsai, what you buy in these kits can no more be described as bonsai than an acorn can be described as an oak table.

For seed to germinate successfully, it is important that it is fresh. This means collecting the seeds yourself or relying on a reputable seed merchant who has stored the seed at the correct temperature and humidity. Tree seed, unlike some vegetable seeds, does not stay viable for very long. In some cases, this is only a matter of months – providing that the seed has been correctly stored. It follows, therefore, that if you buy seed in midsummer from a display subject to summer temperatures, your chances of success are limited.

If you wish to try growing trees or shrubs from seed for use in bonsai, check in the Species Guide (pages 90 to 167) whether the species you are interested in cultivating are suitable for this propagation method. Remember that it will be a few years before a plant is sufficiently developed to be suitable for bonsai training, so you must be able to provide the space and time required to cultivate the material successfully.

Timing the sowing
Nature provides the best possible guide to when to sow seed. Many hardy tree seeds need to go through a period of cold, even freezing conditions before breaking dormancy. It is possible to provide this artificially using a freezer or refrigerator. However, it is preferable to sow seed while it is fresh in early autumn or winter and expose it to the winter weather (while protecting it from birds and rodents).

If a refrigerator is used to break dormancy, it is possible to germinate seed out of season – in midsummer, for example – but this only presents you with a problem later in autumn when the seedlings have not had a full growing season and are often too immature to survive a winter.

Preparation
Some seeds need stratification before sowing. This consists of either burying them in wet sand in pots exposed to the winter frosts or, more easily, placing them in wet sand in a plastic bag in the refrigerator for some months.

Seeds with a hard shell or husk, such as pine or beech, are best soaked in a bowl of water before planting. This helps to soften the shell, but also indicates which seeds are viable. Empty shells float and viable seeds sink, so after soaking discard the "floaters". Be careful, however, as sometimes smaller seeds float simply because of the surface tension of the water. This is easily prevented by adding a few drops of soap or detergent to the water.

GROWING PINES FROM SEED
This demonstration uses seed from the Japanese white pine (*Pinus parviflora*). To collect the seed, place the pine cones in a warm room for some days until they open. Then extract the seeds and soak them as described above. Discard the infertile floating seeds.

Pines are usually grown from seed or by grafting – they have high resin content that inhibits callousing and are not suitable subjects for taking cuttings. Seedlings do not always come true to the parent plant, so grafting is often preferred, but the rootstocks still have to be grown from seed. The development of the seedling into material suitable for bonsai training is shown in Creating a Bonsai on page 66. If you require a large bonsai with a heavy trunk, you will need to allow the young tree to develop in open ground. For small bonsai the tree can be grown on in a pot and potted on into larger size pots as required.

SOWING SEED

1 Fill the seed tray with a seed-sowing soil mixture. In this case, the growing medium for the seeds consists of one part moss peat to one part perlite.

2 You can add a fine layer of sand to help make the seed visible. Create furrows in the surface so that you can sow the seeds evenly and well spaced.

3 Space out the seeds along the furrows. The suitable spacing will vary for different species according to the size of the seed.

4 Cover with coarse grit to a depth between one and two times the size of the seed. Water the tray well and place it outside.

Growth after one year
Cover the tray with wire mesh for protection against birds and rodents until germination. Take care with watering after the seedlings appear in spring, but leave the tray undisturbed for one year.

TRANSPLANTING A SEEDLING

Root trimming
Trim back the long roots to encourage more and finer root development close to the stem base.

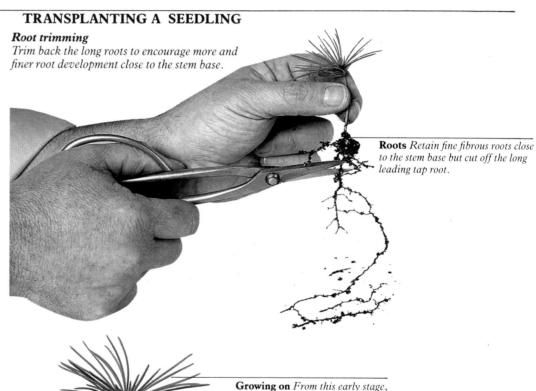

Roots *Retain fine fibrous roots close to the stem base but cut off the long leading tap root.*

Lifting the seedling
Remove the seedling carefully from the tray. You will see that it has developed long, straggly roots.

Potting up the seedling
Fill a 7.5cm (3in) plastic plant pot with free-draining soil mix (one part loam, one part sphagnum moss peat, three parts granite grit). To encourage a radial root system to develop, spread the roots carefully in a wheel-spoke pattern when potting the seedling. Twisted roots will remain tangled as they thicken. If you are maintaining the tree in a pot for possible use as small bonsai, pot on annually into a larger size pot to give the roots more space. If you can plant the tree into open ground after the first year, it develops more quickly into material suitable for bonsai training.

Growing on *From this early stage, the tree must be allowed several years of unrestricted growth while the trunk thickens and the branch structure develops.*

TAKING CUTTINGS

Cuttings are a very easy and reliable propagation method. They also have the advantage that the material used is, in many cases, removed during routine maintenance trimming of bonsai and would otherwise be thrown away. Cuttings are classified as hardwood or softwood. Hardwood cuttings are taken from fully ripened wood, sometimes even wood that is several years old. Softwood cuttings come from the soft new growth of the current season.

When to take cuttings

As a generalization, hardwood cuttings are taken from autumn through winter and softwood cuttings, because they must come from current growth, from around late spring to early summer. However, remarkable results have been achieved by bonsai enthusiasts who, rather than throw out prunings, use the material as cuttings at the supposedly "wrong" time. Remember that any reference book on propagation gives recommendations on when and

how to take cuttings in order to achieve the best possible results and regards the process as an end in itself, whereas for many bonsai enthusiasts cuttings are a by-product. Advice on taking cuttings from individual species is given in the Species Guide (pages 90 to 167), but you can experiment with any material that you have as a result of pruning.

Cultivation

The important thing to keep in mind when you select material for cuttings is that it must be strong and healthy. You should take steps to maintain humidity around the cutting to prevent moisture loss until such time as the cutting has calloused over and begins to root. Humidity can be provided by mist-spraying or by judicious use of plastic or glass cover, for example, a propagator, cold frame or greenhouse. Often with hardwood cuttings even this is unnecessary, as the species that root most readily will grow strongly from material pushed into the ground.

TAKING SOFTWOOD CUTTINGS

This demonstration shows softwood cuttings taken from the dwarf Japanese cedar (*Cryptomeria japonica* 'Yatsubusa'). The selected cutting material is taken off just below the junction of a side shoot. This is the area with the greatest concentration of natural hormones, which encourage the cutting to generate roots.

Although cuttings can be grown in a standard plastic seed tray, the container used here is an earthenware alpine pot. This gives extra depth and the clay walls allow for better drainage and provide more efficient insulation for the soil mixture. If you use a container with large drainage holes, the holes should be covered

with squares of plastic mesh, as for a bonsai pot (see page 53), to prevent the soil from washing through. The soil mixture used as a rooting medium here consists of one part moss peat and one part perlite.

Preparing the pot
Cover the drainage holes with plastic mesh and insert a layer of coarse grit. Fill up the pot with the soil mixture.

1 Select the material for the cutting, hold it gently upright and trim it off cleanly with sharp scissors.

2 Remove side shoots and needles from the lower third of the cutting, to prevent them from rotting under soil level.

3 Use a chopstick, or similar tool, to make a hole in the soil. This enables the cutting to be inserted without damage to the cut end.

Watering and labelling
Water the soil gently but thoroughly. Insert a label with the name of the plant and the date the cuttings were taken.

4 Insert the cutting in the hole and firm down the soil around it to hold it snugly. Repeat the process for as many cuttings as you require, or until the pot is full.

Maintaining the cuttings
Keep the pot of cuttings in an unheated glasshouse or cold frame. They need no further attention other than routine watering. After one year, the cuttings show considerable extension growth and appear strong and healthy. When the cuttings reach this stage, if you lift the pot you should be able to see the roots beginning to grow out through the pot's drainage holes. At this stage, as the pot is becoming crowded, the cuttings are ready to be transplanted into separate pots where they will have more room to develop. Use free-draining soil mix (see page 174) when repotting the cuttings.

Potting up cuttings
Carefully remove a cutting from the pot and trim back the long roots. Replant it in a 7.5cm (3in) plant pot and allow it to grow on for another year. It can then be either planted out in open ground to thicken or potted on into a larger pot.

LAYERING AND GRAFTING

All propagation methods can be used to produce material for bonsai, but some are more appropriate than others. Propagation is a fascinating subject, and if you feel you require more information than is given here, there are various specialist books that can supply further detail of all the possible methods. You can apply propagation techniques to growing new material from a garden-grown plant, as well as using an existing bonsai as the original parent plant. A general handbook on propagation will therefore prove helpful if you intend to propagate a lot of new stock.

You may be familiar with the technique of layering a plant at ground level. This involves various methods of pegging down or burying the end of a shoot in garden soil to encourage it to root while still attached to the parent plant. This is sometimes applied to bonsai stock propagation, but the layer has to be taken from a multi-trunked parent plant growing in the ground.

Air layering is the technique more commonly used for bonsai. This makes it possible to produce a bonsai very quickly, as a well-shaped branch can be selected that can be pruned to a suitable bonsai shape before the process of air layering begins.

Grafting is commonly used in commercial cultivation of trees and shrubs, and it has various advantages in that context. It is a more difficult technique for the beginner or amateur grower to apply with successful results and is explained here only in terms of the basic principles.

AIR LAYERING A HAWTHORN

The material used to demonstrate air layering is a pot-grown maiden tree of flowering hawthorn (*Crataegus oxyacantha* 'Paul's Scarlet'). It was obtained from a garden centre, so was originally intended for garden use and has not been grown or trained to have characteristics particularly suitable for bonsai. The tree is very spindly, but there is a good twiggy section at the top that will yield an attractive small tree that can be developed as bonsai.

The usual method of air layering involves applying sphagnum moss to the stem and wrapping it in clear plastic to make a "parcel" enclosing the air layer. The roots emerge from the stem into the surrounding moss. In this demonstration, a pot of soil is used to surround the stem. The advantage of this method is that when roots have developed, the stem can be cut through at the base of the pot and the rooted tree is already potted without any further disturbance.

The bonsai material
A maiden tree is one in its first year after grafting, with a single, slender trunk. You will be able to find a similar example among garden centre stock.

1 Ring-bark the stem with a very sharp knife. Make two cuts at a distance from each other about one and a half times the diameter of the stem, and remove the bark.

2 Split a plastic pot down the side at one corner and towards the centre of the base. Cut the base to fit around the plant stem and put the pot in place on the trunk.

3 Secure the pot with pieces of wire twisted firmly in place. Insert a free-draining soil mixture (as for cuttings).

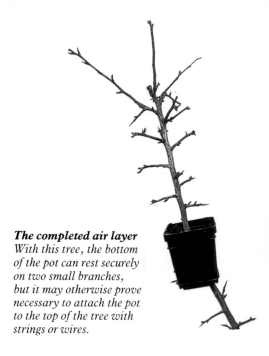

The completed air layer
With this tree, the bottom of the pot can rest securely on two small branches, but it may otherwise prove necessary to attach the pot to the top of the tree with strings or wires.

AIR LAYERING AT LOW LEVEL

In this example, air layering is used to improve the appearance of the tree. The lower part of a maiden tree – the same type of flowering hawthorn as that shown in the previous demonstration – has been air layered to eliminate a fault in the trunk. The tree was originally a grafted plant and the graft made an unattractive feature at about 2.5cm (1in) above soil level.

Air layering at this level enables a new root system to develop above the graft and the original rootstock can then be removed. It is not appropriate to do this while the tree is in flower. The tree will be allowed to grow on with the new root system above the original soil level until early spring, when repotting will take place before the new leaves begin to open from the buds.

You can easily check the progress of the root development after a suitable period of time by removing the pot, which can be reattached by fitting it back around the rootball and replacing the wires.

1 Apply the air layer as in the previous demonstration, with the base of the pot at the original soil level. Here it has been in position for one year.

2 To inspect the roots, unwind the wires holding the pot in place and pull the pot away from the rootball. Replace it until it is time to remove the original root system.

GRAFTING A CRAB APPLE

Grafting is commonly used in bonsai to propagate pines with desirable characteristics, and also for fruiting trees. The reason for grafting fruiting trees is that if they are grown from seed, it can take many years before they become sufficiently mature to produce flowers and fruit. Crab apples (*Malus*), for example, may take between 15 and 20 years to reach this stage. This, coupled with the fact that crab apple trees grown from seed do not often come true to the parent plant, and may have poor flowers or sparse fruit, means that grafting is a good option. A grafted tree will flower and fruit and will have the expected characteristics.

The section of the tree to be grafted onto the rootstock is called the scion. As in this example, a two-year-old crab apple seedling used as stock can have a mature crab apple scion (complete with flower buds) grafted on. This is done in late winter or early spring and the tree will be in flower three months later. When placing the scion in the stock, you need to line up the cambium layers of the two woods, the green layers just below the bark, to ensure an effective graft.

Grafting is particularly well suited to certain species of plants (see page 21) and if you find that you have a particular interest in this technique, you should seek more specialized advice on both the practical detail and suitable rootstocks for the plants you wish to grow.

Preparing the scion
Cut the base of the scion to a wedge shape, using a very sharp grafting knife. You can alternatively use a scalpel or single-edged razor blade to make the cut.

1 Prepare the stock by cutting cleanly across it and then splitting down the stem with a sharp blade. Insert the scion carefully into the split stem.

2 Wind clear plastic tape around the graft to hold it firmly in place. Take the tape over the uncut part of the stock and the upper section of the scion to seal the graft.

3 Plastic tape stretches with the tree's growth, but you can remove it after about a year. This picture shows the completely healed graft two years later.

CHAPTER SIX

COMPENDIUM OF TREES AND SHRUBS FOR BONSAI

Ordered on the same principles as the Bonsai Species Guide (pages 90 to 167), this Compendium lists over 300 trees and shrubs suitable for cultivation as bonsai. The entries are ordered alphabetically by the botanical names, based on genus and species. Sub-species, varieties and cultivars are listed alphabetically following the relevant species entry. Each entry provides a basic description of the tree or shrub, advice on cultivation and the recommended bonsai styles and sizes. The Compendium is a comprehensive extension of the Bonsai Species Guide designed to provide you with a means of selecting from the widest possible choice of material for bonsai.

HOW TO USE THE COMPENDIUM

This compendium lists over 300 trees and shrubs suitable for growing as bonsai. Most are species, but there are also many interesting subspecies, hybrids, varieties, and cultivars. For ease of reference, the compendium includes all the trees in the Bonsai Species Guide, both the featured species and the other forms and related species mentioned there (see pages 90 to 167).

The compendium is arranged in alphabetical order by botanic names. Plants known by two names are included under the one name most widely used, with the synonym given in brackets. The synonyms themselves are included and cross-referenced at the appropriate place. Common names are given throughout. A description of the plant, a summary of its cultivation and propagation requirements, and suggestions for its use as a bonsai are detailed in full for every species. Varieties and cultivars are listed with the relevant species, and both their similarities to the species and the aspects in which they differ are described. Every plant listed here that is also illustrated in the Bonsai Species Guide has a cross reference to the page on which it is shown.

Descriptions

There is a description of every species, outlining natural characteristics such as growth rate, size, and hardiness. The size and shape of leaves are given, as well as unusual colouring and autumn tints. The texture of the bark, and any flowers or fruit produced are also described. For other forms listed under a species, the particular points in which they differ from the species, being for instance dwarf or double-flowered, are outlined.

Cultivation and propagation details

A summary of the particular needs of the plants is given, the information being grouped under the headings of **Position, Watering, Feeding, Repotting, Pruning,** and **Propagation.** Further information on all these aspects of care can be found in *Routine Maintenance* and *Propagation* on pages 168 to 189. Each heading is also identified by a symbol for instant location.

Varieties and cultivars of the species that have the same needs as the species read "Cultivation and propagation as..." and refer back to the species entry. If their care differs in any way from the species — many cultivars, for instance, cannot be propagated from seed, while the species can — these differences will be detailed.

Styles and sizes

A range of styles for each plant is recommended. This is intended to suggest rather than to limit. Other styles are possible, and the choice must depend on the individual tree, but these are the ones most likely to be successful. More information on the styles can be found on pages 46 to

51 of *Creating a Bonsai.* Some plants in the compendium are suited to being used as "accessory plants", grown either in the bonsai container as underplanting for the tree, or separately to set off a bonsai on display. Where this is the case it is mentioned at the end of the styling information.

A range of sizes suitable for the tree is given. This is based on considerations such as natural size, or the fineness of the twig structure or the leaves, and is a consistent guide rather than a formal classification. The sizes are: extra-small, up to 10cm (4in); small, 10-20cm (4-8in); medium, 20-45cm (8-18in); large, 45-90cm (18-36in), and extra-large, over 90cm (36in).

Some varieties and cultivars are suited to the same styles and sizes as their main species, and their entries read "Styles as..." and refer back to the species. The natural characteristics of others may make different styles more appropriate, or they may be dwarf forms more suited to smaller sizes. In these cases their entries give details of the styles and sizes recommended.

Identification *The compendium is arranged by botanic names, and these are given first, in italics. Common names are given below, in bold.*

Description *The natural habit of the tree, its hardiness, and the overall appearance of the leaves are detailed, and any flowers or fruit described.*

Cross-references *Any species that has been illustrated in the species guide has a cross reference to that page.*

Cultivation and propagation *The cultivation requirements and propagation methods are detailed for each species. Symbols for each heading provide instant access to the information.*

Bonsai styling *A range of bonsai styles and sizes that are suitable for each plant are listed.*

Main species entries *Each separate species has a detailed description and full cultivation, propagation and bonsai styling details*

Cultivation as *A. lasiocarpa*.
▣ **Propagation** Grafting.
▣ **Styles** As *A. lasiocarpa*.

Acer buergerianum (A. trifidium)

TRIDENT MAPLE
Deciduous tree. Orange and red autumn colour. (See also page 94.)
▣ **Position** Full sun. Protect from frost.
▣ **Watering** Daily throughout growing season. Keep relatively dry in winter.
▣ **Feeding** Weekly for the first month after leaves appear, then every two weeks until late summer.
▣ **Repotting** Annually in early spring as buds swell. Use free-draining soil mix.
▣ **Pruning** Trim back new shoots throughout growing season. Leaf-cut in midsummer.
▣ **Propagation** Cuttings, seed, air lavering.
▣ **Styles** Suitable for all styles except broom, and for all sizes.

Acer buergerianum formosanum

FORMOSAN TRIDENT MAPLE
Subspecies with thick leathery leaves and more compact growth than the main species. Cultivation, propagation, and styles as for *A. buergerianum*.

Acer buergerianum 'Mino Yatsubusa'

DWARF TRIDENT MAPLE
A dwarf form with a pointed apex and long, narrow, shiny leaves, which appear as if

Alternative forms *Distinguishing features are described. Cultivation, propagation, and styling are referred back to the main species entry where they are identical. Where they differ, the differences are detailed.*

Abies alba

SILVER FIR

Evergreen conifer. Dark-green needle-like leaves, cylindrical cones.
🔲 **Position** Slight shade.
🔷 **Watering** Daily throughout summer.
⬛ **Feeding** Every two weeks from early spring to mid autumn.
⬛ **Repotting** Every second year, in spring or autumn. Use basic soil mix.
✂ **Pruning** Pinch back new shoots throughout growing season.
📘 **Propagation** Seed, layering, cuttings.
📜 **Styles** Formal upright, informal upright, slanting, semicascade, literati, twin-trunk, clump, straight line, sinuous, multiple-trunk, group, saikei. Medium to extra-large sizes.

Abies koreana

KOREAN FIR

Small, slow-growing evergreen conifer. Dark-green leaves. Purple cones even when young.
🔲 **Position** Slight shade.
🔷 **Watering** Daily throughout summer.
⬛ **Feeding** Every two weeks from early spring to mid autumn.
⬛ **Repotting** Every second year, in spring or autumn. Use basic soil mix.
✂ **Pruning** Pinch back new shoots throughout growing season.
📘 **Propagation** Seed, layering, cuttings.
📜 **Styles** Formal upright, informal upright, slanting, semicascade, literati, twin-trunk, clump, straight line, sinuous, multiple-trunk, group, saikei. Medium to extra-large sizes.

Abies koreana 'Compact dwarf'

DWARF KOREAN FIR

Dwarf form. Does not produce cones.
Cultivation as *A. koreana*.
📘 **Propagation** Grafting.
📜 **Styles** As *A. koreana*, suitable for extra-small and small sizes.

Abies lasiocarpa

ALPINE FIR

Evergreen conifer with greyish green needle-like leaves.
🔲 **Position** Slight shade.
🔷 **Watering** Daily throughout summer.
⬛ **Feeding** Every two weeks from early spring to mid autumn.
⬛ **Repotting** Every second year, in spring or autumn. Use basic soil mix.
✂ **Pruning** Pinch back new shoots throughout growing season.
📘 **Propagation** Seed, layering, cuttings.
📜 **Styles** Formal upright, informal upright, slanting, semicascade, literati, twin-trunk, clump, straight line, sinuous, multiple-trunk, group, saikei. Medium to extra-large sizes.

Abies lasiocarpa arizonica

CORK FIR

Form with thick corky bark and silver-grey needle-like leaves.
Cultivation, propagation, and styles as for *A. lasiocarpa*.

Abies lasiocarpa arizonica 'Compacta'

DWARF CORK FIR

Dwarf form of the above, with striking silvery blue-grey foliage.

Cultivation as *A. lasiocarpa*.
📘 **Propagation** Grafting.
📜 **Styles** As *A. lasiocarpa*.

Acer buergerianum (A. trifidium)

TRIDENT MAPLE

Deciduous tree. Orange and red autumn colour. (See also page 94.)
🔲 **Position** Full sun. Protect from frost.
🔷 **Watering** Daily throughout growing season. Keep relatively dry in winter.
⬛ **Feeding** Weekly for the first month after leaves appear, then every two weeks until late summer.
⬛ **Repotting** Annually in early spring as buds swell. Use free-draining soil mix.
✂ **Pruning** Trim new shoots throughout growing season. Leaf-cut in midsummer.
📘 **Propagation** Cuttings, seed, air layering.
📜 **Styles** Suitable for all styles except broom, and for all sizes.

Acer buergerianum formosanum

FORMOSAN TRIDENT MAPLE

Subspecies with thick leathery leaves and more compact growth than the main species.
Cultivation, propagation, and styles as for *A. buergerianum*.

Acer buergerianum 'Mino Yatsubusa'

DWARF TRIDENT MAPLE

A dwarf form with a pointed apex and long, narrow, shiny leaves, which appear as if lacquered red in autumn.
Cultivation, propagation, and styles as for *A. buergerianum*.

Acer campestre

FIELD MAPLE

Small deciduous tree with relatively coarse twig structure. Bright-yellow autumn colour. (See also page 96.)
🔲 **Position** Full sun, slight shade in summer. Protect extra-small sizes from frost.
🔷 **Watering** Daily throughout growing season. Sparingly in winter, but keep moist.
⬛ **Feeding** Every two weeks throughout summer.
⬛ **Repotting** Every two to three years as buds swell. Use basic soil mix.
✂ **Pruning** Trim new shoots throughout growing season. Leaf-cut in midsummer.
📘 **Propagation** Cuttings, seed, air layering.
📜 **Styles** Suitable for all styles except literati. Suitable for medium to large sizes, but can also be grown as extra-small.

Acer davidii

SNAKE BARK MAPLE or PERE DAVID'S MAPLE

Deciduous tree. Heart shaped leaves on red stalks turn rich yellow in autumn. Striking snake-like green and white striped bark.
🔲 **Position** Full sun, slight shade in summer. Protect extra-small sizes from frost.
🔷 **Watering** Daily throughout growing season. Sparingly in winter, but keep moist.
⬛ **Feeding** Every two weeks throughout summer.
⬛ **Repotting** Every two to three years as buds swell. Use basic soil mix.
✂ **Pruning** Trim new shoots throughout growing season. Leaf-cut in midsummer.

📘 **Propagation** Cuttings, seed, air layering.
📜 **Styles** Suitable for all styles except broom. Suitable for medium to large sizes, but can also be grown as extra-small.

Acer ginnala

AMUR MAPLE

Deciduous tree. Visually similar to *A. buergerianum*, and often grown instead of it in colder climates, due to its high tolerance of frost. (See also page 95.)
🔲 **Position** Full sun.
🔷 **Watering** Daily throughout growing season. Keep relatively dry in winter.
⬛ **Feeding** Weekly for the first month after leaves appear, then every two weeks until late summer.
⬛ **Repotting** Annually in early spring. Use free-draining soil mix.
✂ **Pruning** Trim new shoots throughout growing season. Leaf-cut in midsummer.
📘 **Propagation** Cuttings, seed, air layering.
📜 **Styles** Suitable for all styles except broom, and for all sizes.

Acer japonicum

FULL MOON MAPLE

Deciduous tree. Fan shaped leaves, normally with eleven lobes, turn bright yellow, orange, and red in autumn.
🔲 **Position** Full sun, slight shade in summer. Protect extra-small sizes from frost.
🔷 **Watering** Daily throughout growing season. Sparingly in winter, but keep moist.
⬛ **Feeding** Every two weeks throughout summer.
⬛ **Repotting** Every two to three years as buds swell. Use basic soil mix.
✂ **Pruning** Trim new shoots throughout growing season. Leaf-cut in midsummer.
📘 **Propagation** Seed, cuttings, grafting, layering, air layering.
📜 **Styles** Suitable for all styles except broom. Suitable for medium to large sizes, but can also be grown as extra-small.

Acer japonicum 'Aureum'

GOLDEN FULL MOON MAPLE

Yellow leaves, turning orange in autumn.
Cultivation as *A. japonicum*.
📘 **Propagation** Grafting, layering, air layering, cuttings.
📜 **Styles** As *A. japonicum*.

Acer palmatum

JAPANESE MAPLE

Deciduous tree, a classic bonsai subject. Five-lobed leaves turn red in autumn, and bark develops silver colouring with age. (See also page 97.) There are over 250 cultivars.
🔲 **Position** Full sun, slight shade in summer. Protect from severe frost.
🔷 **Watering** Daily throughout growing season. Sparingly in winter, but keep moist.
⬛ **Feeding** Weekly for the first month after leaf buds open, then every two weeks until late summer.
⬛ **Repotting** Every second year in early spring until tree is about 10 years old, then as necessary. Use basic soil mix.
✂ **Pruning** Trim new growth in spring, and leaf-cut in midsummer.

✿ Propagation Seed, cuttings, layering, air layering.
✿ Styles Suitable for all styles except literati, and for all sizes.

Acer palmatum 'Chishio'

JAPANESE RED MAPLE
Crimson spring foliage. Although this was once the most commonly commercially grown bonsai red maple, it has now been largely superseded by 'Deshojo'.
Cultivation as *A. palmatum*.
✿ Propagation Grafting, cuttings, layering, air layering.
✿ Styles As *A. palmatum*.

Acer palmatum 'Deshojo'

JAPANESE RED MAPLE
Brilliant red foliage in spring. The hardiest of the red spring coloured palmatums. (See also page 98.)
Cultivation as *A. palmatum*.
✿ Propagation Grafting, cuttings, layering, air layering.
✿ Styles As *A. palmatum*.

Acer palmatum 'Dissectum'

CUT-LEAF JAPANESE MAPLE
Fine green leaves with seven to eleven lobes turn red in autumn.
Cultivation as *A. palmatum*.
✿ Propagation Grafting, cuttings, layering, air layering.
✿ Styles Informal upright, slanting, semicascade, cascade, twin-trunk, clump. Suitable for all sizes.

Acer palmatum 'Dissectum atropurpureum'

CUT-LEAF PURPLE MAPLE
Purple leaves turn bright orange in autumn. (See also page 99.)
Cultivation as *A. palmatum*.
✿ Propagation Grafting, cuttings, layering, air layering.
✿ Styles Informal upright, slanting, semicascade, cascade, twin-trunk, clump. Suitable for all sizes.

Acer palmatum 'Dissectum atropurpureum' 'Inaba shidare'

CUT-LEAF PURPLE MAPLE
Outstanding cultivar. Leaves are deep purple-red throughout spring and summer, becoming crimson in autumn.
Cultivation as *A. palmatum*.
✿ Propagation Grafting, cuttings, layering, air layering.
✿ Styles Informal upright, slanting, semicascade, cascade, twin-trunk, clump. Suitable for all sizes.

Acer palmatum 'Kagiri Nishiki'

JAPANESE MAPLE 'KAGIRI NISHIKI'
Deep-bluish green leaves have creamy white margins suffused with pink. Vivid rose-crimson autumn colour.
Cultivation, propagation, and styles as for *A. palmatum*.

Acer palmatum 'Kashima'

JAPANESE MAPLE 'KASHIMA'
Very dwarf form. Leaves appear early and are light yellow-green with a reddish margin,

deepening to rich green, then turning bright yellow in autumn.
Cultivation as *A. palmatum*.
✿ Propagation Grafting, cuttings, layering, air layering.
✿ Styles Informal upright, slanting, semicascade, cascade, twin-trunk, clump. Suitable for all sizes.

Acer palmatum 'Katsura'

JAPANESE MAPLE 'KATSURA'
Dwarf yatsubusa form. Foliage is apricot in spring, orange and yellow in autumn.
Cultivation as *A. palmatum*.
✿ Propagation Grafting, cuttings, layering, air layering.
✿ Styles Informal upright, slanting, semicascade, cascade, twin-trunk, clump. Suitable for all sizes.

Acer palmatum 'Kiyohime'

JAPANESE MAPLE 'KIYOHIME'
Very small yatsubusa form. Very early. Horizontal habit with no centre leader.
Cultivation as *A. palmatum*.
✿ Propagation Cuttings, grafting, layering, air layering.
✿ Styles As *A. palmatum*. Particularly suitable for broom, and for smaller sizes

Acer palmatum 'Kotohime'

JAPANESE MAPLE 'KOTOHIME'
Very small yatsubusa form. Strongly vertical habit. One of the smallest-leaved forms.
Cultivation as *A. palmatum*.
✿ Propagation Grafting, cuttings, layering, air layering.
✿ Styles Suitable for all styles except semicascade, cascade, and literati. Suitable for small and extra-small sizes.

Acer palmatum 'Nishiki gawa'

PINE BARK MAPLE
Distinctive corky bark, which becomes very thick and impressive when the tree is still fairly young. Palmatum leaves, red in autumn.
Cultivation as *A. palmatum*.
✿ Propagation Cuttings, grafting, layering, air layering.
✿ Styles Informal upright, slanting, semicascade, cascade, twin-trunk, clump. Suitable for all sizes.

Acer palmatum 'Sango Kaku'

SANGO KAKU MAPLE
Brilliant coral-pink bark, with pink twigs best appreciated in winter. Green leaves have red margins in spring.
Cultivation as *A. palmatum*.
✿ Propagation Grafting, cuttings, layering, air layering.
✿ Styles As *A. palmatum*.

Acer palmatum 'Seigen'

JAPANESE RED MAPLE
Foliage translucent pink and red in spring (when it is extremely wind sensitive), orange and red in autumn. (See also page 99.)
Cultivation as *A. palmatum*.
✿ Propagation Grafting, cuttings, layering, air layering.
✿ Styles As *A. palmatum*.

Acer palmatum 'Shigitatsu Sawa'

JAPANESE MAPLE 'SHIGITATSU SAWA'
Yellow-green leaf with a prominent network of bright-green veins. Red autumn colour.
Cultivation as *A. palmatum*.
✿ Propagation Grafting, cuttings, layering, air layering.
✿ Styles As *A. palmatum*.

Acer palmatum 'Ukigomo'

JAPANESE MAPLE 'UKIGOMO'
Light-green leaves subtly marked with variegations of white and pink. Some leaves are totally white or pink.
Cultivation as *A. palmatum*.
✿ Propagation Grafting, cuttings, layering, air layering.
✿ Styles As *A. palmatum*.

Acer palmatum 'Ukon'

UKON MAPLE
Distinctive lime-green leaves, turning deep yellow and gold in autumn. Branches and twigs also bright lime-green. (See also page 99.)
Cultivation as *A. palmatum*.
✿ Propagation Grafting, cuttings, layering, air layering.
✿ Styles As *A. palmatum*.

Acer trifidium, see *Acer buergerianum*

Ameliancher lamarckii

SNOWY MESPILUS
Deciduous shrub. Scented white flowers in mid spring, purple fruit in autumn.
☼ Position Full sun.
✿ Watering Daily throughout growing season.
✿ Feeding Every two weeks from spring through to autumn.
✿ Repotting Every second year in early spring. Use basic soil mix.
✿ Pruning Trim new growth after flowers fade.
✿ Propagation Seed, cuttings, layering, air layering.
✿ Styles Informal upright, slanting, semicascade, cascade, root-over-rock, twin-trunk, straight line, sinuous, saikei. Suitable for extra-small to large sizes.

Andromeda japonica, see *Pieris japonica*

Andromeda polifolia

BOG ROSEMARY
Lime-hating evergreen shrub. Narrow leaves, heather-like pink flowers in early summer.
☼ Position Slight shade.
✿ Watering Keep soil moist throughout the growing season.
✿ Feeding Every four weeks throughout summer with ericaceous feed.
✿ Repotting Annually in spring. Use lime-free soil mix.
✿ Pruning Trim new growth after flowering.
✿ Propagation Cuttings, division.
✿ Styles Clump, saikei. Suitable for extra-small and small sizes, and for use as an accent plant.

Arundinaria nitida

BAMBOO
Evergreen. Grass-like leaves on strong, arching canes. (See also page 100.)
☼ Position Partial shade. Protect from frost.

Watering Daily at least, but do not allow to stand in water.
Feeding Every two weeks in spring and summer, preferably with high nitrogen feed.
Repotting Every second year in late spring. Use basic soil mix in shallow containers, free-draining in deeper pots.
Pruning Cut back in early spring.
Propagation Division.
Styles Multiple-trunk. Suitable for small and medium sizes.

Arundinaria pygmaea

DWARF BAMBOO

Dwarf species, grows up to 25cm (10in) in nature, much less in a shallow pot.
Position Partial shade. Protect from frost.
Watering Daily at least, but do not allow to stand in water.
Feeding Every two weeks throughout spring and summer.
Repotting Every second year in late spring. Use basic soil mix in shallow containers, free-draining in deeper pots.
Pruning Cut back in early spring.
Propagation Division.
Styles Multiple-trunk. Suitable for extra-small and small sizes.

Azalea indica, see Rhododenron indicum

Berberis buxifolia

BARBERRY

Semi-evergreen shrub. Deep-green box-like leaves with grey undersides. Yellow flowers in spring, purple fruit in autumn.
Position Full sun or shade.
Watering Daily throughout growing season.
Feeding Every two weeks throughout summer.
Repotting Every second year before bud-break in early spring. Use basic soil mix.
Pruning Trim new growth throughout summer.
Propagation Seed, cuttings, division, layering.
Styles Informal upright, slanting, root-over-rock, clasped-to-rock, twin-trunk, clump, straight line, sinuous, group, saikei. Suitable for extra-small to medium sizes.

Berberis darwinii

BARBERRY

Evergreen shrub. Dark-green holly-like leaves. Masses of small golden-orange flowers in very early spring, blue fruit in autumn.
Position Full sun or shade.
Watering Daily throughout growing season.
Feeding Every two weeks throughout summer.
Repotting Every second year before bud-break in early spring. Use basic soil mix.
Pruning Trim new growth throughout summer.
Propagation Seed, cuttings, division, layering.
Styles Informal upright, slanting, root-over-rock, clasped-to-rock, twin-trunk, clump, straight line, sinuous, group, saikei. Suitable for extra-small to medium sizes.

Berberis thunbergii

BARBERRY

Deciduous thorny shrub with red autumn colour. Small yellow flowers in spring, bright-red fruit in autumn.
Position Full sun or shade.
Watering Daily throughout growing season.
Feeding Every two weeks throughout summer.
Repotting Every second year before bud-break in early spring. Use basic soil mix.
Pruning Trim new growth throughout summer.
Propagation Seed, cuttings, division, layering.
Styles Informal upright, slanting, root-over-rock, clasped-to-rock, twin-trunk, clump, straight line, sinuous, group, saikei. Suitable for extra-small to medium sizes.

Berberis thunbergii 'Bagatelle'

DWARF PURPLE BARBERRY

Very hardy dwarf form with compact growth. Foliage is red-purple in spring, turning dark red in summer.
Cultivation as *B. thunbergii*.
Propagation Cuttings, division, layering.
Styles As *B. thunbergii*. Suitable for extra-small and small sizes.

Betula nana

DWARF BIRCH

Deciduous shrub. Tiny leaves with serrated edges turn rich gold in autumn. Copper-coloured trunk. (See also page 102.)
Position Full sun or partial shade. Protect from frost to prevent twig die-back.
Watering Daily throughout growing season. Sparingly in winter, but keep moist.
Feeding Every two weeks from one month after leaves open until end of growing season.
Repotting Every second year in early spring before bud burst. Use basic soil mix.
Pruning Trim new shoots continually.
Propagation Cuttings.
Styles Informal upright, slanting, broom, root-over-rock, clasped-to-rock, twin-trunk, clump, straight line, sinuous, group, saikei. Suitable for extra-small and small sizes.

Betula pendula

SILVER BIRCH

Deciduous tree. Also called European white birch. Heart shaped leaves with gold autumn colour, distinctive silver-white bark. (See also page 103.)
Position Full sun or partial shade. Protect from severe frost to prevent twig die-back.
Watering Daily throughout growing season. Keep moist in winter.
Feeding Every two weeks from one month after leaves open to late summer.
Repotting Every second year in early spring before bud burst, until tree is about 10 years old, then as necessary. Use free-draining soil mix.
Pruning Trim new shoots in spring and at successive flushes of growth. Use a wound sealant.
Propagation Seed.
Styles Informal upright, twin-trunk, group. Suitable for sizes from small to extra-large.

Bougainvillea buttiana

BOUGAINVILLEA

Tender semi-evergreen climber. Oval leaves, deep-red flower-like bracts.
Position Full sun, warm position. Minimum temperature 7°C (45°F).
Watering Daily throughout summer, sparingly in winter.
Feeding Every two weeks throughout summer.
Repotting Every three to four years in spring. Use free-draining soil mix.
Pruning Trim back straggling shoots continually to create a more compact plant.
Propagation Cuttings.
Styles Suitable for all styles except formal upright, broom and literati, and for medium to extra-large sizes.

Bougainvillea buttiana 'Orange King'

ORANGE KING BOUGAINVILLEA

Form with orange flower-like bracts. Cultivation, propagation, and styles as for *B. buttiana*.

Bougainvillea glabra

BOUGAINVILLEA

Tender semi-evergreen climber. Oval leaves, cerise flower-like bracts.
Position Full sun, warm position. Minimum temperature 7°C (45°F).
Watering Daily throughout summer, sparingly in winter.
Feeding Every two weeks throughout summer.
Repotting Every three to four years in spring. Use free-draining soil mix.
Pruning Trim back straggling shoots continually to create a more compact plant.
Propagation Cuttings.
Styles Suitable for all styles except formal upright, broom and literati, and for medium to extra-large sizes.

Bougainvillea glabra 'Magnifica'

BOUGAINVILLEA

Form with rosy purple bracts. Cultivation, propagation, and styles as for *B. glabra*.

Bougainvillea glabra 'Snow White'

WHITE BOUGAINVILLEA

Form with white bracts. Cultivation, propagation, and styles as for *B. glabra*.

Buxus microphylla

JAPANESE BOX

Compact evergreen shrub with small, oblong dark-green leaves.
Position Full sun or shade. Protect from frost and cold winds.
Watering Daily throughout growing season. Do not allow to dry out in winter.
Feeding Every two weeks throughout the growing season.
Repotting Every second year in spring. Use basic soil mix.
Pruning Trim new growth continually.
Propagation Cuttings, division, layering.
Styles Informal upright, slanting, semicascade, root-over-rock, clasped-to-rock, twin-trunk, clump, group, saikei. All sizes.

Buxus sempervirens

COMMON BOX
Evergreen shrub or small tree. Small dark-green leaves. More generally available than *B. microphylla*, but almost indistinguishable.
⊡ **Position** Full sun or shade. Protect from frost and cold winds.
💧 **Watering** Daily throughout growing season. Do not allow to dry out in winter.
▦ **Feeding** Every two weeks throughout the growing season.
▥ **Repotting** Every second year in spring. Use basic soil mix.
✂ **Pruning** Trim new growth continually.
▨ **Propagation** Cuttings, division, layering.
▣ **Styles** Informal upright, slanting, semicascade, root-over-rock, clasped-to-rock, twin-trunk, clump, group, saikei. All sizes.

Calluna vulgaris

HEATHER
Small, lime-hating evergreen shrub. Fine-textured foliage on woody stems, purple flowers. There are many cultivated forms with different coloured foliage and flowers.
⊡ **Position** Full sun.
💧 **Watering** Daily throughout summer.
▦ **Feeding** None. Feeding inhibits this plant from flowering.
▥ **Repotting** Every three to four years. Use lime-free soil mix.
✂ **Pruning** Scissor clip the foliage to keep growth compact.
▨ **Propagation** Cuttings, layering, seed.
▣ **Styles** Informal upright, slanting, semicascade, literati, clasped-to-rock, twin-trunk, clump, multiple-trunk, saikei. Suitable for extra-small and small sizes only. Also used as an accent plant.

Calluna vulgaris 'County Wicklow'

COUNTY WICKLOW HEATHER
Dwarf compact heather with shell-pink double flowers in summer.
Cultivation as *C. vulgaris*.
▨ **Propagation** Cuttings.
▣ **Styles** As *C. vulgaris*.

Calluna vulgaris 'Foxii Nana'

DWARF HEATHER
Fine, moss-like foliage. Light-purple flowers, which appear only rarely.
Cultivation as *C. vulgaris*.
▨ **Propagation** Cuttings.
▣ **Styles** Clasped-to-rock, saikei.

Camellia japonica

COMMON CAMELLIA
Lime-hating evergreen shrub. Shiny leaves. Pink, red, or white flowers in spring.
⊡ **Position** Partial shade. Protect from frost.
💧 **Watering** Daily throughout growing season with lime-free water. Do not allow soil to dry out in winter.
▦ **Feeding** Every two weeks throughout growing season with ericaceous fertilizer.
▥ **Repotting** Every two to three years in late spring. Use lime-free soil mix.
✂ **Pruning** Trim new growth after flowers fade.
▨ **Propagation** Cuttings, layering, seed.
▣ **Styles** Informal upright, slanting, semicascade, cascade, twin-trunk, clump. Suitable for large and extra-large sizes.

Camellia reticulata

CAMELLIA
Lime-hating evergreen shrub. Large single or double flowers in pink or red.
⊡ **Position** Partial shade. Protect from frost.
💧 **Watering** Daily throughout growing season with lime-free water. Do not allow soil to dry out in winter.
▦ **Feeding** Every two weeks throughout growing season with ericaceous fertilizer.
▥ **Repotting** Annually in late spring. Use lime-free soil mix.
✂ **Pruning** Trim new growth after flowers fade.
▨ **Propagation** Cuttings, layering, seed.
▣ **Styles** Informal upright, slanting, semicascade, cascade, twin-trunk, clump. Suitable for large and extra-large sizes.

Camellia sasanqua

CAMELLIA
Lime-hating evergreen shrub. Small, scented white flowers appear in winter and early spring. The smallest and most compact of the camellias, and therefore often used in bonsai cultivation. It requires more winter protection than than other camellias.
⊡ **Position** Partial shade. Protect from frost and cold winds.
💧 **Watering** Daily throughout growing season with lime-free water. Do not allow soil to dry out in winter.
▦ **Feeding** Every two weeks throughout growing season with ericaceous fertilizer.
▥ **Repotting** Every two to three years in late spring. Use lime-free soil mix.
✂ **Pruning** Trim new growth after flowers fade.
▨ **Propagation** Cuttings, layering, seed.
▣ **Styles** Informal upright, slanting, semicascade, cascade, twin-trunk, clump. Suitable for large and extra-large sizes.

Caragana arborescens

CHINESE PEA TREE
Deciduous shrubby tree. Native to Siberia, so very tough, and tolerant of a wide range of temperatures. Compound leaves, yellow pea-type flowers. (See also page 104.)
⊡ **Position** Full sun in- or outdoors.
💧 **Watering** Daily or every two days throughout the growing season. Keep soil relatively dry in winter.
▦ **Feeding** Every two to three weeks throughout growing season.
▥ **Repotting** Every second year in winter or early spring. Use free-draining soil mix.
✂ **Pruning** Trim new shoots as they develop. Prune hard in winter.
▨ **Propagation** Cuttings, seed.
▣ **Styles** Suitable for all styles except formal upright, and for all sizes.

Caragana chamlagu, see *Caragana sinica*

Caragana sinica (C. chamlagu)

MONGOLIAN REDSHRUB
Semi-evergreen shrub. Glossy, oval, serrated dark-green leaves on spiny branches.
⊡ **Position** Full sun in- or outdoors. Protect from frost and freezing winds.
💧 **Watering** Daily or every two days throughout growing season, relatively dry in winter.
▦ **Feeding** Every two to three weeks throughout growing season.

▥ **Repotting** Every second year in winter or early spring. Use free-draining soil mix.
✂ **Pruning** Trim new shoots as they develop. Prune hard in winter.
▨ **Propagation** Cuttings, seed.
▣ **Styles** Suitable for all styles except formal upright, and for all sizes.

Carmona microphylla (Ehretia buxifolia)

FUKIEN TEA
Tender evergreen shrub. Small, shiny dark-green leaves. White flowers followed by red fruit. (See also page 105.)
⊡ **Position** Full sun, slight shade in summer. Minimum temperature 15°C (60°F).
💧 **Watering** Keep soil moist at all times.
▦ **Feeding** Every two weeks from early spring to early autumn. Every four to six weeks throughout winter.
▥ **Repotting** Every second year in early spring. Use basic soil mix.
✂ **Pruning** Trim new growth continually.
▨ **Propagation** Cuttings, seed.
▣ **Styles** All styles and all sizes.

Carpinus betulus

EUROPEAN HORNBEAM
Deciduous tree. Grooved, oval leaves turn yellow in autumn. Striped, ridged grey bark.
⊡ **Position** Sun or slight shade. Protect from frost to avoid twig die-back.
💧 **Watering** Daily in summer. Keep soil moist at all times.
▦ **Feeding** Weekly for first month after leaves appear, then every two weeks to late summer.
▥ **Repotting** Every second year in early spring until tree is about 10 years old, then as necessary. Use basic soil mix.
✂ **Pruning** Trim new shoots in spring.
▨ **Propagation** Seed, cuttings.
▣ **Styles** All styles except formal upright. Suitable for small to extra-large sizes.

Carpinus japonica

JAPANESE HORNBEAM
Deciduous tree. Prominently grooved leaves, long catkins in spring.
⊡ **Position** Sun or slight shade. Protect from frost to avoid twig die-back.
💧 **Watering** Daily in summer. Keep soil moist at all times.
▦ **Feeding** Weekly for the first month after leaves appear, then every two weeks until late summer.
▥ **Repotting** Every second year in early spring until tree is about 10 years old, then as necessary. Use basic soil mix.
✂ **Pruning** Trim new shoots in spring.
▨ **Propagation** Seed, cuttings.
▣ **Styles** All styles except formal upright. Suitable for small to extra-large sizes.

Carpinus laxiflora

LOOSE-FLOWERED HORNBEAM
Smallish glossy leaves, smooth trunk. Loose clusters of flowers form green fruiting 'keys' in autumn. (See also page 106.)
⊡ **Position** Sun or slight shade. Protect from frost to avoid twig die-back.
💧 **Watering** Daily in summer. Keep soil moist at all times.

◧ **Feeding** Weekly for the first month after leaves appear, then every two weeks until late summer.

◧ **Repotting** Every second year in early spring until tree is about 10 years old, then as necessary. Use basic soil mix.

◨ **Pruning** Trim new shoots in spring.

◧ **Propagation** Seed, cuttings.

◪ **Styles** All styles except formal upright. Suitable for small to extra-large sizes.

Carpinus turczaninowii

KOREAN HORNBEAM

Very small leaves on delicate branching twigs. Foliage turns orange-red in autumn.

◧ **Position** Sun or slight shade. Protect from frost to avoid twig die-back.

◧ **Watering** Daily in summer. Keep soil moist at all times.

◧ **Feeding** Weekly for the first month after leaves appear, then every two weeks until late summer.

◧ **Repotting** Every second year in early spring until tree is about 10 years old, then as necessary. Use basic soil mix.

◨ **Pruning** Trim new shoots in spring.

◧ **Propagation** Seed, cuttings.

◪ **Styles** All styles except formal upright. Suitable for small to extra-large sizes.

Castanea

CHESTNUT

Deciduous tree. Large, toothed leaves, white or red flower spikes in spring.

◧ **Position** Full sun.

◧ **Watering** Daily throughout growing season.

◧ **Feeding** Every two to three weeks throughout growing season.

◧ **Repotting** Every second year in spring. Use basic soil mix.

◨ **Pruning** Trim new growth continually.

◧ **Propagation** Seed.

◪ **Styles** Informal upright, slanting, semicascade, twin-trunk, clump, group. Suitable for large and extra-large sizes.

Cedrus atlantica

ATLAS CEDAR

Evergreen conifer. Needle-like leaves, grey bark, cylindrical cones. (See also page 107.)

◧ **Position** Full sun. Protect from extremes of temperature, especially freezing winds.

◧ **Watering** Daily throughout growing season, less frequently the rest of the year. Allow moisture to be absorbed between waterings.

◧ **Feeding** Every two weeks throughout the growing season.

◧ **Repotting** Every three to five years in spring. Use free-draining soil mix.

◨ **Pruning** Pinch back new shoots in spring and at successive flushes of growth.

◧ **Propagation** Seed, cuttings, grafting.

◪ **Styles** Formal upright, informal upright, twin-trunk, group. Suitable for medium to extra-large sizes.

Cedrus atlantica glauca

BLUE ATLAS CEDAR

Blue-grey foliage, pale-grey bark. Cultivation as *C. atlantica*.

◧ **Propagation** Grafting.

◪ **Styles** As *C. atlantica*.

Cedrus brevifolia

CYPRIAN CEDAR

Slow growing evergreen conifer. Very short, dark-green needles.

◧ **Position** Full sun. Protect from extremes of temperature, especially freezing winds.

◧ **Watering** Daily throughout growing season, less frequently the rest of the year. Allow moisture to be absorbed between waterings.

◧ **Feeding** Every two weeks throughout the growing season.

◧ **Repotting** Every three to five years in spring. Use free-draining soil mix.

◨ **Pruning** Pinch back new shoots in spring and at successive flushes of growth.

◧ **Propagation** Grafting.

◪ **Styles** Formal upright, informal upright, twin-trunk, group. Suitable for extra-small to large sizes.

Cedrus deodara

DEODAR or INDIAN CEDAR

Evergreen conifer. Large needles. Drooping branches and leader.

◧ **Position** Full sun. Protect from extremes of temperature, especially freezing winds.

◧ **Watering** Daily throughout growing season, less frequently the rest of the year. Allow moisture to be absorbed between waterings.

◧ **Feeding** Every two weeks throughout the growing season.

◧ **Repotting** Every three to five years in spring. Use free-draining soil mix.

◨ **Pruning** Pinch back new shoots in spring and at successive flushes of growth.

◧ **Propagation** Seed, cuttings, grafting.

◪ **Styles** Formal upright, informal upright, twin-trunk, group. Suitable for medium to extra-large sizes.

Cedrus libani

CEDAR OF LEBANON

Slow-growing, long-lived evergreen conifer. Dark-green leaves carried on spreading, horizontal branches.

◧ **Position** Full sun. Protect from extremes of temperature, especially freezing winds.

◧ **Watering** Daily throughout growing season, less frequently the rest of the year. Allow moisture to be absorbed between waterings.

◧ **Feeding** Every two weeks throughout the growing season.

◧ **Repotting** Every three to five years in spring. Use free-draining soil mix.

◨ **Pruning** Pinch back new shoots in spring and at successive flushes of growth.

◧ **Propagation** Seed, cuttings, grafting.

◪ **Styles** Formal upright, informal upright, twin-trunk, group. Suitable for medium to extra-large sizes.

Celastrus orbiculatus

ORIENTAL BITTERSWEET

Deciduous climber. Yellow autumn colour, green fruit open to reveal golden lining and brilliant-red seeds. (See also page 108.)

◧ **Position** Full sun. Protect small sizes from frost and freezing winds.

◧ **Watering** Daily throughout growing season. Keep moist at all times.

◧ **Feeding** Twice a month in the growing season.

◧ **Repotting** Annually or every second year in early spring. Use basic soil mix.

◨ **Pruning** Trim new growth after flowering and again in late autumn.

◧ **Propagation** Cuttings, layering, air layering.

◪ **Styles** Informal upright, slanting, semicascade, cascade, root-over-rock, clasped-to-rock, twin-trunk, clump, straight line, sinuous. Small and medium sizes.

Celtis sinensis

CHINESE HACKBERRY

Small deciduous tree. Delicate twig structure. Leaves have a polished appearance. Visually similar to *Zelkova serrata*.

◧ **Position** Full sun.

◧ **Watering** Daily throughout summer. Keep moist at other times.

◧ **Feeding** Weekly for first month after buds open, then every two weeks throughout summer.

◧ **Repotting** Annually in early spring. Use basic soil mix.

◨ **Pruning** Trim new shoots as they grow throughout summer.

◧ **Propagation** Seed, cuttings, layering.

◪ **Styles** Formal upright, informal upright, slanting, semicascade, cascade, broom, root-over-rock, clasped-to-rock, twin-trunk, clump, multiple-trunk, group, saikei. All sizes.

Cercidiphyllum japonicum

KATSURA TREE

Deciduous tree. Small leaves, heart shaped with a rounded point, turn brilliant yellow and pink in autumn. Often confused with *Cercis siliquastrum*.

◧ **Position** Sun or half shade.

◧ **Watering** Daily throughout growing season, sparingly in winter.

◧ **Feeding** Every two weeks throughout summer.

◧ **Repotting** Every two to three years in early spring. Use basic soil mix.

◨ **Pruning** Trim back new growth continually.

◧ **Propagation** Seed, cuttings, layering, air layering.

◪ **Styles** Informal upright, slanting, semicascade, cascade, broom, twin-trunk, clump, multiple-trunk, saikei. Suitable for small to extra-large sizes.

Cercis canadensis

AMERICAN REDBUD

Deciduous tree. Bright-green heart shaped leaves, pale-pink flowers in early summer.

◧ **Position** Full sun.

◧ **Watering** Daily throughout the summer, sparingly in winter.

◧ **Feeding** Every two weeks throughout summer.

◧ **Repotting** Every second year in early spring. Use basic soil mix.

◨ **Pruning** Trim back new growth continually.

◧ **Propagation** Seed, cuttings, layering, air layering.

◪ **Styles** Informal upright, slanting, semicascade, cascade, broom, root-over-rock, twin-trunk, clump, multiple-trunk, group. Suitable for medium and large sizes.

Cercis siliquastrum

JUDAS TREE

Deciduous tree. Small, heart shaped leaves. Rose-lilac flowers carried on bare branches in spring.

⬚ **Position** Full sun.
⬚ **Watering** Daily throughout the summer, sparingly in winter.
⬚ **Feeding** Every two weeks throughout summer.
⬚ **Repotting** Every second year in early spring. Use basic soil mix.
⬚ **Pruning** Trim back new growth continually.
⬚ **Propagation** Seed, cuttings, layering, air layering.
⬚ **Styles** Informal upright, slanting, semicascade, cascade, broom, root-over-rock, twin-trunk, clump, multiple-trunk, group. Suitable for medium and large sizes.

Chaenomeles japonica

MAUL'S FLOWERING QUINCE
Deciduous flowering shrub. Oval leaves, brilliant-red flowers on bare branches in early spring, followed by yellow fruit.
⬚ **Position** Full sun. Protect from frost.
⬚ **Watering** Daily throughout growing season, and mist spray except when in flower or fruit. Sparingly in winter, but keep soil moist at all times.
⬚ **Feeding** Every two weeks from the end of flowering until leaves fall.
⬚ **Repotting** Annually or every second year in mid autumn or early spring. Basic soil mix.
⬚ **Pruning** Trim back in mid autumn, and remove basal shoots.
⬚ **Propagation** Seed, cuttings, division, grafting for named hybrids.
⬚ **Styles** All styles except formal upright and broom. Extra-small to medium sizes.

Chaenomeles japonica 'Chojubai'

DWARF FLOWERING QUINCE
Dwarf form. Red or white flowers at intervals throughout the year. (See also page 109.) Cultivation as *C. japonica*.
⬚ **Propagation** Cuttings, division.
⬚ **Styles** As *C. japonica*.

Chaenomeles sinensis (Pseudocydonia sinensis)

CHINESE QUINCE
Small semi-evergreen tree. Glossy leaves turn gold through to purple in autumn. Small pink flowers in spring, followed by fragrant yellow fruit. Attractive flaky textured bark. (See also page 110.)
⬚ **Position** Full sun. Protect from frost.
⬚ **Watering** Daily during growing season, and give plenty of water when fruit is swelling. Sparingly in winter, but keep moist.
⬚ **Feeding** Every two to three weeks throughout growing season.
⬚ **Repotting** Every second year in autumn. Use basic soil mix.
⬚ **Pruning** Allow new shoots to develop and lengthen, then shorten in summer and wire while they are still flexible.
⬚ **Propagation** Seed, cuttings.
⬚ **Styles** Informal upright, twin-trunk, group. Suitable for medium to large sizes.

Chaenomeles speciosa

FLOWERING QUINCE
Deciduous flowering shrub. Oval leaves, red flowers on bare branches in early spring, yellow fruit. Very similar to *C. japonica*.
⬚ **Position** Full sun. Protect from frost.
⬚ **Watering** Daily throughout growing season,
and mist spray except when in flower or fruit. Keep moist at all times.
⬚ **Feeding** Every two weeks from spring through to autumn.
⬚ **Repotting** Annually or every second year in mid autumn or early spring. Basic soil mix.
⬚ **Pruning** Trim back in mid autumn, and remove basal shoots.
⬚ **Propagation** Grafting, cuttings.
⬚ **Styles** Suitable for all styles except formal upright and broom. Suitable for extra-small to medium sizes.

Chaenomeles speciosa 'Nivalis'

WHITE FLOWERING QUINCE
White flowers in early spring. Unusual, as most other forms have pink or red flowers. Cultivation, propagation, and styles as for *C. speciosa*.

Chaenomeles × superba (japonica × speciosa)

FLOWERING QUINCE HYBRIDS
Small to medium-sized flowering shrubs. Oval leaves. The main variation is in the flowers.
⬚ **Position** Full sun. Protect from frost.
⬚ **Watering** Daily throughout growing season, and mist spray except when in flower or fruit. Sparingly in winter, but keep moist.
⬚ **Feeding** Every two weeks from the end of flowering until leaves fall.
⬚ **Repotting** Annually or every second year in mid autumn or early spring. Basic soil mix.
⬚ **Pruning** Trim back in mid autumn, and remove basal shoots.
⬚ **Propagation** Grafting, cuttings.
⬚ **Styles** Suitable for all styles except formal upright and broom. Suitable for extra-small to medium sizes.

Chaenomeles × superba 'Crimson and Gold'

FLOWERING QUINCE
Dark-red flowers with yellow anthers. Cultivation, propagation, and styles as for *C. × superba*.

Chaenomeles × superba 'Etna'

FLOWERING QUINCE
Vermilion flowers. Cultivation, propagation, and styles as for *C. × superba*.

Chaenomeles × superba 'Incendie'

FLOWERING QUINCE
Semi-double orange-red flowers. Cultivation, propagation, and styles as for *C. × superba*.

Chaenomeles × superba 'Pink Lady'

FLOWERING QUINCE
Rose-pink flowers. Cultivation, propagation, and styles as for *C. × superba*.

Chamaecyparis obtusa

HINOKI CYPRESS
Evergreen conifer. Flat, fan-shaped branches, pea-size cones, and scale-like leaves edged with blue on undersides.
⬚ **Position** Full sun, slight shade in summer. Protect from drying winds.
⬚ **Watering** Daily, and mist spray daily, from late spring to early autumn. Keep soil moist at all times.
⬚ **Feeding** Every two weeks from early spring through to mid autumn.
⬚ **Repotting** Every second year in early to mid spring until tree is about 10 years old, then as necessary. Use basic soil mix.
⬚ **Pruning** Pinch out tops of foliage sprays throughout growing season.
⬚ **Propagation** Cuttings, grafting.
⬚ **Styles** Suitable for all styles except broom, and for all sizes.

Chamaecyparis obtusa 'Nana Gracilis'

DWARF HINOKI CYPRESS
Slow-growing, cone-shaped dwarf form with dark-green foliage. Cultivation as *C. obtusa*.
⬚ **Propagation** Grafting, cuttings.
⬚ **Styles** As *C. obtusa*.

Chamaecyparis obtusa 'Yatsubusa'

DWARF HINOKI CYPRESS
Slow-growing, compact, dwarf form with a naturally cone-shaped habit of growth. (See also page 111.) Cultivation as *C. obtusa*.
⬚ **Propagation** Cuttings.
⬚ **Styles** As *C. obtusa*, especially suitable for extra-small to medium sizes.

Chamaecyparis pisifera

SAWARA CYPRESS
Evergreen conifer. Dark-green, scale-like leaves with white markings, very small cones.
⬚ **Position** Full sun, slight shade in summer. Protect from drying winds.
⬚ **Watering** Daily, and mist spray daily, from late spring to early autumn. Keep soil moist at all times.
⬚ **Feeding** Every two weeks from early spring through to mid autumn.
⬚ **Repotting** Every second year in early to mid spring until tree is about 10 years old, then as necessary. Use basic soil mix.
⬚ **Pruning** Pinch out tops of foliage sprays throughout growing season.
⬚ **Propagation** Cuttings.
⬚ **Styles** Suitable for all styles except broom, and for all sizes.

Chamaecyparis pisifera 'Boulevard'

BOULEVARD CYPRESS or BLUE MOSS CYPRESS
Soft steel-blue foliage, with tinges of purple in winter. Cultivation, propagation, and styles as for *C. pisifera*.

Chamaecyparis pisifera 'Plumosa'

CYPRESS 'PLUMOSA'
Frond-like foliage, bright-green when young. There is also a form of this with golden foliage, *C. p.* 'Plumosa Aurea'. Cultivation as *C. pisifera*.
⬚ **Propagation** Cuttings.
⬚ **Styles** Formal upright, informal upright, slanting, twin-trunk, clump, straight line, sinuous, multiple-trunk, saikei. All sizes.

Cornus kousa

KOUSA DOGWOOD
Deciduous shrub. Numerous white flowers appear in early summer. Foliage turns rich bronze and red in autumn.

⊞ **Position** Full sun, slight shade in summer.
💧 **Watering** Daily throughout summer. Do not allow to dry out.
▣ **Feeding** Every two weeks throughout summer.
▣ **Repotting** Every second year in spring. Use basic soil mix.
✄ **Pruning** Trim new shoots after flowers fade.
✿ **Propagation** Cuttings, layering.
✾ **Styles** Informal upright, slanting, semicascade, cascade, root-over-rock, twin-trunk, group, clump, multiple-trunk. Suitable for medium to extra-large sizes.

Cornus officinalis

JAPANESE CORNELIAN CHERRY

Deciduous shrub or small tree. Clusters of yellow flowers appear on bare wood in early spring and are followed by red fruit. Foliage turns red in autumn.
⊞ **Position** Full sun, partial shade in summer.
💧 **Watering** Daily throughout summer, keep moist in winter.
▣ **Feeding** Every two weeks throughout summer.
▣ **Repotting** Every second year in early spring or early autumn. Use basic soil mix.
✄ **Pruning** Trim new shoots after flowers fade.
✿ **Propagation** Layering, seed.
✾ **Styles** Informal upright, slanting, semicascade, cascade, root-over-rock, twin-trunk, clump, multiple-trunk, straight line, sinuous. Medium to extra-large sizes.

Corylopsis pauciflora

BUTTERCUP WINTER HAZEL

Lime-hating deciduous shrub. Small oval leaves, pink when young. Scented yellow flowers in early spring.
⊞ **Position** Full sun.
💧 **Watering** Daily throughout growing season with lime-free water.
▣ **Feeding** Every two weeks throughout growing season with ericaceous fertilizer.
▣ **Repotting** Every second year in early spring. Use lime-free soil mix.
✄ **Pruning** Trim new shoots after flowers fade.
✿ **Propagation** Cuttings, layering, air layering.
✾ **Styles** Informal upright, slanting, root-over-rock, twin-trunk, clump, straight line, sinuous, multiple-trunk, group. Suitable for medium to extra-large sizes.

Corylopsis spicata

SPIKED WINTER HAZEL

Deciduous shrub. Oval leaves, bright-yellow flowers in spring.
⊞ **Position** Full sun, slight shade in summer.
💧 **Watering** Daily throughout summer.
▣ **Feeding** Every two weeks throughout summer.
▣ **Repotting** Every second year after flowering. Use basic soil mix.
✄ **Pruning** Trim new shoots after flowers fade.
✿ **Propagation** Cuttings, layering, air layering.
✾ **Styles** Informal upright, slanting, semicascade, cascade, root-over-rock, twin-trunk, clump, straight line, sinuous, multiple-trunk, group. Medium to extra-large sizes.

Corylus avellana

HAZEL

Deciduous shrub. Large, coarse leaves make it unattractive as a bonsai in summer. Grown for its effect in winter, when its structure and twigs can be seen. Yellow 'lambs' tails' catkins in late winter, nuts in autumn.
⊞ **Position** Full sun, slight shade in summer.
💧 **Watering** Daily throughout summer. Keep soil moist, particularly when nuts are swelling.
▣ **Feeding** Every two weeks throughout the growing season.
▣ **Repotting** Annually in early spring. Use basic soil mix.
✄ **Pruning** Trim back new shoots continually as they grow.
✿ **Propagation** Seed, cuttings, layering.
✾ **Styles** Suitable for all styles except broom and literati, and for medium to extra-large sizes.

Corylus heterophylla

JAPANESE HAZEL

Deciduous shrub similar to *C. avellana*, but with smaller leaves.
⊞ **Position** Full sun, slight shade in summer.
💧 **Watering** Daily throughout summer. Keep soil moist, particularly when nuts are swelling.
▣ **Feeding** Every two weeks throughout the growing season.
▣ **Repotting** Annually in early spring. Use basic soil mix.
✄ **Pruning** Trim back new shoots continually as they grow.
✿ **Propagation** Seed, cuttings, layering.
✾ **Styles** Suitable for all styles except broom and literati, and for medium to extra-large sizes.

Cotinus coggygria

SMOKE TREE

Deciduous shrub. Smooth, rounded leaves, rich orange-red in autumn. Pale, plume-like flowers in summer give appearance of smoke.
⊞ **Position** Sun or shade.
💧 **Watering** Daily throughout summer.
▣ **Feeding** Every two weeks from spring until flowering, then monthly until late summer.
▣ **Repotting** Every second year in early spring. Use basic soil mix.
✄ **Pruning** Trim new growth throughout the growing season.
✿ **Propagation** Cuttings, seed.
✾ **Styles** Informal upright, slanting, semicascade, cascade, twin-trunk, clump, multiple-trunk. Medium to extra-large sizes.

Cotoneaster adpressus

COTONEASTER

Small, flowering deciduous shrub. Pink flowers in early spring. Small leaves have scarlet autumn colour. Bright-red fruit.
⊞ **Position** Full sun. Protect from frost.
💧 **Watering** Daily throughout growing season. Keep moist at all times.
▣ **Feeding** Every two weeks until flowering, then monthly until late summer.
▣ **Repotting** Annually in early spring until the tree is about 10 years old, then as necessary. Use basic soil mix.
✄ **Pruning** Trim old branches in early spring. and new shoots throughout growing season.
✿ **Propagation** Cuttings, seed.
✾ **Styles** Informal upright, slanting, semicascade, cascade, root-over-rock, clasped-to-rock, twin-trunk, clump. Suitable for extra-small to medium sizes.

Cotoneaster adpressus praecox

COTONEASTER

Small deciduous flowering shrub. More brilliant autumn tints and bolder, brighter fruit than *C. adpressus*.
Cultivation, propagation, and styles as for *C. adpressus*.

Cotoneaster congestus

DWARF COTONEASTER

Tiny evergreen shrub with white flowers and red fruit.
⊞ **Position** Full sun. Protect from frost.
💧 **Watering** Daily throughout growing season. Keep moist at all times.
▣ **Feeding** Every two weeks until flowering, then monthly until late summer.
▣ **Repotting** Annually in early spring until the plant is about 10 years old, then as necessary. Use basic soil mix.
✄ **Pruning** Trim old branches in early spring and new shoots throughout growing season.
✿ **Propagation** Cuttings, seed.
✾ **Styles** Informal upright, slanting, semicascade, cascade, root-over-rock, clasped-to-rock, twin-trunk, clump. Suitable for extra-small to medium sizes.

Cotoneaster conspicuus decorus

COTONEASTER

Evergreen shrub. Small leaves, fragrant white flowers, which open fully like wild roses, red fruit. (See also page 113.)
⊞ **Position** Full sun. Protect from frost.
💧 **Watering** Daily throughout growing season. Keep moist at all times.
▣ **Feeding** Every two weeks until flowering, then monthly until late summer.
▣ **Repotting** Annually in late spring until the plant is about 10 years old, then as necessary. Use basic soil mix.
✄ **Pruning** Trim old branches in early spring and new shoots throughout growing season.
✿ **Propagation** Cuttings, seed.
✾ **Styles** Informal upright, slanting, semicascade, cascade, root-over-rock, clasped-to-rock, twin-trunk, clump. Suitable for extra-small to medium sizes.

Cotoneaster horizontalis

ROCKSPRAY COTONEASTER

Deciduous shrub. Small, round, dark-green leaves turning red in autumn, pink flowers in spring, red fruit. (See also page 112.)
⊞ **Position** Full sun. Protect from frost.
💧 **Watering** Daily throughout growing season. Keep moist at all times.
▣ **Feeding** Every two weeks until flowering, then monthly until late summer.
▣ **Repotting** Annually in early spring until the plant is about 10 years old, then as necessary. Use basic soil mix.
✄ **Pruning** Trim old branches in early spring and new shoots throughout growing season.
✿ **Propagation** Cuttings, seed.
✾ **Styles** Informal upright, slanting, semicascade, cascade, root-over-rock, clasped-to-rock, twin-trunk, clump. Suitable for extra-small to medium sizes.

Cotoneaster horizontalis 'Variegatus'

VARIEGATED ROCKSPRAY

Cream and green markings. Pink and red fruit.

Not so vigorous as *C. horizontalis*.
Cultivation, propagation, and styles as for
C. horizontalis.

Cotoneaster microphyllus

COTONEASTER
Evergreen shrub. Slender, pointed, glossy dark-green leaves. White flowers, red fruit.
Position Full sun. Protect from frost.
Watering Daily throughout growing season. Keep moist at all times.
Feeding Every two weeks until flowering, then monthly until late summer.
Repotting Annually in early spring until the plant is about 10 years old, then as necessary. Use basic soil mix.
Pruning Trim old branches in late spring and new shoots throughout growing season.
Propagation Cuttings, seed.
Styles Informal upright, slanting, semicascade, cascade, root-over-rock, clasped-to-rock, twin-trunk, clump. Suitable for extra-small to medium sizes.

Cotoneaster simmonsii

COTONEASTER
Semi-evergreen shrub. Small, leathery leaves, scarlet in autumn. Pink flowers, red fruit.
Position Full sun. Protect from frost.
Watering Daily throughout growing season. Keep moist at all times.
Feeding Every two weeks until flowering, then monthly until late summer.
Repotting Annually in early spring until the plant is about 10 years old, then as necessary. Use basic soil mix.
Pruning Trim old branches in early spring and new shoots throughout growing season.
Propagation Cuttings, seed.
Styles Informal upright, slanting, semicascade, cascade, root-over-rock, clasped-to-rock, twin-trunk, clump. Suitable for extra-small to medium sizes.

Cotoneaster 'Skogholm'

COTONEASTER
Flowering evergreen dwarf shrub. Large oval coral-red fruit. (See also page 113.)
Position Full sun. Protect from frost.
Watering Daily throughout growing season. Keep moist at all times.
Feeding Every two weeks until flowering, then monthly until late summer.
Repotting Annually in early spring until the plant is about 10 years old, then as necessary. Use basic soil mix.
Pruning Trim old branches in early spring and new shoots throughout growing season.
Propagation Cuttings, seed.
Styles Informal upright, slanting, semicascade, cascade, root-over-rock, clasped-to-rock, twin-trunk, clump. Suitable for extra-small to medium sizes.

Crassula arborescens

JADE TREE
Evergreen succulent. Smooth, rounded leaves, pale-pink flowers. (See also page 114.)
Position Full sun, warm location. Minimum temperature 10°C (50°F).
Watering Moderate. Every three to four weeks in cool conditions.
Feeding Monthly from late spring through to early autumn.

Repotting Every second year in spring. Use free-draining soil mix.
Pruning Pinch back new shoots in spring, prune branches throughout growing season. Remove leaves from trunk.
Propagation Cuttings.
Styles Informal upright, twin-trunk, clump. Suitable for medium and large sizes.

Crassula sarcocaulis

CRASSULA
Dwarf evergreen succulent. Grey-green leaves, beautiful but foul-smelling pink flowers.
Position Full sun. Tolerates cold if dry, otherwise winter protection is essential.
Watering Moderate. Every three to four weeks in cool conditions.
Feeding Monthly from late spring through to early autumn.
Repotting Every second year in spring.
Pruning Pinch back new shoots in spring, prune branches throughout growing season. Remove leaves from trunk.
Propagation Cuttings.
Styles Informal upright, twin-trunk, clump. Suitable for extra-small to medium sizes.

Crataegus cuneata

JAPANESE HAWTHORN
Deciduous tree. Small, lobed leaves, white flowers in spring, large rosehip-type fruit.
Position Full sun. Protect smaller sizes from frost.
Watering Daily throughout growing season in generous amounts. Keep moist at all times. Spray regularly against mildew.
Feeding Twice a month during growing season.
Repotting Annually in early spring or early autumn. Use basic soil mix.
Pruning Pinch out terminal shoots in spring. Prune branches after the flowers fade or after leaf fall.
Propagation Cuttings, seed.
Styles Suitable for all styles except formal upright and broom, and for all sizes.

Crataegus laevigata, see *Crataegus oxyacantha*

Crataegus monogyna

COMMON HAWTHORN
Deciduous tree. Strongly fragrant white flowers. Red fruit (haws) in autumn.
Position Full sun. Protect smaller sizes from frost.
Watering Daily throughout growing season in generous amounts. Keep moist at all times. Spray regularly against mildew.
Feeding Twice a month during growing season.
Repotting Annually in early spring or early autumn. Use basic soil mix.
Pruning Pinch out terminal shoots in spring. Prune branches after the flowers fade or after leaf fall.
Propagation Cuttings, seed.
Styles Suitable for all styles except formal upright and broom, and for all sizes.

Crataegus oxyacantha (C. laevigata)

ENGLISH HAWTHORN
Deciduous tree. White flowers, orange-red fruit in autumn.

Position Full sun. Protect smaller sizes from frost.
Watering Daily throughout growing season in generous amounts. Keep moist at all times. Spray regularly against mildew.
Feeding Twice a month during growing season.
Repotting Annually in early spring or early autumn. Use basic soil mix.
Pruning Pinch out terminal shoots in spring. Prune branches after the flowers fade or after leaf fall.
Propagation Cuttings, seed. Grafting is the usual method for hybrids.
Styles Suitable for all styles except formal upright and broom, and for all sizes.

Crataegus oxyacantha 'Paul's Scarlet'

DOUBLE RED-FLOWERING HAWTHORN
Scarlet double flowers. Rarely fruits. (See also page 115.)
Cultivation as *C. oxyacantha*.
Propagation Grafting.
Styles As *C. oxyacantha*.

Cryptomeria japonica

JAPANESE CEDAR
Evergreen conifer. Red-brown bark, which peels away in strips. Needle-like foliage is a bright blue-green.
Position Full sun, slight shade in summer. Protect from frost and drying winds.
Watering Daily, and mist spray daily, throughout growing season.
Feeding Every two weeks from spring through to late autumn.
Repotting Every second year in mid spring. For older trees, every five years in mid spring. Use basic soil mix.
Pruning Pinch back new shoots throughout growing season.
Propagation Seed, cuttings.
Styles Formal upright, clasped-to-rock, twin-trunk, clump, group. Suitable for medium to extra-large sizes.

Cryptomeria japonica 'Yatsubusa'

DWARF JAPANESE CEDAR
Dwarf form with narrow conical habit and compact foliage. (See also page 116.)
Cultivation as *C. japonica*.
Propagation Cuttings.
Styles Formal upright, clasped-to-rock, twin-trunk, clump, group. Particularly good for rock planting and saikei styles. Suitable for extra-small to medium sizes.

Cycas revoluta

CYCAD
Tender evergreen. Fronded leaves, resembling a palm tree.
Position Full sun. Keep warm in winter.
Watering Twice weekly in summer and very sparingly in winter.
Feeding Once a month throughout the spring and summer.
Repotting Every second year in late spring. Use basic soil mix.
Pruning None required.
Propagation Division.
Styles Clump, multiple-trunk. Suitable for small to large sizes.

Cydonia oblonga

COMMON QUINCE

Deciduous tree. Pink and white single flowers, golden fruit in autumn. Similar to Chinese quince *(Chaenomeles sinensis)*.

Position Full sun.

Watering Daily throughout growing season.

Feeding Every two to three weeks throughout growing season.

Repotting Every second year in spring. Use basic soil mix.

Pruning Allow new shoots to develop and lengthen before shortening and wiring.

Propagation Seed, cuttings, layering, air layering.

Styles Informal upright, slanting, semicascade, cascade, twin-trunk, clump, multiple-trunk, straight line, sinuous, group. Medium to extra-large sizes.

Daphne burkwoodii

DAPHNE

Semi-evergreen shrub. Oval leaves, scented pink flowers in early summer.

Position Full sun.

Watering Daily throughout summer.

Feeding Every two weeks throughout summer.

Repotting Every second year in early spring. Use free-draining soil mix.

Pruning Trim new growth after flowers fade.

Propagation Cuttings, layering.

Styles Informal upright, slanting, semicascade, cascade, twin-trunk, clump, multiple-trunk, saikei. Suitable for small and medium sizes.

Daphne odora

DAPHNE

Evergreen shrub. Fragrant pink flowers in winter and early spring.

Position Full sun.

Watering Daily throughout summer.

Feeding Every two weeks throughout summer.

Repotting Every second year in early spring. Use basic soil mix.

Pruning Trim new growth after flowers fade.

Propagation Cuttings, layering.

Styles Informal upright, slanting, semicascade, cascade, twin-trunk, clump, multiple-trunk, saikei. Suitable for small and medium sizes.

Deutzia gracilis

DEUTZIA

Deciduous shrub. Clusters of pure-white flowers in early summer.

Position Full sun, slight shade in summer. Protect from spring frosts.

Watering Daily throughout growing season.

Feeding Every two weeks during growing season.

Repotting Annually in early spring. Use basic soil mix.

Pruning Cut back hard after flowering. Shorten resultant new shoots.

Propagation Cuttings, layering.

Styles Informal upright, slanting, semicascade, cascade, twin-trunk, clump, multiple-trunk. Medium and large sizes.

Deutzia scabra

DEUTZIA

Deciduous shrub. Several cultivars exist. Flowers can be single or double, in shades of white and pink.

Position Full sun, slight shade in summer. Protect from spring frosts.

Watering Daily throughout growing season.

Feeding Every two weeks during growing season.

Repotting Annually in early spring. Use basic soil mix.

Pruning Cut back hard after flowering. Shorten resultant new shoots.

Propagation Cuttings, layering.

Styles Informal upright, slanting, semicascade, cascade, twin-trunk, clump, multiple-trunk. Medium and large sizes.

Deutzia scabra 'Azaleiflora'

DEUTZIA

Small white flowers with reflexed petals. Cultivation, propagation, and styles as for *D. scabra*.

Deutzia scabra 'Nikko'

DEUTZIA

Very dwarf form with white flowers. Cultivation, propagation, and styles as for *D. scabra*.

Deutzia scabra 'Plena'

DEUTZIA

Pink-flushed double flowers. Cultivation, propagation, and styles as for *D. scabra*.

Diospyros kaki

CHINESE PERSIMMON

Deciduous tree. Purple and orange autumn colour, orange tomato-like edible fruit.

Position Full sun.

Watering Daily throughout growing season.

Feeding Every two weeks during growing season.

Repotting Annually in early spring. Use basic soil mix.

Pruning Trim new growth throughout summer.

Propagation Grafting, layering, air layering.

Styles Informal upright, slanting, semicascade, cascade, literati, twin-trunk, clump, straight line, sinuous, group. Suitable for medium to extra-large sizes.

Ehretia buxifolia, see *Carmona microphylla*

Eleagnus multiflora

ELEAGNUS

Deciduous shrub. Green leaves with silvery undersides. Small, scented cream flowers in spring, and oblong, blood-red fruit in midsummer. (See also page 118.)

Position Sun or shade. Protect from frost.

Watering Daily throughout growing season. Sparingly in winter, but keep the soil moist at all times.

Feeding Every two weeks throughout summer.

Repotting Every second year in early spring. Use basic soil mix.

Pruning Trim new shoots as they develop.

Propagation Cuttings.

Styles Informal upright, slanting, semicascade, cascade. Small to large sizes.

Eleagnus pungens

THORNY ELEAGNUS

Evergreen shrub. Shiny leaves with brown speckles on white undersides, scented cream flowers in autumn.

Position Sun or shade. Protect from frost.

Watering Daily throughout growing season. Sparingly in winter, but keep soil moist at all times.

Feeding Every two weeks throughout summer.

Repotting Every second year in early spring. Use basic soil mix.

Pruning Trim new shoots as they develop.

Propagation Cuttings.

Styles Informal upright, slanting, semicascade, cascade. Small to large sizes.

Enkianthus campanulatus

ENKIANTHUS

Lime-hating deciduous shrub. Smallish dark-green leaves turn brilliant yellow, orange-red, and purple in autumn. Creamy white bell-like flowers in spring.

Position Full sun, slight shade in summer.

Watering Daily throughout growing season.

Feeding Every two weeks throughout summer with ericaceous fertilizer.

Repotting Annually in early spring. Use lime-free soil mix.

Pruning Trim back new shoots to shape.

Propagation Cuttings, layering.

Styles Informal upright, slanting, semicascade, root-over-rock, twin-trunk, clump, multiple-trunk, group. Small to large sizes.

Enkianthus cernuus rubens

RED ENKIANTHUS

Lime-hating deciduous shrub. Red flowers in late spring, excellent autumn colour.

Position Full sun, slight shade in summer.

Watering Daily throughout growing season.

Feeding Every two weeks throughout summer with ericaceous fertilizer.

Repotting Annually in early spring. Use lime-free soil mix.

Pruning Trim back new shoots to shape.

Propagation Cuttings, layering.

Styles Informal upright, slanting, semicascade, root-over-rock, twin-trunk, clump, multiple-trunk, group. Small to large sizes.

Enkianthus perulatus

WHITE ENKIANTHUS

Lime-hating deciduous shrub. A compact form more suitable than others for the smaller sizes. White flowers appear with the leaves.

Position Full sun, slight shade in summer.

Watering Daily throughout growing season.

Feeding Every two weeks throughout summer with ericaceous fertilizer.

Repotting Annually in early spring. Use lime-free soil mix.

Pruning Trim back new shoots to shape.

Propagation Cuttings, layering.

Styles Informal upright, slanting, semicascade, root-over-rock, twin-trunk, clump, multiple-trunk, group. Small to large sizes.

Escallonia 'Apple blossom'

ESCALLONIA

Evergreen flowering shrub. Small, glossy leaves, pink and white apple-blossom type flowers in

late summer. Many cultivars and hybrids exist, with flowers in white, pink, or red.
☼ Position Full sun. Protect from frost and freezing winds.
◲ Watering Daily throughout summer. Keep moist in winter.
▤ Feeding Every two weeks in growing season.
▥ Repotting Every second year in early spring. Use basic soil mix.
☑ Pruning Prune back hard after flowering, then trim new shoots as they grow.
▣ Propagation Cuttings, layering.
▤ Styles Informal upright, slanting, semi-cascade, cascade, twin-trunk, clump, multiple-trunk. Suitable for all sizes.

Euonymus alatus
WINGED SPINDLE
Deciduous shrub. Fascinating purple-pink autumn colour, ridged corky 'winged' bark. (See also page 119.)
☼ Position Full light with some sun. Protect smaller sizes from frost.
◲ Watering Daily throughout summer. Keep soil moist at all times. Mist spray throughout the growing season.
▤ Feeding Every two weeks from late spring through to late summer.
▥ Repotting Annually in early spring until the tree is about 10 years old, then as necessary. Use basic soil mix.
☑ Pruning Trim new growth in spring and again two or three times during growing season.
▣ Propagation Cuttings, layering, air layering.
▤ Styles Suitable for all styles except broom, and for all sizes.

Euonymus europeaus
EUROPEAN SPINDLE
Deciduous tree. Scarlet seed capsules.
☼ Position Full light with some sun. Protect smaller sizes from frost.
◲ Watering Daily throughout summer. Keep soil moist at all times. Mist spray throughout the growing season.
▤ Feeding Every two weeks from late spring through to late summer.
▥ Repotting Annually in early spring until the tree is about 10 years old, then as necessary. Use basic soil mix.
☑ Pruning Trim new growth in spring and again two or three times during growing season.
▣ Propagation Seed, cuttings, layering, air layering.
▤ Styles Suitable for all styles except broom, and for all sizes.

Euonymus sieboldianus
JAPANESE SPINDLE
Deciduous tree. Pale-green flowers, pinkish white fruit, red seeds.
☼ Position Full light with some sun. Protect smaller sizes from frost.
◲ Watering Daily throughout summer. Keep soil moist at all times. Mist spray throughout the growing season.
▤ Feeding Every two weeks from late spring through to late summer.
▥ Repotting Annually in early spring until the tree is about 10 years old, then as necessary. Use basic soil mix.
☑ Pruning Trim new growth in spring and again two or three times during growing season.

▣ Propagation Seed, cuttings, layering, air layering.
▤ Styles Suitable for all styles except broom, and for all sizes.

Fagus crenata
JAPANESE WHITE BEECH
Deciduous tree. Foliage turns bronze in autumn. Pale-grey bark. (See also page 120.)
☼ Position Full sun, partial shade in summer. Protect young foliage from wind.
◲ Watering Daily throughout the growing season. Sparingly in winter, but keep soil moist at all times.
▤ Feeding Every two weeks from one month after leaves appear until late summer.
▥ Repotting Every second year in spring until the tree is about 10 years old, then as necessary. Use basic soil mix.
☑ Pruning Pinch back growing tips in spring.
▣ Propagation Seed.
▤ Styles Formal upright, informal upright, slanting, twin-trunk, clump, group. Suitable for sizes from medium up to extra-large.

Fagus japonica
JAPANESE BLACK BEECH
Small deciduous tree. Leaves are oval and bright-green.
☼ Position Full sun, partial shade in summer. Protect young foliage from wind.
◲ Watering Daily throughout the growing season. Sparingly in winter, but keep soil moist at all times.
▤ Feeding Every two weeks from one month after leaves appear until late summer.
▥ Repotting Every second year in spring until the tree is about 10 years old, then as necessary. Use basic soil mix.
☑ Pruning Pinch back growing tips in spring.
▣ Propagation Seed.
▤ Styles Formal upright, informal upright, slanting, twin-trunk, clump, group. Suitable for sizes from medium up to extra-large.

Fagus sylvatica
EUROPEAN BEECH
Large deciduous tree with vivid green leaves and long-lasting bronze autumn colour. Smooth grey bark. (See also page 121.)
☼ Position Full sun, partial shade in summer. Protect young foliage from wind.
◲ Watering Daily throughout the growing season. Sparingly in winter, but keep soil moist at all times.
▤ Feeding Every two weeks from one month after leaves appear until late summer.
▥ Repotting Every second year in spring until the tree is about 10 years old, then as necessary. Use basic soil mix.
☑ Pruning Pinch back growing tips in spring.
▣ Propagation Seed.
▤ Styles Formal upright, informal upright, slanting, twin-trunk, clump, group. Suitable for sizes from medium up to extra-large.

Fagus sylvatica heterophylla
FERN-LEAVED BEECH
Form with deeply cut and lobed leaves. Cultivation as *F. sylvatica*.
▣ Propagation Cuttings, grafting.
▤ Styles As *F. sylvatica*.

Fagus sylvatica 'Riversii'
PURPLE BEECH
Form with dark purple-black leaves. Cultivation as *F. sylvatica*.
▣ Propagation Cuttings, grafting.
▤ Styles As *F. sylvatica*.

Fagus sylvatica 'Rohanii'
PURPLE FERN-LEAVED BEECH
Graceful form with deeply cut purple leaves. Cultivation as *F. sylvatica*.
▣ Propagation Cuttings, grafting.
▤ Styles As *F. sylvatica*.

Ficus benjamina
WEEPING FIG
Tender evergreen. Grown as a houseplant in temperate climates. Pointed, oval leaves on weeping stems. Variegated forms available.
☼ Position Tolerates low light levels. Protect from frost and draughts. Minimum temperature 15°C (60°F).
◲ Watering Generously throughout summer. Keep moist at all other times. Mist-spray to maintain humidity.
▤ Feeding Every two weeks throughout the growing season.
▥ Repotting Every second year in spring. Use basic soil mix.
☑ Pruning Trim new shoots throughout growing season. Cuts exude white milky sap (latex), so seal large cuts.
▣ Propagation Cuttings, air layering.
▤ Styles Suitable for all styles except literati, and for medium and large sizes.

Ficus macrophylla
AUSTRALIAN BANYAN or MORETON BAY FIG
Tender evergreen tree. Buttressed trunk when mature. Glossy, leathery dark-green leaves.
☼ Position Tolerates low light levels. Protect from frost and draughts. Minimum temperature 15°C (60°F).
◲ Watering Generously throughout summer. Keep moist at all other times. Mist-spray to maintain humidity.
▤ Feeding Every two weeks throughout the growing season.
▥ Repotting Every second year in spring. Use basic soil mix.
☑ Pruning Trim new shoots throughout growing season. Cuts exude white milky sap (latex), so seal large cuts.
▣ Propagation Cuttings, air layering.
▤ Styles Suitable for all styles except literati, and for medium and large sizes.

Ficus platypoda
AUSTRALIAN FIG
Tender evergreen tree. Smooth elliptic leaves, small orange-red flowers. In nature often has more than one trunk.
☼ Position Tolerates low light levels. Protect from frost and draughts. Minimum temperature 15°C (60°F).
◲ Watering Generously throughout summer. Keep moist at all other times. Mist-spray to maintain humidity.
▤ Feeding Every two weeks throughout the growing season.
▥ Repotting Every second year in spring. Use basic soil mix.

Pruning Trim new shoots throughout growing season. Cuts exude white milky sap (latex), so seal large cuts.

Propagation Cuttings, air layering.

Styles Suitable for all styles except literati, and for medium and large sizes.

Ficus pumila

CREEPING FIG

Tender evergreen climbing shrub. Oval to heart shaped leaves, small on younger plants.

Position Tolerates low light levels. Protect from frost and draughts. Minimum temperature 15°C (60°F).

Watering Generously throughout summer. Keep moist at all other times. Mist-spray to maintain humidity.

Feeding Every two weeks throughout the growing season.

Repotting Every second year in spring. Use basic soil mix.

Pruning Trim new shoots throughout growing season. Cuts exude white milky sap (latex), so seal large cuts.

Propagation Cuttings, air layering.

Styles Suitable for all styles except literati, and for medium and large sizes.

Ficus retusa

BANYAN FIG

Tender evergreen tree. A banyan type with striking aerial roots, making it a particularly suitable form for clasped-to-rock style. Leaves are small, glossy, and leathery in texture. (See also page 122.)

Position Tolerates low light levels. Protect from frost and draughts. Minimum temperature 15°C (60°F).

Watering Generously throughout summer. Keep moist at all other times. Mist-spray to maintain humidity.

Feeding Every two weeks throughout the growing season.

Repotting Every second year in spring. Use basic soil mix.

Pruning Trim new shoots throughout growing season. Cuts exude white milky sap (latex), so seal large cuts.

Propagation Cuttings, air layering.

Styles Suitable for all styles except literati, and for medium and large sizes.

Ficus rubiginosa

PORT JACKSON FIG or RUSTY-LEAVED FIG

Tender evergreen tree. Undersides of glossy dark-green oval leaves are usually covered with rust-coloured down.

Position Tolerates low light levels. Protect from frost and draughts. Minimum temperature 15°C (60°F).

Watering Generously throughout summer. Keep moist at all other times. Mist-spray to maintain humidity.

Feeding Every two weeks throughout the growing season.

Repotting Every second year in spring. Use basic soil mix.

Pruning Trim new shoots throughout growing season. Cuts exude white milky sap (latex), so seal large cuts.

Propagation Cuttings, air layering.

Styles Suitable for all styles except literati, and for medium and large sizes.

Forsythia intermedia

FORSYTHIA

Deciduous flowering shrub. Coarse growing (except some dwarf forms), so grown primarily for the bright golden-yellow bell shaped flowers in early spring.

Position Full sun.

Watering Daily throughout growing season, sparingly in winter.

Feeding Every two weeks during growing season.

Repotting Every second year in autumn or late winter. Use basic soil mix.

Pruning Prune branches back hard after flowering. Trim shoots to shape.

Propagation Cuttings.

Styles Informal upright, slanting, semi-cascade, cascade, twin-trunk, clump, multiple-trunk. Suitable for all sizes.

Forsythia intermedia 'Minigold'

DWARF FORSYTHIA

Compact dwarf form of *F. intermedia*. Cultivation, propagation, and styles as for *F. intermedia*.

Forsythia ovata 'Tetragold'

DWARF FORSYTHIA

Deciduous flowering dwarf shrub. Golden-yellow flowers, which appear earlier than on other forsythias.

Position Full sun.

Watering Daily throughout growing season, sparingly in winter.

Feeding Every two weeks during growing season.

Repotting Every second year in autumn or late winter. Use basic soil mix.

Pruning Prune branches back hard after flowering. Trim shoots to shape.

Propagation Cuttings.

Styles Informal upright, slanting, semi-cascade, cascade, twin-trunk, clump, multiple-trunk. Suitable for all sizes.

Fortunella hindsii

DWARF ORANGE

Tender evergreen shrub. Glossy oval leaves, small, fragrant white flowers, followed by fruit resembling miniature oranges.

Position Full sun. Warm location, minimum temperature 4°C (40°F).

Watering Daily throughout the summer, weekly in winter.

Feeding Every two weeks throughout summer.

Repotting Every two to three years in spring. Use basic soil mix.

Pruning Trim back new shoots as they grow.

Propagation Seed, cuttings, grafting.

Styles Suitable for all styles except broom and literati, and for extra-small to large sizes.

Fraxinus excelsior

COMMON or EUROPEAN ASH

Deciduous tree. Very hardy. Coarse structure with large compound leaves. White flowers in May, good autumn tints.

Position Full sun.

Watering Daily throughout summer, sparingly in winter.

Feeding Every two weeks throughout summer.

Repotting Every second year in spring. Use basic soil mix.

Pruning Trim shoots back hard continually to keep shape compact.

Propagation Seed, layering, air layering.

Styles Informal upright, slanting, twin-trunk, clump, multiple-trunk. Suitable for large and extra-large sizes.

Fuchsia × *bacillaris (microphylla* × *thymifolia)*

FUCHSIA

Deciduous shrub. Smallish, leathery, ovate leaves. Flowers open bright crimson-red, and darken as they age. The outer petals tend to be reflexed. Not as free-flowering as others.

Position Full sun. Warm location, minimum temperature 7°C (45°F).

Watering Daily throughout growing season. Allow soil to dry out between waterings in winter, but mist spray to keep up humidity.

Feeding Every two weeks throughout the growing season.

Repotting Annually in early spring. Use basic soil mix.

Pruning Pinch back new shoots throughout the growing season.

Propagation Cuttings.

Styles Informal upright, slanting, semicascade, cascade, root-over-rock. Suitable for extra-small to medium sizes.

Fuchsia 'Lady Thumb'

LADY THUMB FUCHSIA

Free-flowering deciduous dwarf form with white and pink flowers.

Position Full sun. Warm location, minimum temperature 7°C (45°F).

Watering Daily throughout growing season. Allow soil to dry out between waterings in winter, but mist spray to keep up humidity.

Feeding Every two weeks throughout the growing season.

Repotting Annually in early spring. Use basic soil mix.

Pruning Pinch back new shoots throughout the growing season.

Propagation Cuttings.

Styles Informal upright, slanting, semicascade, cascade, root-over-rock. Suitable for extra-small to medium sizes.

Fuchsia microphylla

FUCHSIA

Deciduous dwarf form of shrub. Dark-green leaves, small, pendulous red flowers. (See also page 123.)

Position Full sun. Warm location, minimum temperature 7°C (45°F).

Watering Daily throughout growing season. Allow soil to dry out between waterings in winter, but mist spray to keep up humidity.

Feeding Every two weeks throughout the growing season.

Repotting Annually in early spring. Use basic soil mix.

Pruning Pinch back new shoots throughout the growing season.

Propagation Cuttings.

Styles Informal upright, slanting, semicascade, cascade, root-over-rock. Suitable for extra-small to medium sizes.

Fuchsia pumila

DWARF FUCHSIA

Free-flowering deciduous dwarf fuchsia, dark-purple and dark-red flowers.

⚙ **Position** Full sun. Warm location, minimum temperature 7°C (45°F).

💧 **Watering** Daily throughout growing season. Allow the soil to dry out between waterings in the winter months, but mist spray regularly to keep up humidity.

▪ **Feeding** Every two weeks throughout the growing season.

▩ **Repotting** Annually in early spring. Use basic soil mix.

✂ **Pruning** Pinch back new shoots throughout the growing season.

🗲 **Propagation** Cuttings.

🗾 **Styles** Informal upright, slanting, semicascade, cascade, root-over-rock. Suitable for extra-small to medium sizes.

Fuchsia 'Tom Thumb'

TOM THUMB FUCHSIA

Deciduous free-flowering dwarf form. Scarlet and violet flowers.

⚙ **Position** Full sun. Warm location, minimum temperature 7°C (45°F).

💧 **Watering** Daily throughout growing season. Allow soil to dry out between waterings in winter, but mist spray to keep up humidity.

▪ **Feeding** Every two weeks throughout the growing season.

▩ **Repotting** Annually in early spring. Use basic soil mix.

✂ **Pruning** Pinch back new shoots throughout the growing season.

🗲 **Propagation** Cuttings.

🗾 **Styles** Informal upright, slanting, semicascade, cascade, root-over-rock. Suitable for extra-small to medium sizes.

Gardenia jasminoides radicans

GARDENIA

Lime-hating tender evergreen shrub. Shiny dark-green leaves, scented white flowers.

⚙ **Position** Avoid full sun, but give maximum light, with slight shade in summer. Minimum temperature 13°C (55°F).

💧 **Watering** Daily throughout summer, more sparingly in winter, with lime free water.

▪ **Feeding** Every two weeks throughout summer, monthly for the rest of the year, with ericaceous feed.

▩ **Repotting** Every second year in late spring. Use lime-free soil mix.

✂ **Pruning** Trim new growth after flowering and again as required to maintain shape.

🗲 **Propagation** Cuttings, layering, air layering.

🗾 **Styles** Informal upright, slanting, semicascade, cascade, root-over-rock, twin-trunk, clump, multiple-trunk. All sizes.

Gingko biloba

MAIDENHAIR TREE

Deciduous broad-leaved conifer. Gold autumn colour, yellowish fruit. (See also page 124.)

⚙ **Position** Full sun, slight shade for very young specimens. Protect from frost, particularly the roots.

💧 **Watering** Daily throughout growing season. Keep relatively dry in winter.

▪ **Feeding** Twice a month from spring to the middle of summer.

▩ **Repotting** Annually in early spring until the tree is about 10 years old, then every second year. Every three years for aged specimens. Use basic soil mix.

✂ **Pruning** Trim shoots in spring and autumn.

🗲 **Propagation** Seed, air layering, cuttings.

🗾 **Styles** Informal upright, clump. Suitable for medium to extra-large sizes.

Gleditsia triacanthos

HONEYLOCUST

Deciduous tree. Frond-like leaves turn pale yellow in autumn. Three-pointed thorns, long brown seed pods. (See also page 125.)

⚙ **Position** Full sun. Protect from frost to avoid twig die-back.

💧 **Watering** Daily throughout growing season, sparingly in winter.

▪ **Feeding** Every two weeks throughout the growing season.

▩ **Repotting** Every second year in spring. Use basic soil mix.

✂ **Pruning** Trim new shoots as they grow. Prune or remove branches in winter.

🗲 **Propagation** Seed, cuttings.

🗾 **Styles** Informal upright, slanting, semicascade, cascade, twin-trunk. Suitable for small to medium sizes.

Hamamelis japonica

JAPANESE WITCH HAZEL

Deciduous shrub grown for winter effect. Small yellow flowers from midwinter to early spring, good orange colour in autumn.

⚙ **Position** Full sun.

💧 **Watering** Daily throughout summer.

▪ **Feeding** Every two weeks throughout summer.

▩ **Repotting** Every second year, either in late autumn or in early spring after flowering. Use basic soil mix.

✂ **Pruning** Trim new growth to shape throughout the summer.

🗲 **Propagation** Cuttings, layering, air layering, grafting.

🗾 **Styles** Informal upright, slanting, semicascade, cascade, root-over-rock, twin-trunk, clump, multiple-trunk, group. Suitable for medium to extra-large sizes.

Hamamelis mollis

CHINESE WITCH HAZEL

Deciduous shrub similar to *H. japonica*, with earlier, larger, and more fragrant flowers.

⚙ **Position** Full sun.

💧 **Watering** Daily throughout summer.

▪ **Feeding** Every two weeks throughout summer.

▩ **Repotting** Every second year in late autumn, or in early spring after flowering. Use basic soil mix.

✂ **Pruning** Trim new growth to shape throughout the summer.

🗲 **Propagation** Cuttings, layering, air layering, grafting.

🗾 **Styles** Informal upright, slanting, semicascade, cascade, root-over-rock, twin-trunk, clump, multiple-trunk, group. Suitable for medium to extra-large sizes.

Hedera helix

COMMON IVY

Evergreen climber. Glossy dark-green leaves with three to five lobes. Yellowish flowers, berry-like black fruit.

⚙ **Position** Partial shade.

💧 **Watering** Daily throughout growing season.

▪ **Feeding** Every two weeks throughout the growing season.

▩ **Repotting** Every second year in spring or early autumn. Use basic soil mix.

✂ **Pruning** Shoots must be trimmed back hard to form a trunk.

🗲 **Propagation** Cuttings, layering, air layering.

🗾 **Styles** Informal upright, slanting, semicascade, cascade, root-over-rock, twin-trunk, clump. Suitable for all sizes.

Ilex crenata

JAPANESE EVERGREEN HOLLY

Slow-growing evergreen. Small, smooth leaves, insignificant white flowers. Black fruit on female plants in autumn.

⚙ **Position** Sun or shade. Protect from frost and freezing winds.

💧 **Watering** Daily throughout summer, less frequently in winter. Mist spray daily throughout summer unless in full sun.

▪ **Feeding** Every two weeks throughout the growing season.

▩ **Repotting** Every second year in spring. Use basic soil mix.

✂ **Pruning** Constant clipping when young. Trim new shoots as required to maintain shape.

🗲 **Propagation** Cuttings.

🗾 **Styles** Suitable for all styles except broom, and for extra-small to large sizes.

Ilex crenata 'Convexa'

JAPANESE EVERGREEN HOLLY

More compact form, with glossy convex leaves. (See also page 126.)
Cultivation, propagation, and styles as for *I. crenata*.

Ilex crenata 'Stokes'

JAPANESE EVERGREEN HOLLY

Dwarf form with tiny leaves.
Cultivation, propagation, and styles as for *I. crenata*.

Ilex serrata (I. sieboldii)

JAPANESE DECIDUOUS HOLLY

Deciduous tree. Thin, serrated leaves, with a variety of autumn colour from yellow through to purple. Female plants bear red fruit if they are grown near male plants for pollination. (See also page 127.)

⚙ **Position** Sun or shade. Protect from frost.

💧 **Watering** Daily throughout summer. Keep the soil moist at all times to prevent the fruit from dropping.

▪ **Feeding** Every two weeks throughout the growing season.

▩ **Repotting** Annually in early spring until the tree is about 10 years old, then every second year. Use basic soil mix.

✂ **Pruning** Remove all unwanted shoots, and trim others, throughout summer.

🗲 **Propagation** Seed, cuttings, air layering.

🗾 **Styles** All styles and all sizes.

Ilex serrata 'Leucocarpa'

WHITE-BERRIED JAPANESE DECIDUOUS HOLLY

White-fruited form.

Cultivation, propagation, and styles as for
I. serrata.

Ilex serrata 'Subtilis' ('Koshobai')

DWARF JAPANESE DECIDUOUS HOLLY
Miniature form. Unusually small leaves and
fruit. Hermaphrodite, so forms fruit freely, and
acts as a pollinator for female trees of the main
species.
Cultivation, propagation, and styles as for
I. serrata. Suitable for extra-small and small
sizes only.

Ilex sieboldii, see *Ilex serrata.*

Jacaranda mimosifolia, see *Jacaranda ovalifolia*

Jacaranda ovalifolia (J. mimosifolia)

JACARANDA
Tender, lime-hating deciduous tree. Fern-like
leaves, violet flowers in spring.
Position Maximum light, but protect from
direct sunlight. Warm location, minimum
temperature 16°C (60°F).
Watering Daily with lime-free water.
Feeding Every two weeks in summer with
ericaceous fertilizer.
Repotting Every second year in spring. Use
lime-free soil mix.
Pruning Pinch soft terminal shoots to shape.
Propagation Seed.
Styles Informal upright, slanting, semi-
cascade, twin-trunk, clump, multiple-trunk,
saikei. Suitable for small to large sizes.

Jasminum nudiflorum

WINTER JASMINE
Deciduous shrub. Narrow dark-green leaves.
Star-like yellow flowers on bare branches in
winter.(See also page 128.)
Position Full sun, slight shade in summer.
Protect from severe frost.
Watering Daily throughout summer. Keep
moist at all times.
Feeding Two or three times a month from end
of flowering to late summer.
Repotting Annually, preferably in autumn.
Use basic soil mix.
Pruning Trim new shoots in late spring, and
again in autumn. Flowers appear on the previous
year's wood.
Propagation Cuttings, air layering.
Styles Informal upright, slanting,
semicascade, root-over-rock, clasped-to-rock,
twin-trunk, clump. Suitable for extra-small to
medium sizes.

Jasminum officinale

COMMON WHITE JASMINE
Evergreen shrub. Pinnate leaves, scented white
flowers in summer.
Position Full sun. Protect from frost.
Watering Daily throughout growing season.
Feeding Every two weeks throughout the
growing season.
Repotting Every second year in late spring.
Use basic soil mix.
Pruning Trim shoots after flowers fade, and
new shoots in late spring or early autumn.
Propagation Cuttings, air layering.
Styles Informal upright, slanting,
semicascade, root-over-rock, twin-trunk, clump.
Suitable for all sizes.

Juniperus communis

COMMON JUNIPER
Evergreen conifer. Needle-like foliage, with pale
undersides, banded with white on top. Black
fruit. Many cultivars.
Position Full sun, slight shade in summer.
Protect from hard frost.
Watering Daily throughout growing season,
and mist spray in summer.
Feeding Every two weeks from start of
growing season until mid autumn.
Repotting Every second year, preferably in
early spring, until the tree is about 10 years old,
then up to every five years as necessary. Use free-
draining soil mix.
Pruning Pinch back tips of new shoots
throughout growing season.
Propagation Seed, cuttings.
Styles Suitable for all styles except broom,
and for all sizes.

Juniperus × media 'Blaauw'

CHINESE JUNIPER
Evergreen shrub conifer. Grey-blue scale-like
foliage, shaggy bark. (See also page 129.)
Position Full light, slight shade in summer.
Protect from hard frost.
Watering Daily throughout summer, and mist
spray. Keep moist in winter.
Feeding Every two weeks from start of
growing season until mid autumn.
Repotting Every second year, preferably in
early spring, until the tree is about 10 years old,
then up to every five years as necessary. Use free-
draining soil mix.
Pruning Pinch back tips of new shoots
throughout growing season.
Propagation Cuttings.
Styles Suitable for all styles except broom,
and for all sizes.

Juniperus procumbens

CREEPING JUNIPER
Dwarf prostrate evergreen conifer. Tightly
packed needle-like foliage.
Position Full light, slight shade in summer.
Protect from hard frost.
Watering Daily throughout summer, and mist
spray. Keep moist in winter.
Feeding Every two weeks from start of
growing season until mid autumn.
Repotting Every second year, preferably in
early spring, until the tree is about 10 years old,
then up to every five years as necessary. Use free-
draining soil mix.
Pruning Pinch back tips of new shoots
throughout growing season.
Propagation Cuttings.
Styles Suitable for all styles except broom,
and for all sizes.

Juniperus rigida

NEEDLE JUNIPER
Evergreen conifer. Needle-like foliage, green
fruit ripen to purplish-black over two years. (See
also page 130.)
Position: Full sun. Protect from frost.
Watering Daily, and mist spray, throughout
summer. Sparingly in winter, but keep moist.
Feeding Every two weeks from beginning of
spring to early autumn.
Repotting Every second year, preferably in
early to mid spring, until the tree is 10 years old,

then up to every five years as necessary. Use
basic soil mix.
Pruning Pinch out the tops of new growth
throughout growing season. Prune to allow light
in to lower and inner branches.
Propagation Seed, cuttings.
Styles Suitable for all styles except broom,
and for all sizes.

Juniperus sabina

SAVIN JUNIPER
Evergreen. Variable habit. Grey-green,
predominantly scale-like foliage.
Position Full sun, slight shade in summer.
Protect from hard frost.
Watering Daily throughout growing season,
and mist spray in summer.
Feeding Every two weeks from start of
growing season until mid autumn.
Repotting Every second year, preferably in
early spring, until the tree is about 10 years old,
then up to every five years as necessary. Use free-
draining soil mix.
Pruning Pinch back tips of new shoots
throughout growing season.
Propagation Cuttings.
Styles Suitable for all styles except broom,
and for all sizes.

Juniperus sargentii

CHINESE or SARGENT'S JUNIPER
Evergreen conifer. Grey-green needle-like
juvenile foliage, smooth scales when mature.
Blue-black fruit. (See also page 131.)
Position Full sun, slight shade in summer.
Protect from hard frost.
Watering Daily throughout the growing
season, and mist spray in summer. Keep moist in
the winter months.
Feeding Every two weeks from start of
growing season until mid autumn.
Repotting Every second year, preferably in
early spring, until the tree is about 10 years old,
then up to every five years as necessary. Use free-
draining soil mix.
Pruning Pinch back tips of new shoots
throughout growing season.
Propagation Cuttings.
Styles Suitable for all styles except broom,
and for all sizes.

Juniperus squamata 'Meyeri'

BLUE JUNIPER
Evergreen conifer. Greyish blue needles with a
fine 'bloom'. Rough shaggy bark.
Position Full sun, slight shade in summer.
Protect from hard frost.
Watering Daily throughout the growing
season, and mist spray throughout summer.
Feeding Every two weeks from start of
growing season until mid autumn.
Repotting Every second year, preferably in
early spring, until the tree is about 10 years old,
then up to every five years as necessary. Use free-
draining soil mix.
Pruning Pinch back tips of new shoots
throughout growing season.
Propagation Cuttings.
Styles Suitable for all styles except broom,
and for all sizes.

Kadsura japonica

SCARLET KADSURA

Evergreen climber, deciduous in temperate zones. Shiny oval leaves turn red in autumn. White flowers in late summer, red fruit.
⚙ **Position** Full sun. Protect from frost.
💧 **Watering** Daily throughout summer.
▤ **Feeding** Every two weeks throughout the growing season.
▥ **Repotting** Every two to three years, at any time during growing season. Basic soil mix.
✂ **Pruning** Trim shoots throughout summer.
🌱 **Propagation** Cuttings, layering
🎋 **Styles** Informal upright, slanting, semicascade, cascade, root-over-rock, twin-trunk, clump. Medium to extra-large sizes.

Laburnum alpinum

SCOTCH LABURNUM or GOLDEN RAIN TREE

Deciduous tree. Compound leaves, drooping racemes of yellow flowers in late spring and early summer. Very hardy.
⚙ **Position** Full sun.
💧 **Watering** Daily throughout growing season.
▤ **Feeding** Every two weeks throughout the growing season.
▥ **Repotting** Annually in early spring. Use basic soil mix.
✂ **Pruning** Trim shoots to two or three buds.
🌱 **Propagation** Seed.
🎋 **Styles** Informal upright, slanting, semicascade, cascade, twin-trunk, clump, multiple-trunk. Small to extra-large sizes.

Laburnum anagyroides

COMMON LABURNUM or GOLDEN RAIN TREE

Deciduous tree. Compound leaves and drooping racemes of flowers as *L. alpinum*, but racemes are shorter and flower earlier.
⚙ **Position** Full sun.
💧 **Watering** Daily throughout growing season.
▤ **Feeding** Every two weeks throughout the growing season.
▥ **Repotting** Annually in early spring. Use basic soil mix.
✂ **Pruning** Trim shoots to two or three buds.
🌱 **Propagation** Seed.
🎋 **Styles** Informal upright, slanting, semicascade, cascade, twin-trunk, clump, multiple-trunk. Small to extra-large sizes.

Lagerstroemia indica

CRAPE MYRTLE

Deciduous tree. Attractive grey, pink and cinnamon mottled trunk. Flowers in shades of white, pink, or mauve in late summer. (See also page 132.)
⚙ **Position** Full sun. Cool conditions in winter, but protect from frost.
💧 **Watering** Daily from spring to late autumn. Sparingly in winter, but keep moist.
▤ **Feeding** Every two weeks throughout the growing season.
▥ **Repotting** Annually in early spring. Use basic soil mix.
✂ **Pruning** Trim new growth in late spring after flowering, and again in late autumn.
🌱 **Propagation** Cuttings, seed.
🎋 **Styles** Informal upright, slanting, semicascade, root-over-rock. Suitable for medium to extra-large sizes.

Lagerstroemia indica 'Alba'

WHITE CRAPE MYRTLE

Form with white flowers which fade to cream. Cultivation, propagation, and styles as for *L. indica*.

Lagerstroemia indica 'Amabilis'

PURPLE CRAPE MYRTLE

Form bearing magenta flowers. Cultivation, propagation, and styles as for *L. indica*.

Larix decidua

EUROPEAN LARCH

Deciduous conifer. Stems to new shoots light straw-colour. Needle-like foliage is bright green in spring, gold in autumn. (See also page 133.)
⚙ **Position** Full sun. Keep air cool and dry. Protect smaller sizes from frost.
💧 **Watering** Daily throughout growing season. Sparingly in winter, but keep moist.
▤ **Feeding** Every two weeks throughout the growing season.
▥ **Repotting** Annually in early spring, before buds show green. Use basic soil mix.
✂ **Pruning** Pinch back new growth throughout the growing season.
🌱 **Propagation** Seed, cuttings, layering.
🎋 **Styles** Suitable for all styles except broom, and for all sizes.

Larix × eurolepis (decidua × kaempferi)

DUNKELD LARCH

Tough hybrid. New shoots are a pale yellowy orange colour.
⚙ **Position** Full sun. Keep air cool and dry. Protect smaller sizes from frost.
💧 **Watering** Daily throughout growing season. Sparingly in winter, but keep moist.
▤ **Feeding** Every two weeks throughout the growing season.
▥ **Repotting** Annually in early spring, before buds show green. Use basic soil mix.
✂ **Pruning** Pinch back new growth throughout the growing season.
🌱 **Propagation** Seed, cuttings, layering.
🎋 **Styles** Suitable for all styles except broom, and for all sizes.

Larix kaempferi (Larix leptolepis)

JAPANESE LARCH

Deciduous conifer. Has broader leaves than *L. decidua*. New twigs red-orange, darkening to almost purple by winter. (See also page 134.)
⚙ **Position** Full sun. Keep air cool and dry. Protect smaller sizes from frost.
💧 **Watering** Daily throughout growing season. Sparingly in winter, but keep moist.
▤ **Feeding** Every two weeks throughout the growing season.
▥ **Repotting** Annually in early spring, before buds show green. Use basic soil mix.
✂ **Pruning** Pinch back new growth throughout the growing season.
🌱 **Propagation** Seed, cuttings, layering.
🎋 **Styles** Suitable for all styles except broom, and for all sizes.

Larix laricina

TAMARACK or AMERICAN LARCH

Deciduous conifer. Has longer and laxer needles than other larches, and smaller flowers and cones.

⚙ **Position** Full sun. Keep air cool and dry. Protect smaller sizes from frost.
💧 **Watering** Daily throughout growing season. Sparingly in winter, but keep moist.
▤ **Feeding** Every two weeks throughout the growing season.
▥ **Repotting** Annually in early spring, before buds show green. Use basic soil mix.
✂ **Pruning** Pinch back tips of new growth throughout growing season.
🌱 **Propagation** Seed, cuttings, layering.
🎋 **Styles** Suitable for all styles except broom, and for all sizes.

Larix leptolepis, see *Larix kaempferi*

Lespedeza bicolour

JAPANESE BUSH CLOVER

Deciduous shrub. Clover-like leaves, purple-pink flowers in late summer.
⚙ **Position** Full sun. Protect from frost.
💧 **Watering** Daily throughout growing season.
▤ **Feeding** Every two weeks in growing season.
▥ **Repotting** Every second year in spring. Use basic soil mix.
✂ **Pruning** Trim shoots after flowers fade, cut branches back hard to trunk in late autumn.
🌱 **Propagation** Cuttings, seed.
🎋 **Styles** Informal upright, slanting, semicascade, cascade, root-over-rock, clasped-to-rock, twin-trunk, clump. Suitable for extra-small to medium sizes.

Ligustrum ovalifolium

OVAL-LEAF PRIVET

Semi-evergreen shrub. Small oval leaves, white flowers in summer.
⚙ **Position** Full sun or shade.
💧 **Watering** Daily throughout summer.
▤ **Feeding** Every two weeks throughout summer.
▥ **Repotting** Annually in early spring. Use basic soil mix.
✂ **Pruning** Trim shoots after flowering, new growth throughout growing season.
🌱 **Propagation** Cuttings, layering, seed.
🎋 **Styles** Informal upright, slanting, root-over-rock, clasped-to-rock, twin-trunk, clump, group. Suitable for all sizes.

Ligustrum vulgare

COMMON PRIVET

Semi-evergreen shrub. Dark, glossy leaves.
⚙ **Position** Full sun or shade.
💧 **Watering** Daily throughout summer.
▤ **Feeding** Every two weeks throughout summer.
▥ **Repotting** Annually in early spring. Use basic soil mix.
✂ **Pruning** Trim shoots after flowering, new growth throughout growing season.
🌱 **Propagation** Cuttings, layering, seed.
🎋 **Styles** Informal upright, slanting, root-over-rock, clasped-to-rock, twin-trunk, clump, group. Suitable for all sizes.

Liquidambar styraciflua

SWEET GUM

Deciduous tree. Superb orange, red and deep-purple autumn foliage.
⚙ **Position** Full sun.
💧 **Watering** Daily throughout growing season, sparingly in winter.

Feeding Every two weeks throughout summer.
Repotting Every second year in early spring. Use basic soil mix.
Pruning Trim back new shoots as they grow.
Propagation Seed, cuttings.
Styles Suitable for all styles except literati and broom, and for all sizes.

Lonicera japonica

JAPANESE HONEYSUCKLE

Vigorous semi-evergreen climber. Oval leaves. Fragrant white flowers, which fade to yellow, in early summer.
Position Full sun, partial shade in summer. Protect from frost.
Watering Daily throughout growing season. Keep moist at all times.
Feeding Every two weeks throughout summer.
Repotting Every second year in late spring. Use basic soil mix.
Pruning Trim back hard during growing season.
Propagation Cuttings, layering, air layering.
Styles Informal upright, slanting, semicascade, cascade, root-over-rock, clasped-to-rock, twin-trunk, clump, multiple-trunk. Suitable for all sizes.

Lonicera morowii

HONEYSUCKLE

Deciduous shrub. Creamy white flowers changing to yellow, followed by red fruit.
Position Full sun, slight shade in summer. Protect from frost.
Watering Daily throughout growing season. Keep moist at all times.
Feeding Every two weeks throughout summer.
Repotting Every second year in late spring. Use basic soil mix.
Pruning Trim back hard during growing season.
Propagation Cuttings, layering, air layering.
Styles Informal upright, slanting, semicascade, cascade, root-over-rock, clasped-to-rock, twin-trunk, clump, multiple-trunk. Suitable for all sizes.

Lonicera nitida

DWARF HONEYSUCKLE

Evergreen dwarf shrubby honeysuckle. Small leaves. Responds well to constant clipping. (See also page 135.)
Position Full sun, slight shade in summer. Protect from frost.
Watering Daily throughout growing season. Keep moist at all times.
Feeding Every two weeks throughout summer.
Repotting Every second year in late spring. Use basic soil mix.
Pruning Trim back hard during growing season.
Propagation Cuttings.
Styles Suitable for all styles except broom, and all sizes, especially the smallest.

Magnolia stellata

STAR MAGNOLIA

Slow-growing deciduous flowering shrub.

Fragrant white star-like flowers appear in late spring before the leaves.
Position Full sun or shade. Protect flowers from spring frosts.
Watering Daily throughout growing season. Do not allow soil to dry out at any time.
Feeding Every two weeks throughout summer.
Repotting Every three to four years in early spring. Use basic soil mix.
Pruning Shorten new shoots to shape.
Propagation Division, layering.
Styles Informal upright, slanting, semicascade, cascade, twin-trunk, clump, multiple-trunk. Medium and large sizes.

Malus cerasifera

NAGASAKI CRAB APPLE

Deciduous flowering tree. Pink flower buds opening to white, generous display of cherry-like red fruit. (See also pages 136 and 137.)
Position Full sun. Protect roots from frost if grown in a shallow container.
Watering Daily throughout growing season. Be particularly careful to keep moist when in fruit. Spray regularly against mildew.
Feeding Weekly from early spring through to flowering, and from when fruit has developed until autumn.
Repotting Annually in early spring before bud burst. Use basic soil mix.
Pruning Finger prune new shoots in spring and trim long shoots again in autumn.
Propagation Grafting, layering, air layering.
Styles Informal upright, slanting, semicascade, twin-trunk, clump. All sizes.

Malus 'Golden hornet'

GOLDEN HORNET CRAB APPLE

Deciduous flowering tree. White flowers are followed by bright yellow fruit, which remain on the tree after leaf fall.
Position Full sun. Protect roots from frost if grown in a shallow container.
Watering Daily throughout growing season. Be particularly careful to keep moist when in fruit. Spray regularly against mildew.
Feeding Weekly from early spring through to flowering, and from when fruit has developed until autumn.
Repotting Annually in early spring before bud burst. Use basic soil mix.
Pruning Finger prune new shoots in spring and trim long shoots again in autumn.
Propagation Grafting, layering, air layering.
Styles Informal upright, slanting, semicascade, twin-trunk, clump. All sizes.

Malus halliana

HALL'S CRAB APPLE

Deciduous flowering tree. Narrow dark-green leaves. Pink blossom followed by small purple fruit. (See also page 137.)
Position Full sun. Protect roots from frost if grown in a shallow container.
Watering Daily throughout growing season. Be particularly careful to keep moist when tree is in fruit. Spray regularly against mildew.
Feeding Weekly from early spring through to flowering, and from when fruit has developed until autumn.
Repotting Annually in early spring before bud burst. Use basic soil mix.

Pruning Finger prune new shoots in spring and trim long shoots again in autumn.
Propagation Grafting, layering, air layering.
Styles Informal upright, slanting, semicascade, twin-trunk, clump. All sizes.

Malus 'Profusion'

PURPLE CRAB APPLE

Deciduous flowering tree. Purple leaves. Wine-red flowers followed by deep-red fruit.
Position Full sun. Protect roots from frost if grown in a shallow container.
Watering Daily throughout growing season. Be particularly careful to keep moist when tree is in fruit. Spray regularly against mildew.
Feeding Weekly from early spring through to flowering, and from when fruit has developed until autumn.
Repotting Annually in early spring before bud burst. Use basic soil mix.
Pruning Finger prune new shoots in spring and trim long shoots again in autumn.
Propagation Grafting, layering, air layering.
Styles Informal upright, slanting, semicascade, twin-trunk, clump. All sizes.

Malus 'Red jade'

WEEPING CRAB APPLE

Weeping form. Young leaves bright green. Pink and white flowers followed by small red fruit, which remain on the tree throughout the winter.
Position Full sun. Protect roots from frost if grown in a shallow container.
Watering Daily throughout growing season. Be particularly careful to keep moist when tree is in fruit. Spray regularly against mildew.
Feeding Weekly from early spring through to flowering, and from when fruit has developed until autumn.
Repotting Annually in early spring before bud burst. Use basic soil mix.
Pruning Finger prune new shoots in spring and trim long shoots again in autumn.
Propagation Grafting, layering, air layering.
Styles Informal upright, slanting, semicascade, twin-trunk, clump. All sizes.

Malus sieboldii (M. toringo)

CRAB APPLE

Small leaves. Pink buds opening to small white flowers. Tiny yellow or red fruit.
Position Full sun. Protect roots from frost if grown in a shallow container.
Watering Daily throughout growing season. Be particularly careful to keep moist when in fruit. Spray regularly against mildew.
Feeding Weekly from early spring through to flowering, and from when fruit has developed until autumn.
Repotting Annually in early spring before bud burst. Use basic soil mix.
Pruning Finger prune new shoots in spring and trim long shoots again in autumn.
Propagation Grafting, layering, air layering.
Styles Informal upright, slanting, semicascade, twin-trunk, clump. All sizes.

Malus sylvestris

COMMON CRAB APPLE

Small deciduous tree, often with spurs. Toothed oval leaves. Flowers white or suffused with pink, followed by yellow-green or red-flushed fruit.

⚙ **Position** Full sun. Protect roots from frost if grown in a shallow container.
💧 **Watering** Daily throughout growing season. Be particularly careful to keep moist when in fruit. Spray regularly against mildew.
▥ **Feeding** Weekly from early spring through to flowering, and from when fruit has developed until autumn.
▣ **Repotting** Annually in early spring before bud burst. Use basic soil mix.
✂ **Pruning** Finger prune new shoots in spring and trim long shoots again in autumn.
✿ **Propagation** Grafting, layering, air layering, seed.
🌲 **Styles** Informal upright, slanting, semicascade, twin-trunk, clump. All sizes.

Malus toringo, see *Malus sieboldii*

Metasequoia glyptostroboides
_____

DAWN REDWOOD
Deciduous conifer. Conical habit. Flattened, needle-like leaves are a light green, turning to reddish brown in autumn. Shaggy cinnamon-coloured bark.
⚙ **Position** Full sun.
💧 **Watering** Daily throughout growing season.
▥ **Feeding** Every two weeks throughout the growing season.
▣ **Repotting** Every second year in early spring. Use basic soil mix.
✂ **Pruning** Trim back new shoots continually as they grow.
✿ **Propagation** Seed, cuttings.
🌲 **Styles** Formal upright, informal upright, slanting, twin-trunk, clump, multiple-trunk, group. Small to extra-large sizes.

Millettia japonica
_____

JAPANESE MILLETTIA
Evergreen climber. Small, dark-green pinnate leaves, mauve flowers in early summer.
⚙ **Position** Full sun.
💧 **Watering** Plentifully throughout the year.
▥ **Feeding** Every two weeks throughout the growing season.
▣ **Repotting** Annually in early spring. Use basic soil mix.
✂ **Pruning** Trim new growth after flowers fade and throughout summer.
✿ **Propagation** Cuttings, layering, grafting, seed.
🌲 **Styles** Informal upright, slanting, semicascade, cascade, root-over-rock, twin-trunk, clump. Small to large sizes.

Millettia japonica 'Microphylla'
_____

DWARF WISTERIA
Evergreen climber with a neat compact habit. Minute compound leaves are very similar to wisteria in appearance, hence the common name. Seldom flowers.
Cultivation as *M. japonica.*
✿ **Propagation** Division, cuttings, layering.
🌲 **Styles** As *M. japonica,* suitable for extra-small and small sizes.

Morus alba
_____

WHITE MULBERRY
Deciduous. Heart shaped leaves, edible reddish fruit in autumn. (See also page 138.)
⚙ **Position** Full sun. Protect from frost.
💧 **Watering** Daily throughout growing season. Keep moist at all times.

▥ **Feeding** Every two weeks from spring to summer, then with high potash feed from late summer to autumn.
▣ **Repotting** Every second year in early spring. Use free-draining soil mix.
✂ **Pruning** Trim back new growth to two leaves.
✿ **Propagation** Seed, cuttings, air layering, layering.
🌲 **Styles** Informal upright, slanting, semicascade, cascade, root-over-rock, twin-trunk, clump. Suitable for all sizes.

Murraya paniculata
_____

JASMINE ORANGE
Evergreen shrub. Small pinnate leaves. Scented white bell-shaped flowers, orange-like fruit. (See also page 139.)
⚙ **Position** Full sun, slight shade in summer. Indoors in temperate climates. Minimum temperature 17°C (63°F).
💧 **Watering** Daily throughout growing season. Keep slightly moist and humid at all times.
▥ **Feeding** Every two weeks from mid spring to early autumn, every four to six weeks throughout the winter.
▣ **Repotting** Every second year in spring. Use basic soil mix.
✂ **Pruning** Trim new shoots at any time during the growing season.
✿ **Propagation** Cuttings, seed.
🌲 **Styles** Informal upright, slanting, semicascade, cascade, twin-trunk, clump, group. Suitable for all sizes.

Myrtus apiculata
_____

MYRTLE
Small, tender evergreen tree. Cinnamon-coloured bark peels to show cream beneath. Dull-green oval leaves. Small white flowers in summer followed by red and black fruit.
⚙ **Position** Full sun. Protect from cold and frost in winter.
💧 **Watering** Daily throughout summer. Do not allow the soil to dry out at any time.
▥ **Feeding** Every two weeks throughout summer.
▣ **Repotting** Every second year in early spring. Use basic soil mix.
✂ **Pruning** Trim shoots to shape as they grow.
✿ **Propagation** Cuttings, layering.
🌲 **Styles** Informal upright, slanting, semicascade, cascade, twin-trunk, clump, multiple-trunk. Suitable for all sizes.

Myrtus communis
_____

COMMON MYRTLE
Evergreen. Aromatic foliage, white flowers in summer followed by black fruit.
⚙ **Position** Full sun. Protect from cold and frost in winter.
💧 **Watering** Daily throughout summer. Do not allow the soil to dry out at any time
▥ **Feeding** Every two weeks throughout summer.
▣ **Repotting** Every second year in spring. Use basic soil mix.
✂ **Pruning** Trim shoots to shape as they grow.
✿ **Propagation** Cuttings, layering.
🌲 **Styles** Informal upright, slanting, semicascade, cascade, twin-trunk, clump, multiple-trunk. Suitable for all sizes.

Nandina domestica
_____

SACRED or HEAVENLY BAMBOO
Evergreen shrub. Long, narrow leaves, flushed with red during spring and autumn. (See also page 101.)
⚙ **Position** Full sun, partial shade in summer. Protect from frost.
💧 **Watering** Daily throughout summer.
▥ **Feeding** Every two weeks throughout the growing season.
▣ **Repotting** Every second year in spring. Use free-draining soil mix.
✂ **Pruning** Trim new shoots to shape.
✿ **Propagation** Cuttings, division, grafting, seed.
🌲 **Styles** Twin-trunk, clump, multiple-trunk, saikei. Suitable for all sizes.

Nothofagus antarctica
_____

ANTARCTIC BEECH
Deciduous tree. Small, glossy, heart shaped dark-green leaves, which turn bright yellow in autumn.
⚙ **Position** Full sun.
💧 **Watering** Daily throughout summer.
▥ **Feeding** Every two weeks throughout summer.
▣ **Repotting** Every second year in early spring. Use basic soil mix.
✂ **Pruning** Trim new shoots throughout summer. Branch prune in winter.
✿ **Propagation** Seed, cuttings, layering, air layering.
🌲 **Styles** Suitable for all styles except literati, and for all sizes.

Nothofagus obliqua
_____

ROBLE BEECH
Very fast-growing deciduous tree. Oblong leaves with good autumn colour.
⚙ **Position** Full sun.
💧 **Watering** Daily throughout summer.
▥ **Feeding** Every two weeks throughout summer.
▣ **Repotting** Every second year in early spring. Use basic soil mix.
✂ **Pruning** Trim new shoots throughout summer. Branch prune in winter.
✿ **Propagation** Seed, cuttings, layering, air layering.
🌲 **Styles** Suitable for all styles except literati, and for all sizes.

Nothofagus procera
_____

SOUTHERN BEECH
Fast growing deciduous tree. Prominently veined leaves with rich autumn colours.
⚙ **Position** Full sun.
💧 **Watering** Daily throughout summer.
▥ **Feeding** Every two weeks throughout summer.
▣ **Repotting** Every second year in early spring. Use basic soil mix.
✂ **Pruning** Trim new shoots throughout summer. Branch prune in winter.
✿ **Propagation** Seed, cuttings, layering, air layering.
🌲 **Styles** Suitable for all styles except literati, and for all sizes.

Olea europaea
_____

OLIVE
Tender evergreen tree. Shiny, narrow dark-green leaves with light-grey undersides. Insignificant

cream flowers develop into green fruit, ripening to black. Light-grey bark becomes gnarled on old trees.

Position Full sun. Warm location, minimum temperature 7°C (45°F).

Watering Every other day throughout summer, weekly in winter.

Feeding Every two weeks throughout summer.

Repotting Every second year in spring. Use free-draining soil mix.

Pruning Pinch back new shoots throughout the growing season.

Propagation Cuttings, seed.

Styles Suitable for all styles except broom, and for small to extra-large sizes.

Osmanthus delavayi

OSMANTHUS

Evergreen shrub. Small, holly-like leaves, scented white flowers in early spring.

Position Full sun, slight shade in summer.

Watering Daily throughout growing season.

Feeding Every two weeks throughout the growing season.

Repotting Every second year in early spring. Use basic soil mix.

Pruning Trim shoots after flowers fade, and subsequent shoots as they occur.

Propagation Cuttings, grafting, layering.

Styles Informal upright, slanting, semicascade, cascade, twin-trunk, clump, multiple-trunk, group. All sizes.

Parthenocissus tricuspidata

BOSTON IVY

Deciduous climber. Three-lobed leaves turn brilliant red in autumn. Dark-blue fruit.

Position Full sun, slight shade in summer.

Watering Daily throughout summer.

Feeding Every two weeks throughout summer.

Repotting Every second year in early spring. Use basic soil mix.

Pruning Trim new growth back throughout the growing season.

Propagation Cuttings, grafting, layering, seed.

Styles Informal upright, slanting, semicascade, cascade, root-over-rock, twin-trunk, clump. Small to large sizes.

Phyllostachys aurea

GOLDEN BAMBOO

Evergreen. Bright-green young canes become yellow as they mature. (See also page 101.)

Position Partial shade. Keep warm during winter months.

Watering Daily throughout summer. Less frequently at other times, but keep moist.

Feeding Every two weeks throughout summer.

Repotting Every second year in late spring. Use free-draining soil mix.

Pruning Remove new central bud when required height is reached.

Propagation Division.

Styles Clump, multiple-trunk. Suitable for medium to extra-large sizes.

Phyllostachys nigra

BLACK BAMBOO

Clump-forming bamboo. Striking stems, green in first year, deep black by following year.

Position Partial shade. Keep warm during winter months.

Watering Daily throughout summer. Less frequently at other times, but keep moist.

Feeding Every two weeks throughout summer.

Repotting Every second year in late spring. Use free-draining soil mix.

Pruning Remove new central bud when required height is reached.

Propagation Division.

Styles Clump, multiple-trunk. Suitable for medium to extra-large sizes.

Picea abies

NORWAY SPRUCE

Evergreen conifer. Dark-green needle-like leaves, reddish shoots, cylindrical cones.

Position Full sun. Protect smaller sizes from frost.

Watering Daily throughout summer, and mist-spray foliage. Sparingly in winter, but keep soil moist.

Feeding Every two weeks from early spring to mid autumn.

Repotting Every second year in early to mid spring before bud burst, or in autumn. Use free-draining soil mix.

Pruning Finger pinch growing tips throughout spring and summer.

Propagation Seed, cuttings.

Styles Suitable for all styles except broom, and for medium to large sizes.

Picea abies 'Echiniformis'

DWARF SPRUCE

Slow-growing, compact dwarf form with tightly congested foliage.

Cultivation as *P. abies*.

Propagation Cuttings.

Styles As *P. abies*, suitable for extra-small and small sizes.

Picea abies 'Little Gem'

DWARF SPRUCE

Dwarf form. Very compact, with very small leaves. (See also page 140.)

Cultivation as *P. abies*.

Propagation Cuttings.

Styles As *P. abies*, suitable for extra-small to medium sizes.

Picea abies 'Maxwellii'

DWARF SPRUCE

Dwarf form with coarse, spiny needles.

Cultivation as *P. abies*.

Propagation Cuttings.

Styles As *P. abies*, suitable for extra-small to medium sizes.

Picea abies 'Nidiformis'

BIRD'S NEST SPRUCE

Dwarf form with bright, fresh-green buds.

Cultivation as *P. abies*.

Propagation Cuttings.

Styles As *P. abies*, suitable for extra-small to medium sizes.

Picea glauca 'Albertiana Conica'

DWARF ALBERTA WHITE SPRUCE

Slow-growing, compact evergreen dwarf conifer. Conical habit, bright-green foliage.

Position Full sun. Protect smaller sizes from frost.

Watering Daily throughout summer, and mist-spray foliage. Sparingly in winter, but keep soil moist.

Feeding Every two weeks from early spring through to mid autumn.

Repotting Every second year in early to mid spring before bud burst, or in autumn. Use free-draining soil mix.

Pruning Finger pinch growing tips throughout spring and summer.

Propagation Cuttings.

Styles Suitable for all styles except broom, and for small to large sizes.

Picea glehnii

SAKHALIN SPRUCE

Evergreen conifer. Slender conical habit, bluish green leaves, red-brown flaking bark. The preferred spruce species in Japan. Export is now banned, but there are still some stocks, and seed is freely available.

Position Full sun. Protect smaller sizes from frost.

Watering Daily throughout summer, and mist-spray foliage. Sparingly in winter, but keep soil moist.

Feeding Every two weeks from early spring through to mid autumn.

Repotting Every second year in early to mid spring before bud burst, or in autumn. Use free-draining soil mix.

Pruning Finger pinch growing tips throughout spring and summer.

Propagation Seed, cuttings.

Styles Suitable for all styles except broom, and for medium to large sizes.

Picea glehnii 'Yatsubusa'

DWARF SAKHALIN SPRUCE

Dwarf form of *P. glehnii*, almost indistinguishable from *P. abies* 'Little Gem'.

Cultivation as *P. glehnii*.

Propagation Cuttings.

Styles As *P. glehnii*, suitable for extra-small to medium sizes.

Picea jezoensis

YEZO or EDO SPRUCE

Evergreen conifer. Dark-green leaves with white undersides. Young shoots light brown.

Position Full sun. Protect smaller sizes from frost.

Watering Daily throughout summer, and mist-spray foliage. Sparingly in winter, but keep soil moist.

Feeding Every two weeks from early spring through to mid autumn.

Repotting Every second year in early to mid spring before bud burst, or in autumn. Use free-draining soil mix.

Pruning Finger pinch growing tips throughout spring and summer.

Propagation Seed, cuttings.

Styles Suitable for all styles except broom, and for medium to large sizes.

Picea jezoensis hondoensis

HONDO SPRUCE

Shorter leaved variety of *P. jezoensis*.
Cultivation, propagation, and styles as for *P. jezoensis*.

Picea mariana 'Nana'

DWARF BLACK SPRUCE

Dwarf evergreen tree with grey-green needle-like leaves.

◆ **Position** Full sun. Protect smaller sizes from frost.

◆ **Watering** Daily throughout summer, and mist-spray. Sparingly in winter, but keep moist.

◆ **Feeding** Every two weeks from early spring through to mid autumn.

◆ **Repotting** Every second year in early to mid spring before bud burst, or in autumn. Use free-draining soil mix.

◆ **Pruning** Finger pinch growing tips throughout spring and summer.

◆ **Propagation** Cuttings.

◆ **Styles** Suitable for all styles except broom, and for extra-small to medium sizes.

Pieris japonica (Andromeda japonica)

PIERIS

Lime-hating evergreen shrub. Shiny leaves, copper-coloured when young. Panicles of white flowers in spring.

◆ **Position** Slight shade.

◆ **Watering** Daily throughout summer with lime-free water.

◆ **Feeding** Every two weeks with ericaceous fertilizer.

◆ **Repotting** Every three or four years in early spring. Use lime-free soil mix.

◆ **Pruning** Trim back new shoots throughout the growing season.

◆ **Propagation** Cuttings, layering.

◆ **Styles** Informal upright, slanting, semicascade, cascade, root-over-rock, twin-trunk, clump. Small to large sizes.

Pinus densiflora

JAPANESE RED PINE

Evergreen conifer. Blue-green needles growing in pairs, reddish bark.

◆ **Position** Full sun. Protect from frost and cold, drying winds.

◆ **Watering** Daily throughout summer, unless soil is already moist, and mist-spray. Sparingly in winter. Keep fairly dry.

◆ **Feeding** Monthly from midwinter to mid autumn.

◆ **Repotting** Every two to five years in early to mid spring. Use free-draining soil mix.

◆ **Pruning** Finger pinch candles in spring annually, prune branch tips in early autumn every second year.

◆ **Propagation** Grafting, seed.

◆ **Styles** Suitable for all styles except broom, and for all sizes.

Pinus mugo

MOUNTAIN PINE

Small evergreen conifer. Dark-green needles, light-green shoots. (See also page 141.)

◆ **Position** Full sun. Protect from severe frost and freezing winds.

◆ **Watering** Daily throughout summer, unless soil is already moist, and mist-spray. Sparingly in winter. Keep fairly dry.

◆ **Feeding** Every three to four weeks from spring to early winter.

◆ **Repotting** Every three to five years in early to mid spring or late summer. Use free-draining soil mix.

◆ **Pruning** Finger pinch candles throughout the growing season.

◆ **Propagation** Seed. Grafting for dwarf forms.

◆ **Styles** Suitable for all styles except broom, and for all sizes. Dwarf forms are best for clasped-to-rock style and smaller sizes.

Pinus parviflora (P. pentaphylla)

JAPANESE WHITE PINE

Evergreen conifer. Also called Japanese five-needled pine. Twisted bluish needles in bundles of five. Smooth grey bark, small flowers, dark-brown cones. (See also page 142.)

◆ **Position** Full sun. Protect from frost and cold, drying winds.

◆ **Watering** Daily throughout summer, unless soil is already moist, and mist-spray. Sparingly in winter. Keep fairly dry.

◆ **Feeding** Every three to four weeks from spring to early winter.

◆ **Repotting** Every two to five years in early to mid spring. Use free-draining soil mix.

◆ **Pruning** Finger pinch candles in spring annually, prune branch tips in early autumn every second year.

◆ **Propagation** Grafting onto *P. thunbergii*, seed.

◆ **Styles** Suitable for all styles except broom, and for all sizes. Dwarf forms are best for clasped-to-rock style and smaller sizes.

Pinus parviflora 'Kokonoe'

DWARF JAPANESE WHITE PINE

Dwarf yatsubusa form. Thick, slightly twisted dark-green needles. (See also page 143.)
Cultivation as *P. parviflora*.

◆ **Propagation** Grafting.

◆ **Styles** As *P. parviflora*. A very popular cultivar for small and extra-small sizes.

Pinus parviflora 'Miyajima'

DWARF JAPANESE WHITE PINE

One of the cultivars most popular for bonsai, due to its compact growth and small, stiff, straight needles.(See also page 143.)
Cultivation as *P. parviflora*.

◆ **Propagation** Grafting.

◆ **Styles** As *P. parviflora*. Suitable for small and extra-small sizes.

Pinus parviflora 'Nasumusume'

DWARF JAPANESE WHITE PINE

Dwarf yatsubusa form with tiny needles.
Cultivation as *P. parviflora*.

◆ **Propagation** Grafting.

◆ **Styles** As *P. parviflora*, suitable for extra-small and small sizes.

Pinus pentaphylla, see Pinus parviflora

Pinus pumila

DWARF SIBERIAN PINE

Dwarf conifer with blue-green leaves in bundles of five, and red-brown young shoots.

◆ **Position** Full sun. Protect from frost and cold, drying winds.

◆ **Watering** Daily throughout summer, unless soil is already moist, and mist-spray. Sparingly in winter. Keep fairly dry.

◆ **Feeding** Monthly from midwinter through to mid autumn.

◆ **Repotting** Every two to five years in early to mid spring. Use free-draining soil mix.

◆ **Pruning** Finger pinch candles in spring annually, prune branch tips in early autumn every second year.

◆ **Propagation** Grafting, seed.

◆ **Styles** Suitable for all styles except broom, and for all sizes.

Pinus sylvestris

SCOTS PINE

Evergreen conifer. Distinctive spreading outline with flattened top. Short blue-green needles in pairs, flaking orange bark.

◆ **Position** Full sun. Protect from frost and cold winds.

◆ **Watering** Check daily, but water only when soil is drying out. Moderately throughout growing season, sparingly in winter.

◆ **Feeding** Every three to four weeks from spring to early winter.

◆ **Repotting** Every two to five years in early to mid spring. Use free-draining soil mix.

◆ **Pruning** Pinch back candles as needles begin to appear. Remove long shoots throughout growing season. Remove old needles and overcrowded twigs in late summer.

◆ **Propagation** Seed, grafting for cultivars.

◆ **Styles** Suitable for all styles except broom, and for all sizes. Especially suitable for literati, which is the natural style of a mature scots pine.

Pinus sylvestris 'Beuvronensis'

DWARF SCOTS PINE

Very compact dwarf form with short needles. (See also page 144.)
Cultivation as *P. sylvestris*.

◆ **Propagation** Grafting onto *P. sylvestris*.

◆ **Styles** As *P. sylvestris*.

Pinus sylvestris 'Watereri'

DWARF SCOTS PINE

Slow-growing form.
Cultivation as *P. sylvestris*.

◆ **Propagation** Grafting onto *P. sylvestris*.

◆ **Styles** As *P. sylvestris*.

Pinus thunbergii

JAPANESE BLACK PINE

Long, thick, stiff dark-green needles carried in pairs, brown young shoots, craggy bark. (See also page 145.)

◆ **Position** Full sun. Protect from frost and cold winds.

◆ **Watering** Check daily, but water only when soil is drying out. Plentifully if water is quick-draining. Very sparingly in winter.

◆ **Feeding** Every three to four weeks from spring to early winter.

◆ **Repotting** Every two to five years in early to mid spring. Use free-draining soil mix.

◆ **Pruning** Pinch back candles as needles begin to appear. Remove long shoots throughout growing season. Remove old needles and overcrowded twigs in late summer.

◆ **Propagation** Seed.

◆ **Styles** Suitable for all styles except broom, especially suitable for literati. All sizes.

Pinus thunbergii corticosa

CORK-BARKED JAPANESE BLACK PINE

Distinctive corky bark forms broad vertical cracks with wing-like protrusions.
Cultivation as *P. thunbergii*.

◆ **Propagation** Grafting onto *P. thunbergii*.

◆ **Styles** Formal upright, informal upright, slanting, semicascade, cascade, twin-trunk, clump, multiple-trunk. All sizes.

Podocarpus chinensis, see Podocarpus macrophyllus

Podocarpus macrophyllus (P. chinensis)

CHINESE PODOCARPUS
Slow-growing evergreen. Yew-like foliage.
⬚ **Position** Full sun.
⬚ **Watering** Daily throughout growing season.
⬚ **Feeding** Every two weeks from spring to autumn, every four to six weeks in winter.
⬚ **Repotting** Every second year in spring. Use basic soil mix.
⬚ **Pruning** Finger pinch new shoots throughout the growing season.
⬚ **Propagation** Cuttings, layering.
⬚ **Styles** Formal upright, informal upright, slanting, twin-trunk, clump, multiple-trunk, group. Suitable for all sizes.

Potentilla fruticosa

POTENTILLA
Deciduous flowering shrub. Small, divided grey-green leaves, and a shaggy, old-looking bark even when young. Yellow, buttercup-like flowers in summer. There are many cultivars with a variety of habits and flowers.
⬚ **Position** Full sun.
⬚ **Watering** Daily throughout growing season. Do not allow soil to dry out at any time.
⬚ **Feeding** Every two weeks throughout the growing season.
⬚ **Repotting** Every second year in early spring. Use basic soil mix.
⬚ **Pruning** Trim back new shoots continually to keep growth compact.
⬚ **Propagation** Seed, cuttings.
⬚ **Styles** Suitable for all styles except literati, and for extra-small to large sizes.

Potentilla fruticosa 'Kobold'

POTENTILLA
Small, compact form with yellow flowers. Cultivation as *P. fruticosa*.
⬚ **Propagation** Cuttings, grafting.
⬚ **Styles** As *P. fruticosa*, suitable for extra-small to medium sizes.

Potentilla fruticosa 'Manchu'

POTENTILLA
Small, compact form with pure-white flowers. Cultivation as *P. fruticosa*.
⬚ **Propagation** Cuttings, grafting.
⬚ **Styles** As *P. fruticosa*, suitable for extra-small to medium sizes.

Potentilla fruticosa 'Tangerine'

POTENTILLA
Unusually coloured yellow-orange flowers. Cultivation as *P. fruticosa*.
⬚ **Propagation** Cuttings, grafting.
⬚ **Styles** As *P. fruticosa*, suitable for extra-small to medium sizes.

Prunus avium

GEAN or WILD CHERRY
Deciduous flowering tree. With age the smooth grey bark turns red, cracks and peels. White blossom in spring, small reddish-purple fruit in autumn. Foliage turns crimson in autumn.
⬚ **Position** Full sun.
⬚ **Watering** Daily throughout growing season.
⬚ **Feeding** Every two weeks throughout the growing season.
⬚ **Repotting** Every second year in early spring. Use basic soil mix.
⬚ **Pruning** Trim back new growth to create and maintain shape.

⬚ **Propagation** Seed.
⬚ **Styles** Informal upright, slanting, semicascade, cascade, twin-trunk, clump, straight line, sinuous, multiple-trunk, group, saikei. Suitable for all sizes.

Prunus avium 'Plena'

DOUBLE GEAN
Double-flowered form.
Cultivation as *P. avium*.
⬚ **Propagation** Grafting.
⬚ **Styles** As *P. avium*.

Prunus cerasifera

MYROBALAN PLUM
Deciduous flowering tree. Masses of small white flowers appear from late winter through to early spring.
⬚ **Position** Full sun.
⬚ **Watering** Daily throughout growing season.
⬚ **Feeding** Every two weeks throughout the growing season.
⬚ **Repotting** Every second year in early spring. Use basic soil mix.
⬚ **Pruning** Trim back new growth to create and maintain shape.
⬚ **Propagation** Seed.
⬚ **Styles** Informal upright, slanting, semicascade, cascade, twin-trunk, clump, straight line, sinuous, multiple-trunk, group, saikei. Suitable for all sizes.

Prunus cerasifera 'Pissardii'

PURPLE-LEAVED PLUM
Dark-red foliage turns deep purple in autumn. Masses of pink buds opening to white in early spring. Purple fruit.
Cultivation as *P. cerasifera*.
⬚ **Propagation** Grafting, cuttings.
⬚ **Styles** As *P. cerasifera*.

Prunus dulcis

ALMOND
Delicate pink flowers appear on bare wood in late winter and early spring.
⬚ **Position** Full sun.
⬚ **Watering** Daily throughout growing season.
⬚ **Feeding** Every two weeks throughout the growing season.
⬚ **Repotting** Every second year in early spring. Use basic soil mix.
⬚ **Pruning** Trim back new growth to create and maintain shape.
⬚ **Propagation** Grafting.
⬚ **Styles** Informal upright, slanting, semicascade, cascade, twin-trunk, clump, straight line, sinuous, multiple-trunk, group, saikei. Suitable for all sizes.

Prunus 'Hally Jolivette'

HALLY JOLIVETTE CHERRY
Elegant tree with delicate twig structure. Small semi-double white flowers flushed with pink appear in early spring.
⬚ **Position** Full sun.
⬚ **Watering** Daily throughout growing season.
⬚ **Feeding** Every two weeks throughout the growing season.
⬚ **Repotting** Every second year in early spring. Use basic soil mix.
⬚ **Pruning** Trim back new growth to create and maintain shape.
⬚ **Propagation** Grafting.

⬚ **Styles** Informal upright, slanting, semicascade, cascade, twin-trunk, clump, straight line, sinuous, multiple-trunk, group, saikei. Suitable for all sizes.

Prunus incisa

FUJI CHERRY
Free-flowering form. Foliage turns orange in autumn. Pinkish white blossom.
⬚ **Position** Full sun.
⬚ **Watering** Daily throughout growing season.
⬚ **Feeding** Every two weeks throughout the growing season.
⬚ **Repotting** Every second year in early spring. Use basic soil mix.
⬚ **Pruning** Trim back new growth to create and maintain shape.
⬚ **Propagation** Grafting.
⬚ **Styles** Informal upright, slanting, semicascade, cascade, twin-trunk, clump, straight line, sinuous, multiple-trunk, group, saikei. Suitable for all sizes.

Prunus mahaleb

ST. LUCIE CHERRY
Small, heart-shaped bright-green leaves, yellow autumn colour. Masses of fragrant white blossoms in early spring. Black fruit. Does not flower so freely when young.
⬚ **Position** Full sun.
⬚ **Watering** Daily throughout growing season.
⬚ **Feeding** Every two weeks throughout the growing season.
⬚ **Repotting** Every second year in early spring. Use basic soil mix.
⬚ **Pruning** Trim back new growth to create and maintain shape.
⬚ **Propagation** Seed, grafting to hasten flowering.
⬚ **Styles** Informal upright, slanting, semicascade, cascade, twin-trunk, clump, straight line, sinuous, multiple-trunk, group, saikei. Suitable for all sizes.

Prunus mume

JAPANESE FLOWERING APRICOT
Classic bonsai subject. Distinctive angular growth pattern. Single or double flowers in whites, pinks, and reds (sometimes on the same tree) in late winter. Many cultivars available from Japan, where it is also called wild or flowering plum. (See also page 146.)
⬚ **Position** Full sun. Protect from frost to avoid twig die-back and damage to flowers.
⬚ **Watering** Daily throughout growing season. Be particularly careful to keep moist when in flower. Sparingly in winter.
⬚ **Feeding** At least every two weeks in summer.
⬚ **Repotting** Annually in late winter before flowering. Use basic soil mix.
⬚ **Pruning** Trim back hard after flowering. Allow rampant growth in summer and trim back again in autumn.
⬚ **Propagation** Grafting, cuttings, layering.
⬚ **Styles** Suitable for all styles except formal upright and broom, and for all sizes. Literati is the favoured style for this tree.

Prunus padus

BIRD CHERRY
Spikes of small, white, fragrant flowers are followed by small, bitter purple-black fruit.
⬚ **Position** Full sun.
⬚ **Watering** Daily throughout growing season.

◨ **Feeding** Every two weeks throughout the growing season.
◨ **Repotting** Every second year in early spring. Use basic soil mix.
◪ **Pruning** Trim back new growth to create and maintain shape.
◪ **Propagation** Seed.
◪ **Styles** Informal upright, slanting, semicascade, cascade, twin-trunk, clump, straight line, sinuous, multiple-trunk, group, saikei. Suitable for all sizes.

Prunus persica

PEACH
Pale-pink flowers in early spring, followed by familiar edible golden-red fruit. There are many ornamental cultivars, which are more often used for bonsai.
◨ **Position** Full sun.
◪ **Watering** Daily throughout growing season.
◨ **Feeding** Every two weeks throughout the growing season.
◨ **Repotting** Every second year in early spring. Use basic soil mix.
◪ **Pruning** Trim back new growth to create and maintain shape.
◪ **Propagation** Grafting.
◪ **Styles** Informal upright, slanting, semicascade, cascade, twin-trunk, clump, straight line, sinuous, multiple-trunk, group, saikei. Suitable for all sizes.

Prunus persica 'Alboplena'

DOUBLE-FLOWERED PEACH
White double flowers.
Cultivation, propagation, and styles as for *P. persica*.

Prunus persica 'Klara Meyer'

DOUBLE-FLOWERED PEACH
Peach-pink double flowers.
Cultivation, propagation, and styles as for *P. persica*.

Prunus persica 'Russell's Red'

DOUBLE-FLOWERED PEACH
Crimson double flowers.
Cultivation, propagation, and styles as for *P. persica*.

Prunus salicina

JAPANESE PLUM
Small white flowers on bare branches in spring, bright-red autumn foliage.
◨ **Position** Full sun.
◪ **Watering** Daily throughout growing season.
◨ **Feeding** Every two weeks throughout the growing season.
◨ **Repotting** Every second year in early spring. Use basic soil mix.
◪ **Pruning** Trim back new growth to create and maintain shape.
◪ **Propagation** Grafting.
◪ **Styles** Informal upright, slanting, semicascade, cascade, twin-trunk, clump, straight line, sinuous, multiple-trunk, group, saikei. Suitable for all sizes.

Prunus serrulata

FLOWERING CHERRY
The parent of many cultivars bred for garden use, all of which are worth considering for bonsai. Flowers may be single, semi-double, or double, in shades of white, pink, and red, and appear from late winter to late spring.
◨ **Position** Full sun. Protect from frost. Protect flower buds from birds and open flowers from heavy rain.
◪ **Watering** Daily throughout growing season. Sparingly in winter, but keep moist.
◨ **Feeding** Every two weeks from the end of flowering until late summer.
◨ **Repotting** Annually in late spring before bud burst, or in late autumn. Use basic soil mix.
◪ **Pruning** Trim back after flowering. Prune tips of new shoots as they grow in summer.
◪ **Propagation** Grafting.
◪ **Styles** Suitable for all styles except broom, and for all sizes.

Prunus serrulata 'Hisakura'

FLOWERING CHERRY
Deep-pink single flowers.
Cultivation, propagation, and styles as for *P. serrulata*.

Prunus serrulata 'Kanzan'

FLOWERING CHERRY
Purple-pink double flowers.
Cultivation, propagation, and styles as for *P. serrulata*.

Prunus serrulata 'Kiku-shidare Sakura'

FLOWERING CHERRY
Pink double flowers appear before the leaves in early spring. (See also page 148.)
Cultivation, propagation, and styles as for *P. serrulata*.

Prunus serrulata 'Shirotae'

FLOWERING CHERRY
Fragrant white semi-double flowers.
Cultivation, propagation, and styles as for *P. serrulata*.

Prunus spinosa

SLOE
Deciduous tree. Also called blackthorn. Spiny branches. Small white flowers appear on bare branches in early spring. Black fruit. (See also page 147.)
◨ **Position** Full sun.
◪ **Watering** Daily throughout growing season.
◨ **Feeding** Every two weeks throughout the growing season.
◨ **Repotting** Every second year in early spring. Use basic soil mix.
◪ **Pruning** Trim back new growth to create and maintain shape.
◪ **Propagation** Seed.
◪ **Styles** Informal upright, slanting, semicascade, cascade, twin-trunk, clump, straight line, sinuous, multiple-trunk, group, saikei. Suitable for all sizes.

Prunus subhirtella 'Autumnalis'

AUTUMN CHERRY
Slender, graceful branches and twigs. Small, delicate leaves, with brilliant autumn tones. White semi-double flowers appear on bare branches at intervals from late autumn to early spring.
◨ **Position** Full sun.
◪ **Watering** Daily throughout growing season.
◨ **Feeding** Every two weeks throughout the growing season.

◨ **Repotting** Every second year in early spring. Use basic soil mix.
◪ **Pruning** Trim back new growth to create and maintain shape.
◪ **Propagation** Grafting.
◪ **Styles** Informal upright, slanting, semicascade, cascade, twin-trunk, clump, straight line, sinuous, multiple-trunk, group, saikei. Suitable for all sizes.

Prunus subhirtella 'Autumnalis rosea'

PINK AUTUMN CHERRY
Pale-pink semi-double flowers, sometimes in autumn and winter but primarily in spring.
Cultivation, propagation, and styles as for *P. subhirtella* 'Autumnalis'.

Prunus subhirtella 'Fukubana'

PINK SPRING CHERRY
Deep-pink semi-double flowers in early spring.
◨ **Position** Full sun.
◪ **Watering** Daily throughout growing season.
◨ **Feeding** Every two weeks throughout the growing season.
◨ **Repotting** Every second year in early spring. Use basic soil mix.
◪ **Pruning** Trim back new growth to create and maintain shape.
◪ **Propagation** Grafting.
◪ **Styles** Informal upright, slanting, semicascade, cascade, twin-trunk, clump, straight line, sinuous, multiple-trunk, group, saikei. Suitable for all sizes.

Prunus tenella

DWARF RUSSIAN ALMOND
Delicate branches covered with bright-pink flowers in early spring.
◨ **Position** Full sun.
◪ **Watering** Daily throughout growing season.
◨ **Feeding** Every two weeks throughout the growing season.
◨ **Repotting** Every second year in early spring. Use basic soil mix.
◪ **Pruning** Trim back new growth to create and maintain shape.
◪ **Propagation** Grafting, cuttings.
◪ **Styles** Informal upright, slanting, semicascade, cascade, twin-trunk, clump, straight line, sinuous, multiple-trunk, group, saikei. Suitable for all sizes, especially extra-small and small.

Prunus tomentosa

DOWNY CHERRY
Young growth and undersides of leaves have downy texture. Pale-pink or white flowers in early spring, red fruit.
◨ **Position** Full sun.
◪ **Watering** Daily throughout growing season.
◨ **Feeding** Every two weeks throughout the growing season.
◨ **Repotting** Every second year in early spring. Use basic soil mix.
◪ **Pruning** Trim back new growth to create and maintain shape.
◪ **Propagation** Grafting, seed.
◪ **Styles** Informal upright, slanting, semicascade, cascade, twin-trunk, clump, straight line, sinuous, multiple-trunk, group, saikei. Suitable for all sizes.

Pseudocydonia sinensis, see *Chaenomeles sinensis*

Punica granatum

POMEGRANATE

Tender deciduous tree. Shiny oblong leaves, scarlet flowers in late summer to early autumn, followed by yellow-red fruit. (See also page 149.)
⚙ **Position** Full sun. Protect from low temperatures and frost.
💧 **Watering** Daily throughout growing season. Plentifully after flowering as fruit is swelling. Keep moist in winter.
■ **Feeding** Weekly from start of growing season until flowering.
▣ **Repotting** Every second year in early spring until about 10 years old, then as necessary. Use basic soil mix.
✂ **Pruning** Trim non-flowering new shoots throughout growing season.
🌱 **Propagation** Cuttings, seed.
🌲 **Styles** Suitable for all styles except formal upright and broom, and for small through to extra-large sizes.

Punica granatum 'Nana'

DWARF POMEGRANATE

Dwarf form in every respect. Shrub size, with finer growth and smaller flowers and fruit. Cultivation, propagation, and styles as for *P. granatum*. Recommended for extra-small and small sizes.

Pyracantha angustifolia

PYRACANTHA or FIRETHORN

Evergreen shrub. Glossy dark-green oval leaves. Small white flowers in summer are followed by yellow, orange, or scarlet fruit. (See also page 150.)
⚙ **Position** Full light or partial shade. Protect from frost and freezing winds.
💧 **Watering** Daily throughout growing season. Keep moist at all times.
■ **Feeding** Weekly from early spring until flowering, then once fruit has developed every two weeks until mid autumn.
▣ **Repotting** Every second year in early spring. Use basic soil mix.
✂ **Pruning** Shorten new shoots in late spring, and prune older wood in either early spring or late summer.
🌱 **Propagation** Cuttings, air layering, layering, seed.
🌲 **Styles** Informal upright, slanting, semicascade, cascade, root-over-rock, clasped-to-rock, twin-trunk, clump. Suitable for all except extra-large sizes.

Pyracantha coccinea

SCARLET FIRETHORN

Evergreen shrub. Smallish leaves, small white flowers in early summer, bright-red fruit.
⚙ **Position** Full light or partial shade. Protect from frost and freezing winds.
💧 **Watering** Daily throughout growing season. Keep moist at all times.
■ **Feeding** Weekly from early spring until flowering, then once fruit has developed every two weeks until mid autumn.
▣ **Repotting** Every second year in early spring. Use basic soil mix.
✂ **Pruning** Shorten new shoots in late spring, and prune older wood in either early spring or late summer.
🌱 **Propagation** Cuttings, air layering, layering, seed.

🌲 **Styles** Informal upright, slanting, semicascade, cascade, root-over-rock, clasped-to-rock, twin-trunk, clump. Suitable for all except extra-large sizes.

Pyracantha coccinea 'Teton'

DWARF FIRETHORN

Compact dwarf form with yellow-orange fruit. Cultivation, propagation, and styles as for *P. coccinea*. Recommended for smallest sizes.

Quercus cerris

TURKEY OAK

Tough, fast-growing deciduous tree. Lobed, downy leaves are grey-green in spring, turning bronze in autumn.
⚙ **Position** Full sun. Protect from frost.
💧 **Watering** Keep moist.
■ **Feeding** Every two weeks throughout the summer and autumn.
▣ **Repotting** Annually until 10 years old, then every two to three years, in early spring. Use basic soil mix.
✂ **Pruning** Trim new shoots continually.
🌱 **Propagation** Seed, air layering.
🌲 **Styles** Informal upright, slanting, broom, twin-trunk, clump, straight line, sinuous, group. Medium to extra-large sizes.

Quercus palustris

PIN OAK

Deciduous tree. Elegant, slender branches. Sharp-pointed, lobed leaves are bright-green until autumn, when they turn rich scarlet.
⚙ **Position** Full sun. Protect from frost.
💧 **Watering** Keep moist.
■ **Feeding** Every two weeks throughout the summer and autumn.
▣ **Repotting** Annually until 10 years old, then every two to three years, in early spring. Use basic soil mix.
✂ **Pruning** Trim new shoots continually.
🌱 **Propagation** Seed, air layering.
🌲 **Styles** Informal upright, slanting, broom, twin-trunk, clump, straight line, sinuous, group. Medium to extra-large sizes.

Quercus petraea

SESSILE or DURMAST OAK

Closely resembles *Q. robur*, the English oak, but has longer leaves and stalks, and prefers slightly moister conditions.
⚙ **Position** Full sun. Protect from frost.
💧 **Watering** Keep moist.
■ **Feeding** Every two weeks throughout the summer and autumn.
▣ **Repotting** Annually until 10 years old, then every two to three years, in early spring. Use basic soil mix.
✂ **Pruning** Trim new shoots continually.
🌱 **Propagation** Seed, air layering.
🌲 **Styles** Informal upright, slanting, broom, twin-trunk, clump, straight line, sinuous, group. Medium to extra-large sizes.

Quercus robur

ENGLISH OAK

Deciduous tree. Slow-growing and long-lived. Lobed leaves are a bright yellow-green in spring, turning to bronze in autumn. (See also page 151.)
⚙ **Position** Full sun. Protect from frost.
💧 **Watering** Daily throughout growing season.

Sparingly in winter, but keep moist. Spray regularly against mildew.
■ **Feeding** Every two weeks throughout the summer and autumn.
▣ **Repotting** Annually until 10 years old, then every two to three years, in early spring before buds break. Use basic soil mix.
✂ **Pruning** Trim new shoots continually.
🌱 **Propagation** Seed, air layering.
🌲 **Styles** Informal upright, slanting, broom, twin-trunk, clump, straight line, sinuous, group. Medium to extra-large sizes.

Rhododendron indicum (Azalea indica)

SATSUKI AZALEA

Lime-hating evergreen shrub. Smallish, narrow, dark-green leaves. There are many hundreds of Satsuki with flowers in early summer, in shades of white through pinks and reds to purples. Different colours on the same plant are often found, as are striped, speckled or blotched forms.
⚙ **Position** Partial shade. Protect from frost, and from heavy rain when in flower.
💧 **Watering** Daily throughout growing season, and mist-spray, with lime free water. Keep the soil moist at all times.
■ **Feeding** Every two weeks from early spring until flowering, then monthly from the end of flowering through to early autumn. Use ericaceous fertilizer.
▣ **Repotting** Annually or as necessary after flowering. Use lime-free soil mix.
✂ **Pruning** Remove flowers as soon as they fade. Remove all new shoots after flowers fade. Prune secondary shoots until midsummer.
🌱 **Propagation** Cuttings, air layering.
🌲 **Styles** Suitable for all styles except broom, and for all sizes.

Rhododendron indicum 'Chinzan'

SATSUKI 'CHINZAN'

Small, narrow glossy leaves, and small deep-pink flowers with red throats. Cultivation, propagation, and styles as for *R. indicum*.

Rhododendron indicum 'Hakurei'

SATSUKI 'HAKUREI'

Small, glossy dark-green leaves with a narrow, pointed shape. Creamy white flowers. (See also page 153.) Cultivation, propagation, and styles as for *R. indicum*.

Rhododendron indicum 'Kaho'

SATSUKI 'KAHO'

Large trumpet-type flowers in pale, soft shades of pink. (See also page 152.) Cultivation, propagation, and styles as for *R. indicum*.

Rhododendron indicum 'Kazan'

SATSUKI 'KAZAN'

Small-leaved form with a compact habit. Small red flowers. Cultivation, propagation, and styles as for *R. indicum*.

Rhododendron indicum 'Kinsai'

SATSUKI 'KINSAI'

Small narrow leaves, deeply cut red flowers. Cultivation, propagation, and styles as for *R. indicum*.

Rhododendron indicum 'Korin'

SATSUKI 'KORIN'

Compact form with small pink flowers. Cultivation, propagation, and styles as for *R. indicum*.

Rhododendron kiusianum

KURUME AZALEA

Dwarf evergreen or semi-evergreen form. Also called Kirishima azalea. Flowers in shades of pink, red, and purple.
Position Partial shade. Protect from frost, and from heavy rain when in flower.
Watering Daily throughout growing season, and mist-spray, with lime free water. Keep the soil moist at all times.
Feeding Every two weeks from early spring until flowering, then monthly from the end of flowering through to early autumn. Use ericaceous fertilizer.
Repotting Annually or as necessary after flowering. Use lime-free soil mix.
Pruning Remove flowers as soon as they fade. Remove all new shoots after flowers fade. Prune secondary shoots until midsummer.
Propagation Cuttings, air layering.
Styles Suitable for all styles except broom, and for all sizes.

Rhododendron obtusum

JAPANESE KURUME AZALEA

Evergreen or semi-evergreen. Small shiny leaves, red flowers. (See also page 153.)
Position Partial shade. Protect from frost, and from heavy rain when in flower.
Watering Daily throughout growing season, and mist-spray, with lime free water. Keep the soil moist at all times.
Feeding Every two weeks from early spring until flowering, then monthly from the end of flowering through to early autumn. Use ericaceous fertilizer.
Repotting Annually or as necessary after flowering. Use lime-free soil mix.
Pruning Remove flowers as soon as they fade. Remove all new shoots after flowers fade. Prune secondary shoots until midsummer.
Propagation Cuttings, air layering.
Styles Suitable for all styles except broom, and for all sizes.

Ribes sanguineum

FLOWERING CURRANT

Deciduous flowering shrub. Small, lobed leaves have a characteristic pungent smell. Racemes of pink flowers in early spring.
Position Full sun or shade.
Watering Daily throughout growing season.
Feeding Every two weeks throughout summer.
Repotting Every second year in early spring. Use basic soil mix.
Pruning Cut back hard after flowering, then shorten subsequent shoots as they grow.
Propagation Cuttings, layering.
Styles Informal upright, slanting, semicascade, cascade. Suitable for extra-small to medium sizes.

Robinia pseudoacacia

FALSE ACACIA

Deciduous tree. Pinnate leaves, white pea-type flowers in early summer, rough bark.

Position Full sun.
Watering Daily throughout growing season.
Feeding Every two weeks throughout the growing season.
Repotting Every second year in spring. Use basic soil mix.
Pruning Trim back new growth continually throughout growing season to create and maintain shape.
Propagation Seed, cuttings, layering.
Styles Informal upright, slanting, semicascade, cascade, twin-trunk, clump, multiple trunk, group. All sizes.

Sageretia theezans

SAGERETIA

Tender evergreen shrub. Small oval leaves on slender branches. White flowers in summer, followed by blue fruit. Rough bark scales off in patches. (See also page 154.)
Position Full sun, slight shade in summer. Minimum temperature in summer 18°C (65°F), in winter 12°C (54°F). Needs high humidity.
Watering Daily throughout summer. Keep soil moist in winter.
Feeding Every two weeks throughout summer, monthly in winter.
Repotting Every second year in spring. Use basic soil mix.
Pruning Trim new shoots at any time during growing season.
Propagation Cuttings.
Styles Suitable for all styles and sizes.

Salix babylonica

WEEPING WILLOW

Deciduous tree. Long, narrow leaves on slender, flexible, hanging branches. (See also page 155.)
Position Full sun, slight shade in summer. Protect from severe frost.
Watering Daily throughout growing season, more often in hot weather. Stand in shallow water in midsummer. Keep moist in winter.
Feeding Every two weeks from early spring through to late summer.
Repotting Twice annually, in early spring and again in midsummer. Use basic soil mix.
Pruning Trim previous year's growth in early spring after repotting.
Propagation Cuttings.
Styles Informal upright, slanting, semicascade, cascade, root-over-rock, twin-trunk, saikei. Medium to extra-large sizes.

Salix helvetica

SWISS WILLOW

Bushy shrub with small, downy grey-green leaves. Yellow catkins in early spring.
Position Full sun, slight shade in summer. Protect from severe frost.
Watering Daily throughout growing season, more often in hot weather. Stand in shallow water in midsummer. Keep moist in winter.
Feeding Every two weeks from early spring through to late summer.
Repotting Twice annually, in early spring and again in midsummer. Use basic soil mix.
Pruning Trim previous year's growth in early spring after repotting.
Propagation Cuttings.
Styles Informal upright, slanting, semicascade, cascade, root-over-rock, twin-trunk, saikei. Extra-small to medium sizes.

Sasa veitchii

DWARF VARIEGATED BAMBOO

Evergreen grass. Narrow leaves on purple-green canes, become variegated in autumn and winter. Not suitable for cultivation as a bonsai, but commonly used as an accent plant.
Position Slight shade.
Watering Water plentifully.
Feeding Weekly throughout summer.
Repotting Annually in late spring. Use free-draining soil mix.
Pruning Remove central shoot to control height, cut down stems to ground level in early summer.
Propagation Division.
Styles Use as an accent plant only.

Schefflera actinophylla

UMBRELLA TREE

Tender evergreen tree grown as a houseplant in temperate climates. Light-grey trunk with a tendency to produce aerial roots. Shiny, bright-green leaves on long stalks.
Position Bright light. Warm location, minimum temperature 16°C (60°F).
Watering Twice weekly throughout summer. Every two weeks in winter.
Feeding Monthly throughout summer.
Repotting Every second year in spring. Use free-draining soil mix.
Pruning Prune top shoots back hard in order to encourage branching.
Propagation Cuttings.
Styles Informal upright, clasped-to-rock, twin-trunk, clump, multiple-trunk, group, saikei. Suitable for small and medium sizes.

Sequoia sempervirens

CALIFORNIAN REDWOOD

Evergreen conifer. Conical habit. Spongy red-brown bark. Flattened, needle-like leaves. The world's tallest tree, standing 115 metres (376 feet), is a Californian redwood.
Position Full sun.
Watering Daily throughout growing season.
Feeding Every two weeks throughout the growing season.
Repotting Every three to four years in early spring. Use basic soil mix.
Pruning Shorten new shoots as they grow to create and maintain shape.
Propagation Seed, cuttings.
Styles Formal upright, informal upright, slanting, twin-trunk, clump, multiple trunk, group. Small to extra-large sizes.

Sequoiadendron giganteum

WELLINGTONIA

Evergreen conifer. Conical habit, drooping branches. Bright-green scale-like foliage, thick spongy bark. (See also page 156.)
Position Full sun, partial shade in summer. Protect from frost and freezing winds.
Watering Daily during growing season, and mist-spray in summer. Sparingly in winter.
Feeding Every two weeks from spring through to autumn.
Repotting Every second year in early spring. Use basic soil mix.
Pruning Pinch out new growth continually.
Propagation Cuttings, seed.
Styles Formal upright, twin-trunk, group. Suitable for medium to extra-large sizes.

Serissa foetida

TREE OF A THOUSAND STARS

Evergreen shrub. Small oval leaves, masses of small white flowers appear in summer. Bark and roots have an unpleasant smell. (See also page 157.)
☼ **Position** Full sun. Warm location, minimum temperature 12°C (54°F).
💧 **Watering** Daily throughout growing season, and mist-spray except when in flower to maintain high humidity. Keep soil relatively dry in winter.
▤ **Feeding** Every two weeks throughout the growing season, monthly in winter.
▦ **Repotting** Every second year in early spring. Use basic soil mix.
✂ **Pruning** Trim new shoots after repotting.
✍ **Propagation** Cuttings.
⚘ **Styles** Suitable for all styles except formal upright and broom, and for extra-small to medium sizes.

Sophora japonica

JAPANESE PAGODA TREE

Deciduous tree. Pinnate leaves, white pea-type flowers in late summer on older trees.
☼ **Position** Full sun.
💧 **Watering** Daily throughout growing season.
▤ **Feeding** Every two weeks throughout the growing season.
▦ **Repotting** Every second year in early spring. Use basic soil mix.
✂ **Pruning** Trim new growth continually to create and maintain shape.
✍ **Propagation** Seed, cuttings, grafting.
⚘ **Styles** Informal upright, slanting, semicascade, cascade, twin-trunk, clump, multiple-trunk, group. All sizes.

Sorbus aucuparia

ROWAN or MOUNTAIN ASH

Deciduous tree. Pinnate leaves turn gold and orange in autumn. White flowers in spring, clusters of bright-red fruit in autumn. (See also page 158.)
☼ **Position** Full sun.
💧 **Watering** Daily throughout growing season. Sparingly in winter, but keep moist.
▤ **Feeding** Every two weeks throughout the growing season.
▦ **Repotting** Annually or every second year in spring before bud burst. Use basic soil mix.
✂ **Pruning** Trim new shoots continually to create and maintain shape.
✍ **Propagation** Seed, grafting for cultivars.
⚘ **Styles** Suitable for all styles except formal upright and broom, and for all sizes.

Sorbus cashmiriana

CASHMIRIANA MOUNTAIN ASH

Deciduous tree. Dark-green pinnate leaves, white flowers and fruit.
☼ **Position** Full sun.
💧 **Watering** Daily throughout growing season. Sparingly in winter, but keep moist.
▤ **Feeding** Every two weeks throughout the growing season.
▦ **Repotting** Annually or every second year in early spring. Use basic soil mix.
✂ **Pruning** Trim new shoots continually to create and maintain shape.
✍ **Propagation** Seed. Grafting for cultivars.
⚘ **Styles** Suitable for all styles except formal upright and broom, and for all sizes.

Sorbus commixta

KOREAN MOUNTAIN ASH

Deciduous tree. Copper-coloured young growth. Brilliant autumn foliage, small red fruit.
☼ **Position** Full sun.
💧 **Watering** Daily throughout growing season. Sparingly in winter, but keep moist.
▤ **Feeding** Every two weeks throughout the growing season.
▦ **Repotting** Annually or every second year in early spring. Use basic soil mix.
✂ **Pruning** Trim new shoots continually to create and maintain shape.
✍ **Propagation** Seed. Grafting for cultivars.
⚘ **Styles** Suitable for all styles except formal upright and broom, and for all sizes.

Sorbus 'Joseph Rock'

JOSEPH ROCK MOUNTAIN ASH

Deciduous tree. Orange, copper and purple autumn foliage. White flowers, yellow fruit.
☼ **Position** Full sun.
💧 **Watering** Daily throughout growing season. Sparingly in winter, but keep moist.
▤ **Feeding** Every two weeks in growing season.
▦ **Repotting** Annually or every second year in early spring. Use basic soil mix.
✂ **Pruning** Trim new shoots continually to create and maintain shape.
✍ **Propagation** Grafting.
⚘ **Styles** Suitable for all styles except formal upright and broom, and for all sizes.

Spiraea japonica

JAPANESE SPIRAEA

Deciduous shrub. Small, toothed oval leaves, flat heads of pink flowers from midsummer on.
☼ **Position** Full sun.
💧 **Watering** Daily throughout growing season.
▤ **Feeding** Every two weeks throughout the growing season.
▦ **Repotting** Every second year in spring. Use basic soil mix.
✂ **Pruning** Trim back new growth hard after flowering and again throughout summer.
✍ **Propagation** Cuttings.
⚘ **Styles** Informal upright, slanting, semicascade, cascade, clump, saikei. Suitable for extra-small to medium sizes.

Spiraea thunbergii

SPIRAEA

Early-flowering deciduous shrub. Narrow, toothed leaves. Small white flowers in spring.
☼ **Position** Full sun.
💧 **Watering** Daily throughout growing season.
▤ **Feeding** Every two weeks throughout the growing season.
▦ **Repotting** Every second year in spring. Use basic soil mix.
✂ **Pruning** Trim back new growth hard after flowering, and again throughout summer.
✍ **Propagation** Cuttings.
⚘ **Styles** Informal upright, slanting, semicascade, cascade, clump, saikei. Suitable for extra-small to medium sizes.

Stewartia grandiflora, see *Stewartia pseudocamellia*

Stewartia monodelpha

STEWARTIA

Lime-hating deciduous dwarf shrub or small tree. Oval leaves turn brilliant scarlet and purple in autumn. White flowers in summer. Shiny copper bark. (See also page 159.)
☼ **Position** Full sun, partial shade in summer. Protect from frost.
💧 **Watering** Daily throughout growing season with lime-free water. Do not allow the soil to dry out at any time.
▤ **Feeding** Every two weeks throughout the growing season with ericaceous fertilizer.
▦ **Repotting** Every second year in early spring. Use lime-free soil mix.
✂ **Pruning** Trim new growth continually to create and maintain shape.
✍ **Propagation** Cuttings, seed.
⚘ **Styles** Formal upright, group. Suitable for small to medium sizes.

Stewartia pseudocamellia (S. grandiflora)

STEWARTIA

Lime-hating deciduous shrub or small tree. White flowers in summer, good red-yellow autumn foliage, flaking bark.
☼ **Position** Full sun, partial shade in summer. Protect from frost.
💧 **Watering** Daily throughout growing season with lime-free water. Do not allow the soil to dry out at any time.
▤ **Feeding** Every two weeks throughout the growing season with ericaceous fertilizer.
▦ **Repotting** Every second year in early spring. Use lime-free soil mix.
✂ **Pruning** Trim new growth continually to create and maintain shape.
✍ **Propagation** Cuttings, seed.
⚘ **Styles** Formal upright, group. Suitable for small to medium sizes.

Styrax japonica

SNOWBELL

Lime-hating deciduous shrub or small tree. Oval leaves carried on fan-shaped branches. White bell-like flowers in early summer.
☼ **Position** Full sun.
💧 **Watering** Daily throughout growing season.
▤ **Feeding** Every two weeks throughout the growing season with ericaceous fertilizer.
▦ **Repotting** Every second year in early spring. Use lime-free soil mix.
✂ **Pruning** Trim continually throughout summer to create and maintain shape.
✍ **Propagation** Cuttings, layering, seed.
⚘ **Styles** Informal upright, slanting, root-over-rock, twin-trunk, clump. All sizes.

Syringa velutina

KOREAN LILAC

Deciduous shrub. Oval leaves, strongly scented lilac-pink flowers in mid spring.
☼ **Position** Full sun.
💧 **Watering** Daily throughout growing season.
▤ **Feeding** Every two weeks throughout the growing season.
▦ **Repotting** Every second year in spring. Use basic soil mix.
✂ **Pruning** Trim new growth after flowers fade and again as necessary throughout summer.
✍ **Propagation** Cuttings, division, layering.
⚘ **Styles** Informal upright, slanting, semicascade, cascade, root-over-rock, clasped-to-rock, twin-trunk, multiple-trunk, group, saikei. Extra-small to medium sizes.

Tamarix juniperina

TAMARISK

Deciduous shrub or small tree. Scale-like foliage, purplish or brownish pink flowers in spring and summer. (See also page 160.)
☼ **Position** Full sun, slight shade in summer. Protect from severe frost.
💧 **Watering** Water plentifully, keep soil moist at all times.
▪ **Feeding** Every two weeks throughout the growing season.
▪ **Repotting** Annually or every second year in mid spring. Use free-draining soil mix.
✂ **Pruning** Cut back hard in autumn.
✲ **Propagation** Cuttings, layering.
☰ **Styles** Informal upright, slanting, semicascade, cascade, root-over-rock, clasped-to-rock, twin-trunk, clump. Suitable for small to large sizes.

Taxodium distichum

SWAMP CYPRESS

Deciduous conifer. Light-green needle-like leaves, orange autumn colour, red-brown bark.
☼ **Position** Full sun, slight shade in summer.
💧 **Watering** Daily throughout growing season. Stand in shallow water in summer, keep moist in winter.
▪ **Feeding** Every two weeks throughout the growing season.
▪ **Repotting** Every second year in late spring. Use free-draining soil mix.
✂ **Pruning** Finger pinch new shoots throughout growing season.
✲ **Propagation** Seed, cuttings, layering.
☰ **Styles** Formal upright, informal upright, slanting, root-over-rock, clasped-to-rock, twin-trunk, clump, multiple-trunk, group. Suitable for all sizes.

Taxus baccata

ENGLISH YEW

Evergreen tree. Dark-green needle-like leaves, bright pinkish-red fruit on female trees. (See also page 161.)
☼ **Position** Partial shade.
💧 **Watering** Daily throughout growing season, and mist-spray. Sparingly in winter, but keep soil moist.
▪ **Feeding** Twice a month throughout the growing season.
▪ **Repotting** Every three or four years in spring. Use free-draining soil mix.
✂ **Pruning** Finger pinch new shoots throughout growing season; wait until after flowering if fruit is required.
✲ **Propagation** Cuttings, layering, air layering.
☰ **Styles** Suitable for all styles except broom, and for all sizes.

Taxus cuspidata

JAPANESE YEW

Evergreen tree. Very similar to *T. baccata*, the English yew. Leaves are a brighter green, with paler undersides. Female trees bear deep-pink fruit with distinctive protruding seed. (See also page 162.)
☼ **Position** Partial shade.
💧 **Watering** Daily throughout growing season, and mist-spray. Reduce watering in winter, but keep soil moist.
▪ **Feeding** Twice a month during growing season.

▪ **Repotting** Every three or four years in spring. Use free-draining soil mix.
✂ **Pruning** Finger pinch new shoots throughout growing season; wait until after flowering if fruit is required.
✲ **Propagation** Cuttings, layering, air layering.
☰ **Styles** Suitable for all styles except broom, and for all sizes.

Taxus cuspidata 'Nana'

DWARF JAPANESE YEW

Dwarf form with dense foliage. Cultivation, propagation, and styles as for *T. cuspidata*. Extra-small and small sizes.

Thymus serpyllum

THYME

Dwarf evergreen shrub with small, aromatic leaves and mauve, pink or white flowers.
☼ **Position** Full sun.
💧 **Watering** Daily throughout growing season.
▪ **Feeding** Every two weeks throughout the growing season.
▪ **Repotting** Every second year at any time. Use basic soil mix.
✂ **Pruning** Clip to shape.
✲ **Propagation** Cuttings.
☰ **Styles** Suitable for all styles as extra-small. Otherwise used as an accent or accessory plant, particularly on rocks, for saikei, and as ground cover for groups.

Tilia cordata

SMALL-LEAVED LIME

Deciduous tree. Lime-green heart-shaped leaves. Smooth grey trunk. Scented cream flowers in summer.
☼ **Position** Full sun or shade.
💧 **Watering** Daily throughout growing season.
▪ **Feeding** Every two weeks throughout the growing season.
▪ **Repotting** Every second year in early spring. Use basic soil mix.
✂ **Pruning** Constantly trim back new shoots to create and maintain shape.
✲ **Propagation** Seed, cuttings.
☰ **Styles** Suitable for all styles except literati, and for all sizes.

Tsuga canadensis

EASTERN HEMLOCK

Evergreen conifer. Graceful, with needle-like leaves. Similar to *T. heterophylla*, but in nature usually grows with two or more trunks.
☼ **Position** Partial shade. Protect from freezing winter winds.
💧 **Watering** Daily throughout growing season, and mist-spray in summer. Keep moist during the winter months.
▪ **Feeding** Twice a month during growing season.
▪ **Repotting** Every second year in spring. Use free-draining soil mix.
✂ **Pruning** Finger pinch new shoots throughout growing season.
✲ **Propagation** Seed, cuttings. Grafting for named cultivars.
☰ **Styles** Suitable for all styles except broom, and for small to extra-large sizes.

Tsuga canadensis 'Nana'

DWARF HEMLOCK

Delicate, compact dwarf form. Cultivation as *T. canadensis.*

✲ **Propagation** Grafting.
☰ **Styles** as *T. canadensis*. Suitable for small and medium sizes.

Tsuga canadensis 'Pendula'

DWARF HEMLOCK

Weeping dwarf form. Slender, arching growth. Bright green new growth shows against deeper green of older foliage.
Cultivation as *T. canadensis.*
✲ **Propagation** Cuttings, grafting.
☰ **Styles** as *T. canadensis*. Suitable for small and medium sizes.

Tsuga heterophylla

WESTERN HEMLOCK

Evergreen conifer. Delicate, graceful habit of growth. Short, glossy needle-like leaves, light-green when young, becoming darker. (See also page 163.)
☼ **Position** Partial shade. Protect from freezing winds.
💧 **Watering** Daily throughout growing season, and mist-spray in summer. Keep moist during the winter months.
▪ **Feeding** Twice a month during growing season.
▪ **Repotting** Every second year in spring until about 10 years old, then as necessary. Use free-draining soil mix.
✂ **Pruning** Finger pinch new shoots just before they harden throughout growing season.
✲ **Propagation** Seed, cuttings.
☰ **Styles** Suitable for all styles except broom, and for small to extra-large sizes.

Ulmus × elegantissima 'Jacqueline Hillier'

JACQUELINE HILLIER ELM

Deciduous tree with neat, dense habit. Small, toothed leaves.
☼ **Position** Full sun. Protect from frost.
💧 **Watering** Daily throughout growing season, more frequently if necessary in very hot weather. Keep moist in winter.
▪ **Feeding** Weekly for the first month after leaf buds open, and then every two weeks until the late summer.
▪ **Repotting** Annually in early spring. Use free-draining soil mix.
✂ **Pruning** Trim new shoots throughout the growing season.
✲ **Propagation** Cuttings, grafting.
☰ **Styles** Suitable for all styles and sizes.

Ulmus glabra

WYCH or SCOTCH ELM

Deciduous tree. Dull-green leaves turn yellow in autumn. Grey-brown bark.
☼ **Position** Full sun. Protect from frost.
💧 **Watering** Daily throughout growing season, more frequently if necessary in very hot weather. Keep moist in winter.
▪ **Feeding** Weekly for first month after leaf buds open, then every two weeks until the late summer.
▪ **Repotting** Annually in early spring. Use free-draining soil mix.
✂ **Pruning** Trim new shoots throughout the growing season.
✲ **Propagation** Seed, cuttings, root cuttings.
☰ **Styles** Suitable for all styles and sizes.

Ulmus parvifolia

CHINESE ELM

Deciduous tree. Small, serrated, bright-green leaves which last into winter, long flexible roots. The best elm for bonsai cultivation. (See also page 164.)

Position Full light and sun. Protect roots from frost in winter.

Watering Daily throughout growing season, more frequently if necessary in very hot weather. More sparingly in winter, but keep moist at all times.

Feeding Weekly for first month after leaf buds open, then every two weeks until the late summer.

Repotting Annually in early spring until about 10 years old, then as necessary. Use free-draining soil mix.

Pruning Trim back new shoots in spring.

Propagation Cuttings, root cuttings.

Styles Suitable for all styles and sizes.

Ulmus parvifolia 'Hokkaido'

HOKKAIDO ELM

Tiny bright-green leaves on delicate twigs. Cultivation as *U. parvifolia*.

Propagation Cuttings.

Styles As *U. parvifolia*, suitable for extra-small to medium sizes.

Ulmus parvifolia variegata

VARIEGATED CHINESE ELM

Green and creamy white variegated form. Cultivation, propagation, and styles as for *U. parvifolia*.

Ulmus procera

ENGLISH ELM

Deciduous tree. Dark-green leaves, bright-yellow autumn colour, fissured grey-brown bark. (See also page 165.)

Position Full light and sun. Protect smaller sizes from frost.

Watering Daily throughout growing season, more frequently if necessary in very hot weather. Keep moist in winter.

Feeding Weekly for first month after leaf buds open, then every two weeks until the late summer.

Repotting Annually in early spring until about 10 years old, then as necessary. Use free-draining soil mix.

Pruning Trim new shoots throughout the growing season. Leaf-cut in midsummer.

Propagation Cuttings, root cuttings, suckers.

Styles Suitable for all styles and sizes.

Vitis vinifera

GRAPE VINE

Deciduous climber. Dark-green lobed leaves, green or purple edible fruit in autumn.

Position Full sun.

Watering Daily throughout growing season.

Feeding Every two weeks throughout summer.

Repotting Every second year in early spring. Use basic soil mix.

Pruning Trim new shoots throughout the growing season.

Propagation Cuttings, grafting, layering.

Styles Informal upright, slanting, semicascade, cascade, root-over-rock. Suitable for all sizes.

Weigela florida

WEIGELA

Deciduous shrub. Oval leaves, trumpet-shaped rose-pink flowers in early summer.

Position Slight shade.

Watering Daily throughout growing season.

Feeding Every two weeks in growing season.

Repotting Every second year in early spring. Use basic soil mix.

Pruning Trim shoots after flowers fade, and shorten new shoots back as they appear throughout the summer.

Propagation Cuttings, layering.

Styles Informal upright, slanting, semicascade, cascade, twin-trunk, clump, group. Suitable for medium and large sizes.

Wisteria floribunda

JAPANESE WISTERIA

Deciduous climber. Bright-green pinnate leaves, long racemes of scented bluish purple flowers in late spring. (See also page 166.)

Position Full sun. Protect from frost.

Watering Daily throughout growing season. Stand in shallow water in hot weather. Keep moist in winter.

Feeding Weekly from end of flowering to midsummer and from early to late autumn.

Repotting Every three years as soon as flowering is finished. Use basic soil mix.

Pruning Trim new shoots in spring after flowers fade and again in early summer, midsummer, and autumn.

Propagation Grafting, cuttings, layering, air layering.

Styles Informal upright, slanting, semicascade, cascade, root-over-rock. Suitable for medium to extra-large sizes.

Wisteria sinensis

CHINESE WISTERIA

Very vigorous deciduous climber. Similar to *W. floribunda*, with shorter flowering racemes, and more strongly scented flowers.

Position Full sun. Protect from frost.

Watering Daily throughout growing season. Stand in shallow water in hot weather. Keep moist in winter.

Feeding Weekly from end of flowering to midsummer and from early to late autumn.

Repotting Every three years as soon as flowering is over. Use basic soil mix.

Pruning Trim new shoots in spring after flowers fade and again in early summer, midsummer, and autumn.

Propagation Grafting, cuttings, layering, air layering.

Styles Informal upright, slanting, semicascade, cascade, root-over-rock. Suitable for medium to extra-large sizes.

Zelkova serrata

JAPANESE ELM

Deciduous tree. Serrated oval leaves turn yellow, red and bronze in autumn. Smooth grey bark. (See also page 167.)

Position Full sun, slight shade in summer. Protect from frost to avoid twig die-back.

Watering Daily throughout summer. Keep moist at other times.

Feeding Weekly for the first month after leaf buds open, and then every two weeks through the summer.

Repotting Annually in early spring until about 10 years old, then as necessary. Use basic soil mix.

Pruning Trim new shoots. Remove large leaves throughout the growing season.

Propagation Seed, cuttings, air layering.

Styles Suitable for all styles except literati, and especially for broom and group. Suitable for all sizes.

Zelkova serrata variegata

VARIEGATED JAPANESE GREY-BARKED ELM

Green and creamy white variegated form. Cultivation, propagation, and styles as for *Z. serrata*.

Zelkova serrata 'Yatsubusa'

DWARF ZELKOVA

Compact form with leaves approximately a quarter the size of those on the species Cultivation as *Z. serrata*.

Propagation Cuttings.

Styles As *Z. serrata*.

Zelkova serrata 'Yatsubusa variegata'

VARIEGATED DWARF ZELKOVA

Green and creamy white variegated form. Cultivation as *Z. serrata*.

Propagation Cuttings.

Styles As *Z. serrata*.

GLOSSARY

Accent plant A separate planting, often seasonal, of small herbaceous plants, bulbs or grasses, displayed in conjunction with bonsai when on formal display.

Accessory plant or **planting** This term covers the same meaning as accent plant, but can also refer to additional plants within the confines of the bonsai pot as underplanting for the tree or trees, particularly in larger groups and saikei plantings.

Adult foliage The mature leaves of a tree that has one type of young foliage and a distinctly different leaf shape in maturity.

Air layering A propagation method in which conditions are created that encourage roots to form on the trunk or branch of a tree.

Apex In general terms, the top or summit of an object or shape. In bonsai, the term commonly refers to the top portion of the tree and horticulturally it can also mean the tip of a shoot or branch.

Aspect A position facing in a particular direction; for plants, particularly relating to factors such as the direction of sunlight and prevailing winds.

Broad-leaved The description of trees and shrubs that have flat, relatively broad leaves, as compared to needle-shaped or scale-like foliage.

Bud break The stage when a leaf bud has opened just enough to show a green tip. This is followed by bud burst, when the leaves begin to unfurl and separate.

Callus Corky-textured tissue that forms over a wound on a trunk or branch, for example, where a branch or twig has been pruned out.

Cambium A narrow continuous layer of cell tissue growing between the bark and wood of woody plants. In live wood, the cambium layer is green and moist.

Collected tree A naturally dwarfed tree taken from the wild for training as bonsai.

Compound leaf A leaf composed of two or more separate but similar parts, called leaflets.

Conifer A tree that bears cones containing the tree seeds. Most conifers are evergreen trees. Examples commonly grown as bonsai are cedars, junipers, pines and spruces.

Cross A hybrid plant, the result of deliberate cross-fertilization between species or varieties.

Crown The upper part of a tree where the branches spread out from the trunk.

Cultivar A variant plant produced in cultivation. Named cultivars are identified by the name of the parent species followed by the cultivar name in single quotation marks: for example, *Acer palmatum* 'Deshojo'.

Cut-leaved The description of a tree or shrub with leaves shaped in distinct segments.

Deciduous The description of a tree or shrub that loses its leaves annually, usually remaining bare-stemmed over winter and developing new foliage in spring.

Die-back The death of young shoots or branch tips, due to extreme weather conditions or any of several fungus diseases.

Divided leaf A leaf formed of separate sections emerging from a common base.

Division A method of propagating shrubby plants by dividing the rootball and replanting the separated sections.

Dwarf The description of a variety or cultivar that is smaller than the species plant, though it has the same basic characteristics. Dwarfing may also occur in species through natural causes; dwarf cultivars are bred to be small.

Ericaceous A term referring to plants of the family *Ericaceae*, generally indicating lime-hating plants that must be given lime-free soils and fertilizers.

Evergreen The description of a tree or shrub that retains leaves throughout the year.

Fruit The part of a plant that carries the seed; the term generally includes fleshy fruits and berries, pod-like seed cases and nuts.

Genus The unit of classification for a group of closely related plants. In a plant's botanical name, the genus is identified by the first word in the full name: for example, *Acer*.

Germination The point when a seed starts into growth, subsequently developing roots and shoots.

Habit The characteristic growth pattern of a plant: for example, a tree may have an upright, branching or prostrate habit.

Hardy A term applied to plants capable of withstanding winter frost. Hardiness is relative to local climate and the degrees of frost to which the plant may be exposed.

Hermaphrodite The description of a plant that has both male and female reproductive organs and is therefore self-fertilizing.

Humidity The degree of moisture in the atmosphere.

Internodal distance The length of a portion of stem between two nodes, or leaf joints.

Juvenile foliage The young leaves of a tree that produces one type of foliage in new or young growth and mature leaves of a distinctly different shape.

Larva A mobile wingless grub that is the second stage in the lifecycle of an insect.

Leader Generally, the main shoot at the tip of a branch that extends the branch growth. In bonsai, this term usually indicates the uppermost continuation of the trunk.

Lifting The process of taking a plant out of the ground; that is, digging it up with its entire rootball.

Loam A soil consisting of a balanced mixture of clay, sand and decomposed organic matter. Typically, it has a loose, workable texture.

Mist-spraying The practice of providing humid conditions for a plant using a mechanical sprayer that emits water as a spray of very fine particles.

Needle A type of leaf that is narrow and relatively hard-textured.

New wood A twig, branch or stem originating in the current season's growth.

Nitrogen One of the essential elements of plant nutrition, identified by the chemical symbol N. It promotes above-ground growth, particularly the green tissue in stems and leaves.

Node The points on a twig or branch where leaf buds and leaves appear. A node may also be the source of a new shoot.

NPK The chemical symbols for nitrogen (N), phosphorus (P) and potassium (K), an abbreviation that may be used in denoting the relative proportions of these elements as ingredients of a fertilizer.

Nursery bed Prepared ground in which seedlings or young plants are grown until they reach a stage when they can be lifted for bonsai use or other purposes.

Old wood A twig, branch or stem that originated in the previous growing season or earlier.

Ornamental tree A general term referring to a tree bred or grown for the beauty of its foliage and flowers, rather than for functional reasons.

Peat Partly decomposed organic matter, originating from the natural decomposition of vegetation in bogs, marshes or heathland. As an ingredient of a potting soil, peat assists moisture retention.

Perlite A substance used to provide ventilation and moisture retention in a potting soil or other growing medium. It is a form of volcanic rock heat-treated to create coarse, lightweight granules.

Phosphorus One of the essential elements of plant nutrition, identified by the chemical symbol P. It encourages root development and also ripening of fruits and seeds.

Pinching out or **back** A technique used in growing or shaping a tree that consists of pulling off soft new shoots with finger and thumb.

Potassium One of the essential elements of plant nutrition, identified by the chemical symbol K. It encourages strong new growth, development of flower buds and fruit formation. In plant cultivation, the term potash is commonly used for this element, meaning a substance containing potassium; for example, as an ingredient of a fertilizer.

Pot-bound The condition of a pot-grown plant when the root growth has filled the pot to the extent of eliminating all air spaces.

Prostrate The habit of a plant that tends to grow along the ground rather than upright.

Pruning The practice of cutting or pinching back the shoots, leaves and stems of a tree or shrub to control the growth rate and shape the plant.

Raceme An elongated flowerhead composed of individual flower stalks growing from a central stem.

Reflexed Bent downwards and backwards, a description that may be used of some types of foliage or flower petals.

Repotting The practice of taking a pot-grown plant out of its pot at regular intervals and replanting to refresh the soil and encourage renewed root growth.

Rootball The mass of roots and soil seen when a plant is taken out of its pot or lifted from the ground.

Root pruning The practice of cutting back the roots of a pot-grown plant to make room in the container for fresh soil and encourage new root growth.

Rootstock The root system and main stem used as the basis of a new plant in propagation by grafting.

Scion A woody stem or small section of a tree or shrub used to propagate a new plant by grafting on a rootstock. The scion holds the characteristics of the new plant; the rootstock enables it to grow strongly.

Scorching Damage caused to foliage by the action of strong sun or wind. Also, damage to roots that can be caused by an overdose of fertilizer.

Species The unit of classification for a plant having particular characteristics. In the botanical name of the plant, the species is identified by the second word of the name: for example, *Acer palmatum*.

Sphagnum moss A type of moss native to damp locations such as bogs and marshes. It is highly water-absorbent and has various uses in plant cultivation, particularly in air layering, or as a binding for large wounds to keep them moist.

Standard A tree or shrub grown or trained with a single stem up to 1.8m (6ft) below the branching head.

Stock See **Rootstock**

Stratification The process of preparing tree seed for sowing by dispersing the seeds in sand and subjecting them to cold conditions, outdoors or artificially in a freezer or refrigerator. This encourages germination.

Succulent The description of a plant that has fleshy stems or leaves capable of retaining relatively large amounts of moisture.

Sub-species A unit of plant classification denoting a wild or naturally occuring variant of a species.

Suckering The growth of a plant that produces new shoots at the base or below ground travelling out from the plant base.

Synonym An alternative botanical name for a plant, usually an old or invalid classification.

Systemic The description of an insecticide or fungicide that acts by entering the sap of the plant and counter-attacking infestation or disease from within over a period of time.

Tap root A long root that anchors a plant by growing vertically downward. The term is often used in referring to the first undivided root of a seedling.

Tender The description of a plant that cannot withstand frost and is likely to die if kept outdoors in cold conditions. Tenderness is relative to the local climate in which the plant is grown.

Topiary The practice of pruning full-size trees or shrubs into ornamental shapes.

Tufa rock A type of easily worked limestone useful for work plantings because it is very porous and retains moisture.

Variety A naturally occurring variant of a species.

Viability The ability of a seed to germinate.

Winter kill The death of a plant due to frost or freezing winds.

Woody The description of a plant stem that has hardened and will not die off in winter conditions or during the plant's dormancy.

Wound sealant A compound formulated to seal a cut in a branch or trunk, preventing sap bleeding and moisture loss, and to promote healing.

Yatsubusa A particular type of dwarf form. Internodal distances are shorter than commonly found on a dwarf, and nodes have more buds than usual, resulting in denser growth.

INDEX

Page numbers in *italics* refer to illustrations

ACKNOWLEDGMENTS

Author's acknowledgments I would like to thank four people without whom this book would not have materialised. First of all my wife Christine whose encouragement, and help with the nursery, enabled me to devote time to this project. Secondly, Nigel Osborne and Judy Martin for their professional help but also for the nagging that enabled deadlines to be met, and finally Paul Goff whose bonsai and photographic expertise resulted in the sparkling photographs throughout this book. Thanks also to the following people who helped in so many ways; Mark Abbott; Dan Barton; Martin Bradder; Petra Engelke; Reiner Goebel; Hoka-en; Bill Jordan; Dorothy Koreshoff; Mike Limb; Mike Lorimer; Geoff Owen; Roy Payne; Marcel Sallin; Roy Stenson; Hotsumi Terakawa; Corin Tomlinson; Harry Tomlinson (senior); Paul Tomlinson; William Valavanis.

Photography

All photography by Paul Goff except: 7 *above right* author; 8/9 *main* author; 17 author; 40 author; 41 author; 42 Bill Jordan (England); 43 author; 95 Reiner Goebel (Canada); 156 Dan Barton (England); 180/181 Bill Jordan (England).

Illustration
David Ashby

Tree Credits

6 61cm (21in) high, 25 years old. Container — glazed Japanese Tokoname oval; 7 41cm (16in) high, 15 years old. Grown from a cutting by the author; 10 *top* Details p159. Owner — author/*bottom* 46cm (18in) high. Planted on tufa rock for 5 years by the author; 11 56cm (22in) high, 15 years old. Planted on tufa rock 6 years ago by the author; 14 Details p99. Container — unglazed Japanese Tokoname rectangle. Created from garden centre material by the author; 15 46cm (18in) high, 24 years old. Created from seedlings by the author. Container — unglazed Japanese Tokoname oval; 16 61cm (24in) high. Planted by the author 5 years ago. Container — unglazed Japanese Tokoname oval suiban; 18 *top* Details p129. Created by the author from garden centre material as a demonstration at the Federation of British Bonsai Societies International Bonsai Convention 1985/*bottom* Details p121. Created from collected hedge material by the author; 20 Details p153. Created over 8 years, by the author; 21 25cm (10in) high. Planting and slab created by Bill Jordan (England); 22 15cm (6in) high, 8 years old. Created from seedling by the author. Container — unglazed Japanese Tokoname oval; 23 Details p127. Owner — author; 24 30cm (12in) high. From seedlings, planted on tufa for 20 years by the author; 26 Details p142. Owner — author; 29 30cm (12in) high. Dwarf Japanese white pine, satsuki azaleas, cotoneaster, planted by the author. Container — unglazed Japanese Tokoname oval suiban; 30 *top* 38cm (15in) high. Sargents juniper, Korean hornbeam 'Chojubai' quince, acorus and cotula. Planted on Ibigawa rock by the author. Container —

unglazed Japanese Tokoname oval/*bottom* Japanese larch, 25cm (10in) high, 23 years old. Planted as a group from seedlings 20 years ago by the author. Container — unglazed Japanese Tokoname narrow rectangle; 31 8cm (3in) high, 6 years old. Created by Paul Tomlinson (England) from a cutting. Container — glazed Japanese Tokoname cascade; 32 30cm (12in) high, 15 years old. Owner — author. Container — 'Onyx' glazed German oval handmade by Petra Engelke; 33 Picture life size, 4 years old. Created from a cutting by Roy Payne (England). Container — glazed Japanese Tokoname oval; 34 Details p152. Owner — author; 35 *top left* 23cm (9in) high, 12 years old. Created from a graft by the author. Container — glazed Japanese Tokoname oval/*top right* 15cm (6in) high, 8 years old. Created from a cutting by the author. Container — glazed Japanese Tokoname oval; 36 Details p165. Collected and trained by Paul Goff (England). Container — glazed English oval handmade by Bryan Albright; 37 *top left* 51cm (20in) high, 15 years old. Grown from seedlings. Owner — author. Container — unglazed Japanese Tokoname oval/*top right* Details p120. Owner — author/*bottom left* 15cm (6in) high, 6 years old. Owner — author. Container — glazed Japanese Tokoname oval; 38 Details p146/147. Owner — author; 39 *top* 51cm (20in) high, 35 years old. Owner — author. Container — unglazed Japanese Tokoname rectangle/*bottom left* Details p151, autumn foliage on front cover. Styled from a collected tree by the author. In 1986, after only 2 years of training this tree received awards at the International Bonsai and Suiseki Exhibition in Osaka, Japan, and the Federation of British Bonsai Societies National Exhibition/*bottom right* 30cm (12in) high, 12 years old. From seedlings. Owner — author. Container — unglazed Japanese Tokoname oval; 40 Main picture courtesy of Reiner Goebel (Canada) of his private collection; 42 Gold medal winning displays by Bill Jordan (England); 46 *left* 30cm (12in) high, 10 years old. Created from a seedling by the author. Container — unglazed Japanese Tokoname rectangle/*right* Details p103. Owner — Martin Bradder (England); 47 *top* Details p148. Owner — author/*bottom left* Details p141. Grown from a seedling for 14 years by the author and initially styled by John Naka as a demonstration on his lecture tour of Britain in 1984. Subsequent care and wiring by the author/*bottom right* 51cm (20in) high, 10 years old. Created from a garden centre plant by the author. Container — unglazed Japanese Tokoname square cascade; 48 *top middle* Details p145. Owner — author/*top right* Details p95. Owner — author/*bottom left* 30cm (12in) high, 15 years old. Japanese trained tree from seed. Owner — Geoff Owen (England). Container — glazed Japanese Tokoname oval; 49 *left* See note to p29/*right* Details p98. Owner — author; 50 *top* See note to p20/*bottom left* 51cm (20in) high, 15 years old. Japanese trained tree. Owner — author. Container — glazed English rectangle handmade by Bryan Albright/*bottom right* Details p109. Japanese trained tree. Owner — author; 51 *top* Details p99. Created from young grafts by the author/*bottom* Details p88/89; 94 Owner — author; 95 *top* Created by

Reiner Goebel (Canada)/*bottom* Owner — author; 96 Created by Roy Stenson (England); 97 Created from seedling by author; 98/99 All owned by author; 100/101 All owned by author; 102 Created by Roy Stenson (England), 103 Owner — Martin Bradder (England); 104 Owner — author; 105 Owner — Hoka-en (Holland); 106 Owner — Hoka-en (Holland); 107 Planted by the author as a demonstration at the British Bonsai Convention in 1982; 108 Owner — author; 109 Owner — author; 110 Owner — author; 111 Planted 2 years ago by the author; 112 Japanese trained. Owner — author; 113 *top* Grown by the author from a cutting/*bottom* grown from a cutting by Roy Stenson (England). Container also by Roy Stenson; 114 Grown from a cutting by the author's father. Harry Tomlinson Snr.; 115 Developed from a graft by the author; 116/117 Planted as a demonstration to the Manchester Bonsai Society (England) four years ago by the author; 118 Japanese trained. Owner — author; 119 Owner — author; 120 Owner — author; 121 Created from collected hedge material by the author; 122 Owner — Hoka-en (Holland); 123 Grown from a cutting by Mike Lorimer, (England); 124 Owner — author; 125 In first year of bonsai training by the author; 126 Created from garden centre material by the author; 127 Owner — author; 128 Japanese styled. Owner — author; 129 Created by the author from garden centre material as a demonstration at the Federation of British Bonsai Societies International Bonsai Convention 1985; 130 Carved and styled by the author; 131 Owner — Mike Limb (England); 132 Owner — Hoka-en (Holland); 133 Grown from a seedling by the author; 134 Grown from a seedling by the author; 135 Grown from collected material by Mark Abbot (England). Container by Gordon Duffett; 136/137 All owned by the author; 138 Owner — Martin Bradder (England); 139 Owner — Hoka-en (Holland); 140 Styled and planted on rock 5 years ago by the author; 141 See notes to p47; 142/143 Owner — author: 144 In its first year of training by the author from garden centre material. (Subsequent training will involve removal of at least half the branches.); 145 Owner — author; 146/147 All owned by the author; 148 Owner — author; 149 Owner — author; 150 Owner — author; 151 See notes above to p39; 152 Owner — author; 153 *top* Created over 8 years by the author/*bottom* Owner — Corin Tomlinson (England); 154 Owner — Hoka-en (Holland); 155 grown from cuttings by the author; 156 Created from garden centre material by Dan Barton (England); 157 Owner — Hoka-en. (Holland); 158 In first year of training by the author; 159 Planted on the slab two years ago by the author; 160 Carved and styled from an old stump by Hotsumi Terakawa (Japan/Holland); 161 Created from garden centre material by the author. Shown after pruning but before wiring and refinement; 162 Japanese trained. Owner — author; 163 Owner — author; 164 Created from a cutting by the author; 165 Collected and trained by Paul Goff (England). See p36 for autumn foliage and new container; 166 Owner — author; 167 Planting by the author; 171 Garden display Paul Goff (England).